Isabel Vincent

See no Evil

The
Strange
Case
of
Christine
Lamont
and
David
Spencer

Isabel Vincent

See no Evil

First published in Canada by
Reed Books Canada
204 Richmond St. W., Suite 300
Toronto, Ontario
M5V 1V6

Copyright © 1995 by Isabel Vincent

All rights reserved

No part of this publication may be reproduced, stored in a retrieval system, or transmitted, in any form or by any means (photocopying, electronic, mechanical, recording, or otherwise) without written permission of the publisher.

Canadian Cataloguing in Publication Data
Vincent, Isabel, 1965–
   See no evil: the strange case of Christine Lamont and David Spencer

Includes index.
ISBN 0-433-39619-9

1. Lamont, Christine. 2. Spencer, David. 3. Terrorism — Brazil.
4. Diniz, Abilio dos Santos — Kidnapping, 1989. 5. Kidnapping — Brazil.
6. Canada — Foreign relations — Brazil. 7. Brazil — Foreign relations — Canada.
I. Title.

HV6604.B732D58 1995   364.1'54'0922   C95-930909-8

Acknowledgements

   Little Drummer Girl
   by John le Carre copyright © David Cornwell 1983.
   Reprinted by permission.

Printed and bound in Canada by Metropole Litho Inc.

Com um abraço, para os meus pais.

Acknowledgements

Many people throughout Latin America, Canada, and the United States contributed to this book. They are journalists, diplomats, former Central American guerrillas, political exiles, intelligence officials, politicians, and ordinary people whose jobs — or worse — whose lives might be in jeopardy if they were mentioned by name. I would like to thank all of them for allowing me into their offices and, in some cases, living rooms, front porches, and neighbourhood bars to discuss the contents of this book.

In Brazil, I owe thanks and a huge *abraço* to the SBT (Sistema Brasileiro de Televisão) staff and, especially, to Boris Casoy in São Paulo, for his insights into Brazilian politics and the media. Thank you to the staffs of O *Globo* in Brasília and *Folha de São Paulo*, particularly Claudio Julio Tognolli, who helped me with contacts in the São Paulo security forces and was not averse to using the famous Brazilian *jeitinho* when things seemed impossible to arrange. Thanks to the staff at the Globo Television Network in Rio de Janeiro, who allowed me to spend several hours in their library examining videotapes. Thank you to the staff of the Canadian Embassy in Brasília, the Canadian Consulate in São Paulo and the Brazilian Embassy in Ottawa. I also owe a great deal to Carmen dos Santos at the Penetenciária Feminina and Walter Hoffgen at the Penetenciária do Estado who are probably sick of journalists making the rounds of their jails, but who always took the time to speak to me when I showed up. Thanks also to Waldomiro Bueno Filho of the DEIC (Departamento Estadual de Investigaçoes Criminosas) in São Paulo, for being candid about several unpopular aspects of this case.

Thank you to Jens Glusing, my colleague from *Der Spiegel* with whom I spent many enjoyable hours on the road in Central and South America, arguing about the Latin American left. In Rio de Janeiro, Nélida Piñón is my guardian angel. Her love and unconditional support are the main reasons that Rio has felt like home over these last four years. Heloisa Leuzinger, who set up appointments, checked facts, steered me in the right direction about the case in Brazil, and called me every day to make sure I was eating properly, has been an invaluable assistant and a dear friend. To Candace Piette of the BBC, who kindly put me up at her flat in São Paulo and listened to all of my problems (both literary and otherwise), *um abraço grande*. Thank you also to Paulo Henrique Amorim of Globo in New York, who one day took out his notebook and gave me a wealth of contacts and information on Brazil, and who took care of me in Haiti. Thank you also to César Ottoni, Carmen Ferreira and Fabiano Maciel for their insights into Brazilian politics and to Pedro Lobo in Rio de Janeiro for his friendship and photographic skills.

In Brazil, I owe my biggest debt to Jeb Blount, who encouraged me to write this book in the first place. His enthusiasm was infectious, and his love and support will not be forgotten. He was always generous with sources and shared with me his brilliant insights into Latin American politics and economics.

Thank you to David Spencer and Christine Lamont, who despite not cooperating with me on this book, agreed to talk to me for several hours at a time about the Latin American left.

In Nicaragua, I want to thank the staff at *La Barricada* for allowing me to wander through their archives at will, and the staff at *La Prensa*, especially Roberto Orozco, for being so generous with classified information on the bunker explosion and with contacts in Managua. In El Salvador, I am grateful to the former FMLN militants who, despite their fear, agreed to speak to me about the bunker explosion. In both countries, several Latin American diplomats were extremely helpful with information on terrorism.

In Miami, Glenn Garvin of the *Miami Herald* was extremely generous with his contacts and time, as was the staff at Kroll Associates. Thanks also to Donna DeCesare in New York, with whom I drove all over El Salvador last March and discussed the ideas for this book.

In Canada, I want to thank my sources at the RCMP and the Department of Foreign Affairs, whom I unfortunately cannot name

SEE NO EVIL

here. Thank you to Margaret Cannon, John Bentley Mays, Jack Kapica, Eve Drobot, Valerie Hussey, and Ricky Englander for their support during the difficult writing of this book in Toronto. Thank you to Tony Pereira for putting up with a day-long interview and offering me Brazilian hospitality at his home in Sudbury. I also want to thank Keith and Marilyn Lamont, Bill Spencer, and David Humphreys for agreeing to speak to me and facilitating interviews with Christine and David's supporters in Canada. I also owe thanks to *Globe and Mail* editor-in-chief William Thorsell for sending me to Latin America in the first place, and to the late Jay Scott, who was always incredibly generous and encouraging of my work. Rick Cash in the *Globe* library has been an invaluable source of information and an enthusiastic supporter.

Dean Cooke has been a wonderful agent, believing in this upstart reporter from the very beginning. Thanks to Oliver Salzmann for his encouragement and to my editor David Kilgour, whose enthusiasm and good advice always came through loud and clear, even over bad international telephone lines. Thank you to editor Edward O'Connor for his insights into the manuscript. Thank you to Bonnie Robinson and David Megginson for their warmth and hospitality in Ottawa, and to Kate Fillion in Toronto for her support and sound advice. I also want to thank the staff at Faema on Davenport Avenue for serving their potent, double espresso with great warmth and humour every afternoon while I was writing this book in Toronto.

Thank you to George and Franklynne Vincent, who kindly allowed me to use their attic to write most of the manuscript. To my nephew Matthew I say, I'm finally finished, sweetheart, so you can put your toys back up in the attic. It's all yours.

Finally, I want to thank my dear friend Jamie Cooper, who tried to talk me out of the whole thing when I first told him what I was doing. Ironically, I don't think I could have finished this book without him. He ended up providing much of the framework for the section on international terrorism, and his love and support kept me going through some very difficult times.

ISABEL VINCENT
Rio de Janeiro, December 1994

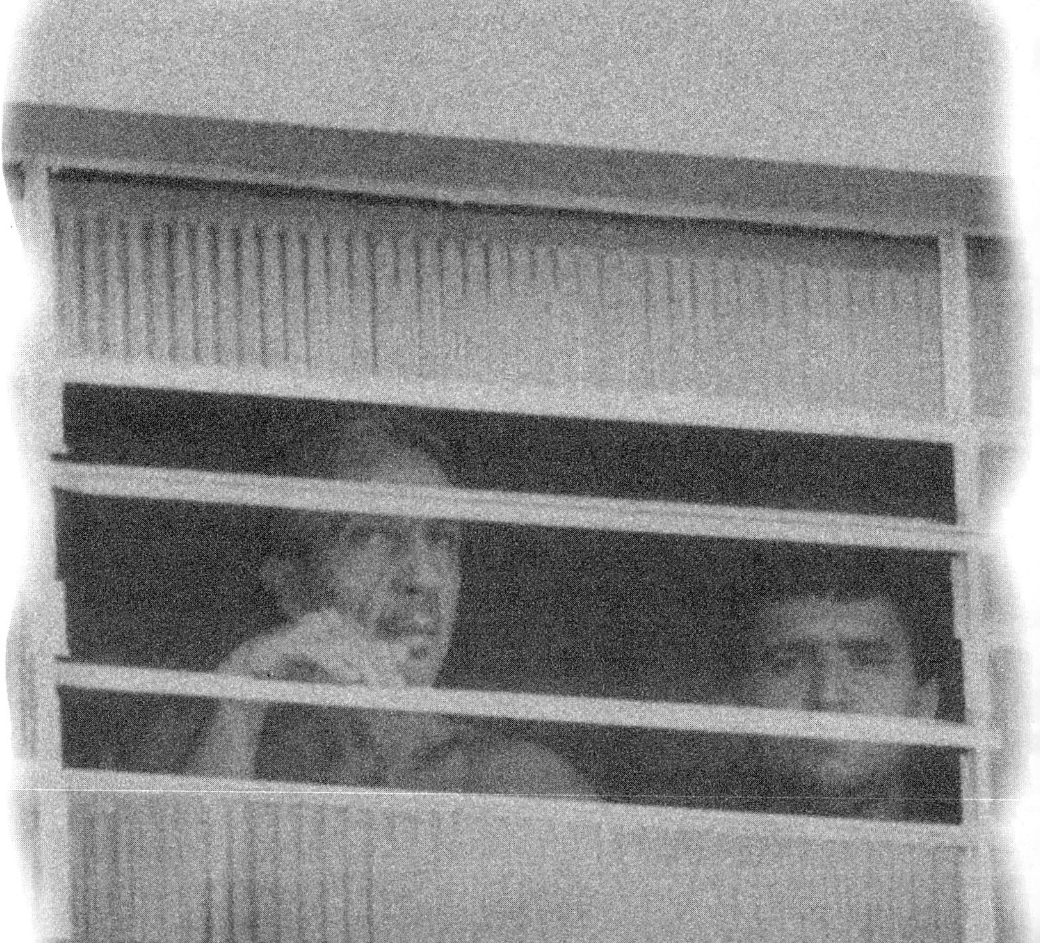

One

Sunday, December 17, 1989, was voting day in Brazil. Across the country, millions of Brazilians were getting ready to go to their local polling stations to vote for their first directly elected leader in nearly three decades.

But although that Sunday was charged with so much historical importance, few Brazilians remember it as the dawn of a new democratic era. In fact, several years later many are hard-pressed to recall press footage showing the two presidential candidates, Fernando Affonso Collor de Mello and Luis Inácio Lula da Silva, engaging in any of the normal telegenic exercises — marking ballots, kissing babies — associated with the final hours of a presidential election campaign.

For most of that weekend, the country's media were preoccupied with a bigger story. Globo, the country's largest television network, frequently interrupted its regular programming to report live from a tree-lined, middle-class suburb of São Paulo where journalists fumbled with microphone cords and negotiated a jumble of police cars, crowds, and media vans to report on the most notorious kidnapping in Brazil's history.

Abílio dos Santos Diniz, executive vice-president of the Pão de Açucar supermarket chain and one of the country's wealthiest men, was holed up in a makeshift underground cell on Praça Hachiro

SEE NO EVIL

Miyazaki, number 59 — an unassuming, beige, two-storey house that was cordoned off with yellow and black police tape. For thirty-six hours, two hundred men from São Paulo's elite Anti-Kidnapping Division, a specially trained cadre of the Civil Police, surrounded the suburban house and tried to convince six heavily armed terrorists to free Diniz and give themselves up peacefully. In Brazil, where for years a rash of high-powered kidnappings had terrorized the country's wealthiest executives, big-city police forces had developed highly trained squads that specialized in combatting urban terrorism and kidnappings.

Millions of Brazilians watched fascinated as Globo carried the negotiations live. "We're going to kill," said the Argentine leader of the group, who was known to police by his codename Juan. Through the open slats in an upstairs bathroom window, TV viewers could see the harried Juan pointing a gun at Diniz's head. The ashen-faced Diniz stood motionless and his eyes were closed. Juan was nervous and perspiring so much that the sweat glued his dishevelled brown hair to his forehead. He stuck his hand out one of the window's slats and awkwardly threw a balled-up note to journalists and the police. In the note, Juan demanded an airplane, arms, and an armoured car in exchange for Diniz's liberty. On the street below, Diniz's distraught family members kneeled in front of the house, sobbing, clutching rosaries, and frantically reciting their prayers.

"You're not going to kill anyone, Juan. You and your friends are going to come out peacefully and nobody's going to get hurt," said Nelson da Silveira Guimarães, a hardened São Paulo cop and chief of the Civil Police's Anti-Kidnapping Division.

Guimarães was right, but it took the intervention of Dom Paulo Evaristo Arns, São Paulo's white-haired cardinal and well-known human rights advocate, to convince the kidnappers to give themselves up. Dom Paulo, whose presence had been specifically requested by the kidnappers, was flown to the house in a police helicopter to convince the kidnappers that they would not be tortured or gunned down by police. Before the media arrived en masse, São Paulo police had reportedly tried to shoot their way into the house. A video made by the Civil Police after the stand-off shows several bullet holes scattered throughout the house. Cardinal Arns was joined by diplomats from Canada, Argentina, and Chile, who also participated in the negotiations.

According to subsequent press reports, São Paulo police had already tortured five members of the ten-member group a few days earlier to find the location of the house where Diniz was being held. Juan, the nom de guerre for Humberto Eduardo Paz and one of those tortured, was brought to the house in the early hours of December 16 in order to help police negotiate the surrender of the five other kidnappers, who were holding Diniz at gunpoint inside. Juan, who arrived at the scene of the crime handcuffed and under the watch of two young police officers, nevertheless managed to escape into the house at dawn to join his five comrades.

"I will personally guarantee the life and integrity of all of you if you surrender," said the stout, bespectacled cardinal, awkwardly balancing himself on the roof of the house next door as he tried to grasp another note from Juan.

Just as polls were closing across the country in the late afternoon, a hush fell over the crowd on Praça Hachiro Miyazaki. The police officers surrounding the house instinctively reached for their weapons as the kidnappers began to file out one at a time, throwing their guns on the ground as they stepped into the courtyard to be frisked by two heavily armed members of the anti-kidnapping squad.

The first to emerge through the wrought-iron gates of the driveway at 5:02 p.m. were two earnest Canadians who looked as if they were coming out of a university classroom rather than the well-equipped bunker where Diniz had been a prisoner for the last six days — held for $30 million U.S. in ransom.

Despite the muggy, late spring weather in São Paulo that day, Christine Lamont, thirty, was dressed in a rumpled print shirt, black cotton skirt, black tights, and very sensible black shoes. She and her boyfriend, David Spencer, twenty-six, didn't look like the international terrorists the São Paulo police portrayed them to be.

"Look at him, he's so young," remarked a Globo television reporter in her on-air commentary when David emerged from the house. He had his hands up and looked away as a police officer efficiently rummaged through his pockets, scattering the contents — a comb, wallet, loose change — on the sidewalk in front of the house.

Grim and apprehensive, Christine and David turned away from the glare of the bright television lights as they climbed into the police bus waiting on the street. For security reasons, São Paulo police had ordered three helicopters and twenty police cars to follow the bus loaded with the kidnappers for the twenty-kilometre drive to Civil Police headquarters in downtown São Paulo.

As the last of the kidnappers boarded the bus, Oscar Matsuo, an officer with the Special Rescue Forces of São Paulo's Civil Police, waved his 9-mm pistol at the crowd in a sign of victory. The crowd, made up of journalists, curious neighbours, and Diniz's family and closest friends, broke into spontaneous applause as Diniz, unsteady on his feet but physically unharmed, staggered through the front gate. After nearly a week in captivity, he was bedraggled and unshaven, and his complexion matched his soiled grey pyjama top. His family members later said he looked as if he had aged ten years.

Glued to their television screens, Brazilians breathed a collective sigh of relief. Some even cried when they saw the dazed Diniz embracing his brother Alcides. São Paulo police were praised for a job well done. "It's indeed rare to see the Brazilian police acting in such an intelligent way," ran a typical article in the following week's *Veja* magazine, noting that the entire rescue operation had been carried out efficiently and without any bloodshed.

The rescue of Diniz on election day was considered a good omen in Brazil, an economic powerhouse that had fallen on hard times after the 1980s debt crisis. Once Latin America's wealthiest and most promising country, Brazil also had the biggest foreign debt in the Third World and one of the greatest disparities between rich and poor. After more than two decades of military rule, corruption and statist economic policies, this country of 150 million people, was reeling from high inflation, a deep recession, and soaring crime rates. So for many Brazilians, weary of their country's negative image abroad, the resolution of the Diniz kidnapping occurring on the same day their country embraced democracy symbolized hope for the future. "*Agora, o Brasil vai dar certo*" ("Brazil's finally going to get it right") was more than a political rallying cry that day. Perhaps for the first time in decades, Brazilians were starting to believe in the potential of their country to be a great world power. That night, with the majority of the votes counted, Brazil's new president prepared his acceptance speech. Young and handsome, his arms raised in victory, forty-year-old Fernando Affonso Collor de Mello promised to wipe out inflation and poverty, privatize inefficient state industries, and open up Latin America's largest economy to foreign investment. A black belt in karate, the new president said he was going to kick Latin America's largest nation into the First World. In Brazil, most people believed him.

■

Eight thousand kilometres away, in Canada, the Diniz kidnapping predictably garnered more press coverage than the outcome of Brazil's historic elections. The reaction across the country was one of shocked disbelief. Two Canadians involved in a kidnapping. . . where? National prime-time newscasts showed the Globo footage of Christine, daughter of upper-middle-class parents in Langley, British Columbia, step gingerly through the house gates, escorted by a stocky Brazilian plainclothes officer. David, originally from Moncton, New Brunswick, squinted at the harsh television lights and seemed on the verge of tears as he followed his girlfriend into the red and white police bus.

"I couldn't believe it, but that night when the news came on I thought they were guilty as hell. It certainly looked like that," said Bill Spencer, David's father, recalling the day he found out that his son had been arrested for kidnapping in Brazil. Mr. Spencer, who watched Christine, then David file out of the São Paulo house on the TV set in his Moncton living room, says he had no idea his son was even in Brazil at the time.

"David had always been concerned with the poor. I can understand him working with street kids, but to confine and kidnap someone is just not in character for him," he says. "But why are you asking me? What's my opinion worth? I'm the parent."

The night of her daughter's arrest, Marilyn Lamont was sitting at the dining-room table in her spacious Langley home writing Christmas cards. Dr. Keith Lamont was upstairs and didn't hear the phone ring. "There was this woman's voice telling me that she was with External Affairs in Ottawa, that she was phoning to tell me that she had received news from São Paulo that Christine had been arrested," recalled Mrs. Lamont, who at first thought the call was some kind of tasteless practical joke. "There was no emotion in her voice or the slightest element of surprise or concern."

Christine's parents were perplexed although, unlike Mr. Spencer, they remained adamant that their daughter had to be innocent. Four days after the surrender, Marilyn and Keith Lamont arrived in São Paulo, where they told Brazilian reporters that the last they'd heard of their daughter, she was working in Nicaragua as a translator. They seemed too shocked to say anything more, except that they were surprised to find that the prison authorities in São Paulo were very cooperative — even friendly.

Their first encounter with their daughter in a São Paulo jail was extremely tense. Christine reportedly told her lawyer that she would only see her parents on the condition that they not ask her any questions about the kidnapping. Dr. and Mrs. Lamont, who were escorted by Canadian consular officials to the Penitenciária Feminina, readily agreed to the rather odd request and, with great difficulty, somehow managed to sidestep the issue of the kidnapping at their first meeting with Christine. To this day, it is not known if Christine and her parents have ever really discussed why she was in Brazil or how she got mixed up in the country's most sensational kidnapping.

Christine and David were accused of extortion by kidnapping, a crime that carries a sentence of eight to fifteen years on conviction in Brazil. An indictment sent to a criminal court in São Paulo stated that Christine and David had rented the house on Praça Hachiro Miyazaki where Diniz was held and that David had ordered repairs to one of the vehicles used in the December 11 kidnapping of the fifty-three-year-old supermarket magnate. David had also bought the building materials used to make Diniz's cramped 1.5-metre by 3-metre underground cell, accessible through a dried-up artesian well under the kitchen. Moreover, both Christine and David were travelling under false passports and had used forged documents and false identities to rent at least two houses in São Paulo.

Christine was travelling under the name of Langley friend Lisa Lynne Walker and David under the name of Paul Joseph Gomes Mendes, a former president of Simon Fraser University's student council. Police said that in the kidnap hideout David was known by the codename Modesto and Christine by the name Susana. When speaking about the case nearly six years later, a São Paulo Civil Police officer who investigated the kidnapping couldn't remember Christine's real name. "What was her name?" asked Waldomiro Bueno Filho. "Sorry, I get confused. She had so many aliases that I can't remember her real name."

According to Brazilian press reports and Diniz himself, both David and Christine carried weapons during the thirty-six-hour stand-off. At the house, police seized "a huge quantity of weapons" and ammunition, as well as radio surveillance equipment so sophisticated that the Anti-Kidnapping Division's chief Guimarães remarked nearly five years later, "I couldn't believe it. They had better radios than the São Paulo police force." Guimarães believes the equipment was used by the kidnappers to track the movements of the São Paulo police on the day of the kidnapping and during the subsequent investigation.

Christine and David had no previous criminal record. When they lived in Vancouver, they worked for Central American solidarity groups and campaigned for human rights in El Salvador. In 1989, they claimed, they travelled to Nicaragua and later to Argentina and Brazil to help the oppressed and work for social change. David met the self-confessed leader of the kidnap group, Humberto Paz, in Buenos Aires in August 1989 and found that they shared the same political viewpoints and passion for social justice. According to David, Humberto was in the process of forming a pan–Latin American organization to promote social change and help the poor, and he asked David and Christine to rent a house for the organization's members in São Paulo.

In fact they rented two houses, in both instances with forged documents and false identification. They posed as gem merchants and used forged letters of reference from a Vancouver jewellery import–export firm that Christine and her sister Heather had worked for.

At their trial, which began in January 1990, David and Christine provided testimony that flatly contradicted the charges against them. They told the court that they had had nothing to do with the kidnapping and didn't even know that Diniz was being held in a cubicle under their kitchen for nearly a week. Although David admitted to buying building materials, he said he had no idea that his friends were excavating the basement to construct a cell. He also said that he and Christine had no idea that there was a large cache of arms in the basement. How were they to know what their housemates were doing when they were out all day sightseeing in São Paulo? they asked.

"If at any point I would have heard of plans for a kidnapping or anything illegal I would have immediately said to Christine, 'Let's get the hell out of here,'" said David in a 1992 interview for "Presumed Innocent," a documentary by CBC television's current affairs program *The Fifth Estate*.

In the same interview, David said he had taken up arms to defend himself and Christine against São Paulo's notoriously violent police during the stand-off.

"Their only crime was to be inside the house, afraid to leave," said Canadian journalist Victor Malarek in the *Fifth Estate* documentary.

Christine and David claim they are innocent. They maintain that their only interest was to work for Latin America's poor, and that they were just unwitting dupes who were caught up in something they didn't understand.

Although they knew few details of the kidnapping and of Christine and David's involvement in it, like any caring parents, the Lamonts rushed to their daughter's defence. Powerless in the face of Brazilian bureaucracy, they turned to the Canadian government for help. They hired David Humphreys, an Ottawa lobbyist, who expertly turned what had started out as a run-of-the-mill consular case into a huge political issue in Canada. The plight of Christine and David became an international human rights issue taken up by prominent Canadian politicians, such as British Columbia MP Svend Robinson, and became a subject of some heated debate in the House of Commons. The Lamonts and Mr. Spencer demanded that Canada intervene in the case. They collected signatures on a petition and held vigils for Christine and David in Vancouver. The pleas for the release of the two Canadians grew more urgent when, in December 1991, an appeals court in São Paulo overturned the lower court's ruling on sentencing and handed down twenty-eight-year sentences for the two Canadians and the other members of the group.

Now their families lobbied even harder for an expulsion order from Brazil that would see the two returned to Canada as free citizens. The families argued that Christine and David were the victims of corrupt Brazilian justice and that there had been several legal irregularities in the trial proceedings that would not have been tolerated in Canada. For an expulsion, the Canadian prime minister would have to formally ask the Brazilian president to free the prisoners. The Brazilian ministry of justice and the president would then have to give their formal approval and release the Canadians. In Brazil this rare legal manoeuvre is usually granted only for humanitarian reasons, in cases where foreign prisoners in Brazil have developed a terminal illness and want to spend their last days close to their families in their home countries. Even if the Canadian government had decided to ask for an expulsion, there is no guarantee that President Fernando Collor would have approved it. Collor, who had little support in a fractious congress made up of nineteen political parties, and who had become incredibly unpopular as a result of a severe anti-inflation shock plan in the early days of his government, was unlikely to agree to an expulsion. The Diniz kidnapping had become a political hot potato. Few Brazilian politicians wanted to be associated with helping the international terrorists involved in the affair.

In Canada, the Tory government refused to seek an expulsion because legal experts in the Department of External Affairs had determined that David and Christine had received a fair trial in Brazil. Nevertheless, the Mulroney government tried to boost its flagging popularity on what was by then — thanks to dogged lobbying by the Lamonts — a politically charged issue by reaching a compromise. Taking their cue from External Affairs, Canadian diplomats in Brazil lobbied for an exchange-of-prisoners treaty that would allow Christine and David to serve out the rest of their sentences in Canadian jails. Still, even this option required that the Brazilian government, and more specifically the Brazilian president, intervene. Although the Lamonts and Mr. Spencer were becoming successful in their lobbying efforts on Parliament Hill, Brazil was another matter.

The Progressive Conservative government's unyielding position on the case only fuelled the outrage of Christine and David's supporters in Canada. Even the Canadian press crumbled. Many respected Canadian journalists swallowed up the distortions in the Humphreys-led media campaign as fact, without doing any independent research. Few reporters made any effort to understand the complexities of the Brazilian justice system or the Latin American radical left. They were so quick to classify this case as a violation of human rights that few bothered to find out exactly whose rights had been violated.

"This would never have happened if the Canadian press had just done its job covering this case, but I guess we just don't have the same aggressive culture of the press as they do in the United States," said a Canadian media analyst.

Almost everyone cited a report on urban violence in Brazil published by Amnesty International in 1990, which detailed the torture of the five members of the Diniz kidnapping group by São Paulo police a few days before the weekend stand-off. Canadian supporters of Christine and David say that the case should have been thrown out at once because part of the evidence had been obtained through torture. But this evidence was not used in the appeals court trial and was discounted by the judge in the first trial.

Moreover, few Canadian journalists spoke with officials at Amnesty International in Ottawa, who would have given them a detailed explanation of why the organization was not going to touch David and Christine's case in Brazil.

"We're certainly monitoring the case, but it's only a criminal justice matter, not a case of political prisoners," said John Tackaberry, a spokesman for Amnesty International in Ottawa. However, the most interesting thing that Tackaberry and other human rights workers I interviewed said was that legitimate human rights workers never travel on false passports.

Still, though, the distortions about the false passports and justice in Brazil were taken as gospel truth. Tackaberry says he was swamped with calls from people from all over the country demanding to know what Amnesty International was doing to free the Canadians in Brazil. "People would call up and try to make us feel guilty for not helping these poor Canadians," says Tackaberry. "So I would ask them what they knew about the case, which was always the stuff the parents had told the press. Then I would give them the facts, and they wouldn't call back again."

Neither the Lamonts nor most of the Canadian media at the time seemed to understand the facts in this case. "What is it about the Brazilian justice system that can't see through the circumstantial evidence?" asked Malarek in the *Fifth Estate* documentary. This was only one of many accounts that provided a sympathetic picture of the two Canadians as victims of a corrupt Third World justice system, rotting away in dark, disease-infested jails in São Paulo.

Again, it didn't matter that the situation was more complicated than this, that Christine and David's jail cell in São Paulo were more like college dorm rooms than Third World hell-holes or that the Canadian government had thoroughly reviewed the case and found that, contrary to popular belief, David and Christine had been given a fair hearing. Even a senior Liberal government bureaucrat in the newly named Department of Foreign Affairs wasn't going to let the facts get in the way of a good political issue. In a lengthy off-the-record discussion in

SEE NO EVIL

April 1994, the bureaucrat in question told me that "for humanitarian reasons" Canada was going to intervene to get David and Christine out of jail as soon as possible because their situation was surely akin to that depicted in *Midnight Express*, Alan Parker's frightening film about an American who winds up in a nasty Turkish prison for drug smuggling.

Perhaps the Liberal government, which had won the 1993 election partly on a promise to free the two Canadians, felt it would look heroic in the eyes of the Canadian public by working to liberate the convicted kidnappers and bringing them home as national heroes. Or perhaps the Liberals had boxed themselves into such a tricky political corner that despite the possible guilt of the pair, they now had no choice but to try to bring them home, and fast.

■

When I arrived in Brazil in July 1991 to take over *The Globe and Mail's* South American bureau, I had read very little about the case, but my gut instinct, based on the tiny number of clippings I had seen, told me that those two Canadians, holed up in São Paulo prisons, had to be innocent.

I wrote my first story about the case in December 1991, when the two lost their appeal and their sentences were increased to twenty-eight years. In an interview with one of their lawyers after the decision was handed down, I found out that many believed that the decision of the appellate court had been politically motivated. In Brazil, the Diniz kidnapping had in fact become intertwined in a complicated political web. The São Paulo political machine was using the Diniz case as a model of police efficiency. Brazil had suffered a recent wave of kidnappings, and although few of them gained the same notoriety as the Diniz case, the Civil Police used them to improve its image.

Luis Antônio Fleury Filho, who in 1989 was the secretary of public security overseeing the São Paulo police, had clearly used the Diniz case in his successful bid for governor of São Paulo state in 1990. Furthermore, some political enemies of left-wing presidential candidate Luis Inácio Lula da Silva, known in Brazil as Lula, had tried to link the kidnappers to Lula's Workers Party (PT). This was particularly evident on the eve of the second round of voting in the 1989 election when battle lines were clearly drawn between Lula and Collor. According to

Brazilian press reports, Civil Police officials planted PT election paraphernalia in a safe house used by the kidnappers. One of the Chilean kidnappers, Ulisses Gallardo Acevedo, said that he was forced by police to wear a T-shirt blazoned with the PT logo when he was interrogated. He said police photographed him wearing the T-shirt on the eve of the run-off vote. However, the photograph was not issued to the press until nearly three months after the elections.

But political machinations aside, we are still talking about the kidnapping and forcible confinement of a human being for monetary gain — a fact that many of Christine and David's supporters and many on the left both in Canada and in Latin America conveniently forget about. For Christine and David's politically correct supporters, torture is something that repressive elements of the right-wing inflict on leftist activists. The abduction and confinement of a prominent member of the Brazilian elite by leftist freedom fighters don't count as torture because, well, he somehow deserves this sort of treatment. For the militant left, especially in Latin America, the elite is uniformly morally repugnant and devoid of humanity.

■

Despite the complexities of their case, David and Christine might indeed be out of jail today if it hadn't been for an accidental explosion nearly half a continent away.

On May 23, 1993, a bunker stocked with arms belonging to the FPL, a radical faction of El Salvador's Farabundo Marti National Liberation Front (FMLN), exploded in an auto repair shop owned by well-known Basque separatists in the Nicaraguan capital of Managua. In addition to a sizeable cache of arms, the blast unearthed more than three thousand documents and false passports. Among the documents were passports belonging to David and Christine, credit cards, false press credentials and drivers' licences, and phony letters written to convince their families in Canada that they were still living in Nicaragua when they were, in fact, already in Brazil. In addition to the documents, police found lists of Latin American industrialists, detailing their daily movements and sources of income.

Romeu Tuma, former head of the Brazilian Federal Police and the Latin American director of Interpol, called the Managua find "the missing link" between a series of recent high-profile kidnappings in Latin

America and an international Marxist terrorist network with ties to the Basque separatist group ETA (the acronym stands for Euzkadi Ta Askatasuna or Basque Homeland and Freedom).

Indeed, the honeymoon with the Canadian press began to sour. The coup de grace came on July 24, 1993, when *The Toronto Star* published a two-and-a-half-page article on the Managua bunker explosion, complete with photos of doctored Ontario drivers' licences featuring pictures of David and Christine under their aliases, Paul Joseph Mendes and Lisa Lynne Walker. There were also letters to be sent to family in Canada bearing Post-it notes with neatly printed instructions in Spanish to mail them at staggered intervals. Nicaraguan police even found Christine's CN Tower pass after the explosion.

Soon after the blast, the left-wing Managua daily *Barricada* plastered the photographs of the two Canadians on the front page. Brazilian authorities vowed to re-open the investigation into the Diniz kidnapping. David and Christine and their lawyers in Brazil seemed dumbfounded. In a statement read by one of his lawyers, David said that he and Christine had given all of their personal documents to a Sandinista named Steve while they were in Buenos Aires in 1989. It seemed a rather feeble explanation, but it was all that they would say. Today neither David, Christine, nor their lawyers will comment very much on the Managua explosion. In my first interview with Christine, she refused to speak about the bunker except to say that she knew nothing about it and had never been to the Managua neighbourhood where the explosion took place.

In Canada, their supporters fumbled for excuses. Some said the explosion was a CIA plot to make Christine, David, and the Central American left look bad. Indeed, in Nicaragua, the rumour mill was working overtime after the blast, which made everyone from officials in Violetta Chamorro's government to the Sandinistas look very bad in the eyes of the international community. Following the blast, fifteen more bunkers were uncovered in addition to eight "safe houses" that Interpol said were occupied by a host of Central American guerrilla groups that used Managua as a base of operations.

Nearly a year after the explosion, two Mexican industrialists whose names were on the list from the bunker of Latin America's 150 most "kidnap-able" victims were abducted in Mexico City. Alfredo Harp Helu, president and major stockholder of the financial conglomerate

Banamex–Accival and the first Mexican to be kidnapped after the blast, was held for $30 million U.S. in ransom.

I arrived in El Salvador the day of Harp's kidnapping and tried to interview FPL militants in San Salvador. Spooked by the Harp abduction, not only would no one speak about the explosion of the *"buzon de Santa Rosa"* (the Santa Rosa bunker), as it came to be known in Latin America, but I was told by some members of the FMLN that any kind of investigation into the bunker and the list of potential kidnap victims would be dangerous. The day after the bunker exploded a leading FPL militant was found shot in San Salvador, killed with a bullet to the head. Salvadorean police found the phone number of the Managua bunker in his pocket along with pay stubs for the salary of a man named Abel Martinez, the security guard at the bunker, who is currently in jail in Nicaragua.

The Managua blast marked an important turning point in the history of the Latin American left. Why were leftist freedom fighters engaging in high-powered kidnappings, many of them planned and orchestrated by Basque terrorists in exile? Analysts said that the blast exposed the vulnerability of these groups. After the fall of the Berlin Wall in 1989, the radical left around the world was groping for a new definition and a new source of funding to wage the revolution. With the decline of the Soviet Union and the economic crisis in Cuba following more than thirty years of a U.S.-imposed trade embargo, the left had to look for other sources of funding. Interpol and some private terrorism consultants say that the plans to kidnap Latin American business leaders were hatched at a "conference" in Hamburg, Germany in 1988. In September of that year, Germany was the site of an important International Monetary Fund and World Bank meeting that was the object of protests by several leftist groups from around the world.

Kidnapping to raise money for Marxist and separatist causes is nothing new, but the Managua explosion was significant because it provided proof of the shadowy alliances among international terrorist groups and of their very active presence in Latin America. For years, radical Marxist and separatist groups around the world had used kidnapping as a quick way to make money to support their causes. Terrorism experts had suspected that groups like ETA, factions of Chile's MIR and Argentina's MTP regularly collaborated on such cases. ETA and the Irish Republican Army regularly collaborate on arms purchases because "it's cheaper to buy in bulk," according to John Carroll, a private consultant and former director of information services at Kroll Associates, a private investigation firm based in Miami.

In Canada, the explosion also marked a turning point in the campaign to free David and Christine. For some of their supporters, the evidence was incontrovertible. Many broke ranks with the family. When I called David Humphreys from Brazil after the bunker explosion he seemed at a loss for words.

The parents were quick to come to the defence of their children. Mr. Spencer said that he had no doubt his son had written the letters so that his family back home in Canada wouldn't worry. He explained that when he was serving as a cook with the Canadian Forces in the Far East during the Second World War, "it was standard procedure to pre-date and postdate letters."

But was it standard procedure to lie?

Even the Lamonts, who have worked indefatigably since 1989 to prove their daughter's innocence, were thrown for a loop. "I'll never forget the telephone call I made to Christine Lamont's parents to tell them about the documents. I spoke to her mother and there was only silence on the other end of the phone. Then she composed herself and said there had to be an explanation," said Tim Johnson, a reporter for the *Miami Herald* stationed in Managua. He was one of the first to investigate the bunker explosion.

A few months after the explosion, Christine confessed to a Canadian consular official in São Paulo that she was worried that her father was angry at her because she hadn't received any letters from him. The consular official suspected that the contretemps between father and daughter had to do with the Managua explosion. "It was very difficult for Christine to explain the whole Managua incident to her parents," said a Canadian diplomat formerly stationed in São Paulo. "We got the feeling that things turned a little bit sour at that point."

In Canada, the story, which had been major news for several years, was starting to grow stale — at least the version of the story that Christine, David, and their parents were trying to sell. At *The Globe and Mail*, editors refused to run stories on the pair unless there was a new development in their case in Brazil. Many editors realized that "news" in this case was simply being churned out as a result of an expensive public relations campaign. "It's a dead story now," said one of my editors at the *Globe* following the Managua blast. "Everyone knows they're guilty."

But this story is long from over. With further appeals pending in the Brazilian courts, Christine and David's fate still hangs in the balance. The kidnap group with which they were affiliated is still doing good business in Latin America. Brazilian and Mexican executives, who drive around in bulletproof cars with a legion of armed security guards, live in fear of the shadowy group of terrorists who continue to strike against some of the wealthiest targets in the region.

Furthermore, this is not a case that's easily summed up with a simple innocent or guilty verdict. The central question for me has always been, Are David and Christine guilty of a ruthless, calculating crime or are they simply two innocents abroad? Were they guided by some vague notion of working for social justice in an area of the world still marked by glaring disparities between rich and poor, where the remnants of *la revolución* still have a romantic appeal?

There are those in Canada who see David and Christine as heroes, brutally and wrongly jailed for their beliefs, but steadfast in their commitment to the struggle for justice and human rights in Latin America. "This case is about genuinely sincere and politically aware people who wanted to change the world," says Blaine Donais, a Toronto-based lawyer. As a law student in Saskatoon, Donais tried to make a case for the expulsion of David and Christine by using the Charter of Rights and Freedoms to compel the Canadian government to take action.

Many Canadians want to believe they are innocent because their cause, vague though it might be, was so just, so politically correct. If educated, well-brought-up Canadians take the trouble to go all the way to the Third World, then they must be heroic and altruistic, with noble intentions. We need heroes, and our national pride is somehow tied up with ennobling Christine and David's journey into the heart of Latin America. After all, who has ever heard of a Canadian terrorist, anyway?

Perhaps, to use a film analogy, we want them to be like Sissy Spacek and Jack Lemmon in *Missing*, the Costa-Gavras movie about two committed North Americans searching for truth and justice in Pinochet-era Chile. *Missing* has all of the things that politically correct North Americans love: leftist idealists fighting a repressive and corrupt foreign government, torture, sexy Latin American revolutionaries, and, yes, a love story.

On the surface, the Christine Lamont/David Spencer story has all of the same elements. No doubt it would be a big success at the box office, but there are a few problems. Truth, in Latin America at least, is much stranger and definitely more complicated than fiction. For starters, the Latin American militant left is practically dead, the Cold War is over, there is only one Latin American dictatorship left (and it's run by a Marxist–Leninist), and Christine and David's jails are not really such dark and nasty hell-holes. There is, however, the love story. . . .

For nearly six years many Canadians wrapped Christine and David in a protective veil of goodwill. Christine and David said they had seen no evil and most Canadians could see no evil in this case. Over the last year, my requests for interviews among their supporters were almost always met with the question, "How are you going to use your information?" or "How is this going to help them?" In a brief interview given while he was in São Paulo in April 1994 for Christine's thirty-fifth birthday, Dr. Lamont said that he would like journalists like me to do "favourable pieces" on Christine and David. I was struck with the word "favourable." Whatever happened to the old-fashioned journalistic concept of just being fair?

Last year, a young journalism student from Carleton University in Ottawa who was doing a masters thesis on Christine and David called me at my office in Rio de Janeiro to get my views on the case. He prefaced his remarks with, "Everyone knows that they were victims of Brazilian corruption. They're innocent." I declined comment at the time. I wasn't going to convince someone so set in his ways. This future journalist from one of Canada's finest schools of journalism had already made up his mind, irrespective of the facts. What struck me as sad was the fact that he wasn't the exception, but the rule in Canada. Most Canadian journalists had made up their minds long before they ever started researching the story. Many of them came to Brazil with their stories already written. They simply plugged in the facts that suited their arguments; they omitted those that didn't fit.

Some might call it media manipulation or a conspiracy of the Lamont and Spencer families, working with David Humphreys. I call it incompetence and laziness. Judging by much of the Canadian reporting on the case, many Canadian journalists just didn't do their homework. They took what the parents told them at face value and created the Lamont/Spencer myth.

SEE NO EVIL

With the story so firmly entrenched in the Canadian media, nobody seemed interested in asking probing questions. Even other journalists questioned my motives for writing this book. "What are you going to use this information for? I thought you told me that they got a raw deal," said Vancouver journalist Kim Bolan.

Most people would agree that David and Christine did indeed get "a raw deal" with the twenty-eight-year sentences. But painting them as pathetic victims of some corrupt banana-republic justice system has probably done more harm than good — both in Canada and in Brazil. David Humphreys' media campaign has been based mostly on distortions and half-truths, and has played upon Canadians' ignorance of Latin America. In Canada, "human rights" and "social justice" became throwaway phrases — they took on twisted, convoluted meanings in the interests of liberating two Canadians who have never taken full responsibility for their actions.

In Brazil, Canadian lobbying efforts to repatriate the two have met largely with derision and outrage, mostly by well-connected politicians and journalists who feel their country has been the victim of Canadian imperialism. Brazilians are passionately nationalistic and don't appreciate a G-7 power — even one as middling as Canada — interfering in their affairs.

In fact, the Lamont/Spencer case has demonstrated just how racist and xenophobic Canadians can be. The Lamonts were initially successful in their campaign because they built on Cold War myths of banana-republic countries, ruled by evil, right-wing dictators, who kept order by employing paramilitary death squads to rub out their political opponents. Set against this backdrop, Canadians, who are known around the world for tolerance and fair-mindedness, came to seem incredibly arrogant.

"This whole case became sad and then eventually disgusting," said a Canadian diplomat who has followed the case since 1989. "The problem really started with a lack of knowledge between Canada and Brazil. It wasn't hard for the Lamonts to do what they did. All they did was exploit a basic weakness in the system. In this case arrogance precluded Canadians from learning the truth, even when it was staring them in the face."

Indeed, the Lamonts told us Christine and David were innocent. They told us that the Brazilian press, the police, and the judicial system were corrupt. They told us that Christine and David were rotting away in disease-infested, overcrowded Brazilian jails. They told us that the Tory government wasn't willing to lift a finger to help them because Christine and David were too far left for the Conservatives. They told us Christine and David were victims.

And we believed them.

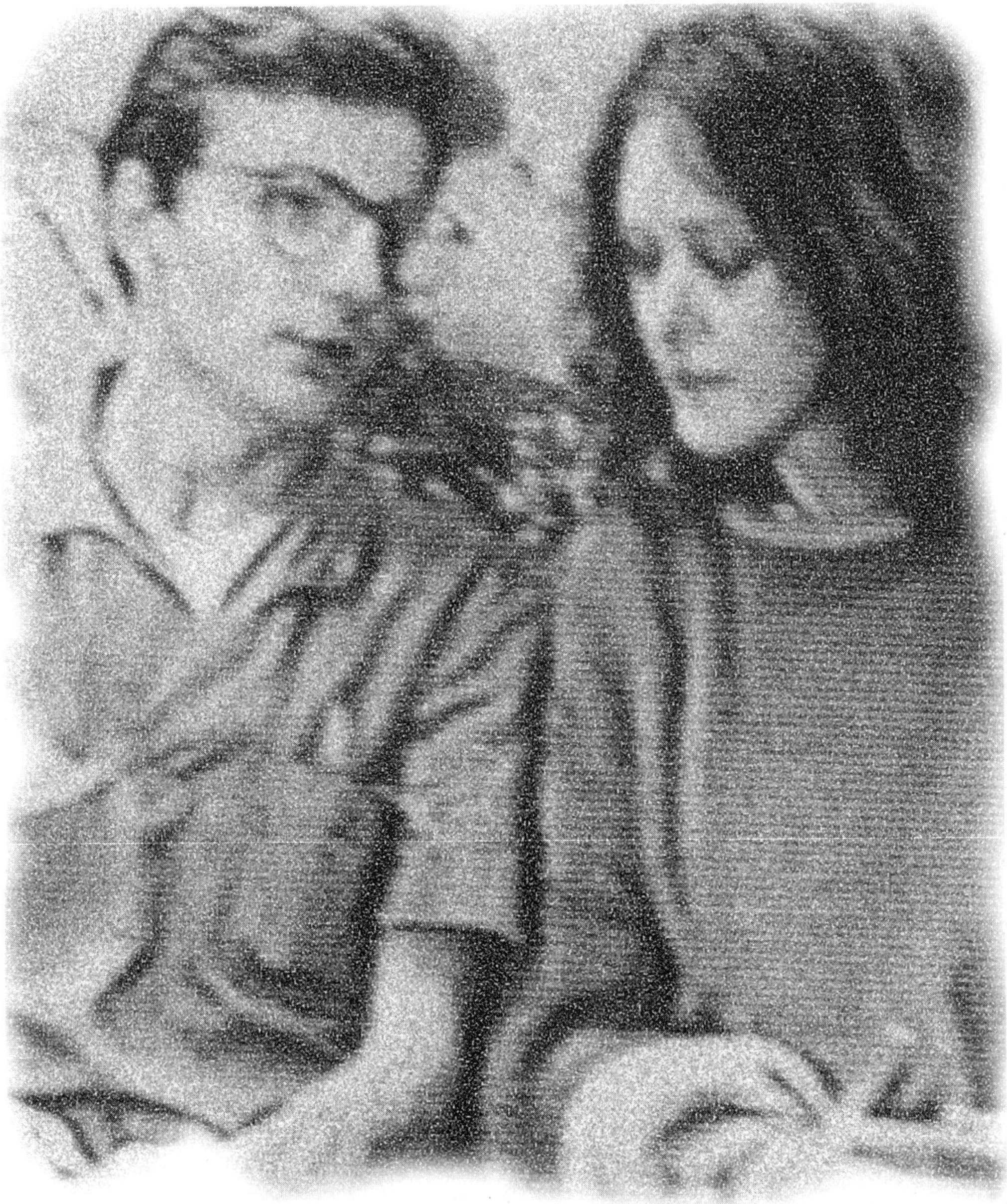

Two

Vancouver's Commercial Drive is a long way from the working-class Carandiru neighbourhood in São Paulo where David and Christine are serving their twenty-eight-year sentences in separate prisons.

True, Commercial Drive, where the Canadians began the journey into the heart of Latin American revolutionary politics that would eventually take them to São Paulo, is about as working class as you'll get in any big Canadian city. But it's really no match for the bleak, smog-choked squalor of Carandiru. In the Commercial Drive district, elderly Chinese women, clutching too many plastic shopping bags, wait for the Victoria Street bus in the shadow of the British Columbia Sugar Refining Company. Chinese laundries and acupuncture clinics share city blocks with Portuguese bakeries and Salvadoran grocery stores. There are also health food stores where you can buy organically grown produce (for a huge mark-up) and vintage clothing shops frequented by young Vancouverites wearing a lot of black.

More than any other place in Vancouver, Commercial Drive has become a kind of unofficial hub for the city's trendy left. The La Quena Coffee House on Commercial near Napier is one of their favourite meeting spots.

Started in 1982 by a Chilean political exile, La Quena looks more like a throwback to the 1960s; long-haired teenagers in tie-dyed T-shirts and Birkenstocks smoke dope and read their poetry in the middle of the afternoon to anyone who will listen.

At lunch time, chain-smoking Latin American leftists, many of them exiles who arrived in Canada in the 1980s to escape persecution by brutal military regimes, mingle with Che Guevara wannabes, clean-cut university students from upper-middle-class Vancouver families, sporting snug-fitting black jeans and colourful, woven Guatemalan knapsacks.

At La Quena, Cuba is still held up as a model for socialist revolution in the Third World, and the Cold War is still a hot topic every lunch-hour over alfalfa-sprout-and-cream-cheese sandwiches and cups of black organic coffee, imported from Chiapas, Mexico in support of the Zapatista National Liberation Army rebels.

The cafe organizes fundraisers for a host of politically correct causes, most of them Latin American. When I visited in April 1994, there were posters of Ruben Zamora, a former Salvadoran rebel who ran for president in that year's elections, pasted on just about every available wall space. Volunteers who run the cafe were planning a Chilean Rainforest Evening, a seminar on the plight of Guatemala's internal refugees, and something called a Total Hemp Crawl. Al Fossen, a local artist who was helping to organize the last event, told me that he was campaigning for the decriminalization of marijuana.

I asked Al, a greying leftie who has been a volunteer at La Quena since 1986, if he knew David and Christine. He said that he had never met them personally, but that the cafe had already sponsored several fundraisers and vigils for the pair, who he believes are victims of a corrupt Brazilian justice system. Like many of La Quena's regulars, he believes that David and Christine were pawns in a sophisticated political game to discredit the Brazilian left.

"They're heroes here," said Al, whose business card reads "Hempsters, Marijuana Users' Club." And then, looking around the coffee shop, he dropped his voice to a conspiratorial whisper. "They say that David and Christine organized fundraisers for the FMLN. I heard they once even raised money to buy food for an FMLN battalion during the war." That was in the late 1980s, when El Salvador was still being torn apart by a brutal war, and the FMLN exiles in Vancouver "controlled La Quena," according to Al.

Al says he doesn't associate much with the Salvadorans in the neighbourhood. A few doors away from La Quena, a Salvadoran immigrant recently opened a *pupuseria*, a lunch counter which sells *pupusas*, or Salvadoran burritos. "I hate the owner. He's a fascist pig. Can you believe it? He supported ARENA in the election," fumed Al, referring to the rightist party that has been traditionally linked to death squads. It's a measure of the "evil" influence of neoliberal reforms sweeping Latin America today that even political exiles from the region no longer have the good sense to be leftist anymore, said Al.

José, an unemployed Salvadoran immigrant and La Quena regular for more than ten years, has been eavesdropping on our conversation from a nearby table. "The problems in my country all came from outside forces of imperialism," he said, and then sizing me up in a quick glance, added in Spanish, "I knew David and Christine. They were my friends."

Over several cups of black coffee, he fondly recalled working on fundraisers and going to the movies with *"mis amigos canadienses."* He remembered both of them as being very intelligent, especially David, whom he characterized as being more active in Salvadoran politics than Christine. And every time I asked him a difficult question about what he thought David and Christine were doing hanging around with terrorists in Argentina and Brazil, he laughed and gave me the kind of equivocal answer that I had grown accustomed to in the murky world of Salvadoran politics. "They knew exactly what they were doing," he said with a smile.

Years of waging an underground struggle against brutal right-wing regimes that were often supported by the United States had made many Latin American guerrillas and those in solidarity with them extremely suspicious of anyone asking too many questions about their activities. Evasiveness was an initiation rite — something you needed to learn to be a good revolutionary in Latin America in the 1980s.

"Why should anyone tell you anything? Why should anyone trust you? How are you going to help them? Unless you can offer them something in return, everyone here is always going to lie to you to protect themselves and their comrades," warned my Salvadoran friend Horacio, a journalist and former rebel who has just returned to El Salvador after living in exile in Mexico for several years.

Nevertheless I persisted with José, a stout, tired-looking man in his mid-thirties who seemed as if he really wanted to talk about David and Christine and the changes going on in his country. José said he was disappointed that many former leftist militants in El Salvador were now embracing social-democratic policies, in some cases trading in their AK-47s for cellular phones to wage the struggle on the political battlefield.

In El Salvador and throughout most of Latin America, the militant left was crumbling. Even the FMLN's military strategist and revolutionary hero, Joaquín Villalobos, was now playing party politics and criticizing the militant left in the country for being too disorganized and, horror of horrors, too left wing.

"There is no longer an FMLN," said Villalobos in an interview with the *Miami Herald* in October 1994, adding that the five factions within the guerrilla Front, which managed to stay united and extremely disciplined during the twelve-year civil war, were dissolving under the pressures of peace-time politics. Today, the FMLN is so fractured that its leaders are hardly on speaking terms, and the formal dissolution of the Front is now complete.

Villalobos described the choice for the FMLN as being between "a viable social–democratic left or one that is nonviable, Marxist–Leninist–communist, now in the process of extinction."

But José, who is very much an orthodox leftist, disagrees with Villalobos, whom he described as a political opportunist. "The problem with the left in El Salvador is too much corruption. If you move away from the party line, you should be punished. We need someone like Fidel Castro running the country. In Cuba, if you're corrupt, they simply shoot you," said José, who has worked at a variety of odd jobs in Vancouver since leaving El Salvador in the early days of the civil war.

I tried again to steer the conversation to David and Christine. If they were so intelligent, how could they not be aware that they were involved in a terrorist group? "If David and Christine said that they didn't know what was going on, then it must be true," laughed José.

When I asked him if he had been a fighter in El Salvador, he responded in that frustratingly enigmatic tone: "We were all fighters in El Salvador. All of us. We fought with our conscience."

"But don't you think it's odd that two middle-class kids from Canada would get involved with guerrilla movements in Latin America?" I asked.

Looking around at the earnest university students busily tacking up Latin American solidarity posters at La Quena that spring afternoon, I realized it was a stupid question. These were precisely the kind of people who would be caught up with the righteousness and romance of the revolution. Indeed, the history of the Latin American revolutionary left after the Second World War is full of what Mexican historian Jorge Castañeda calls in his book *Utopia Unarmed* "an intellectualized middle class outraged by an intolerable estrangement from the society it lives in, and the abyss separating that class from the vast, undifferentiated universe of the poor." Che Guevara, Latin America's most famous guerrilla and, according to Castañeda, the "icon of the armed Latin American left," who waged the struggle in Cuba and died exporting it to Bolivia in 1967, was, after all, from a good middle-class Argentine family.

> *If ever there was an illustration of the anguish evoked in sensitive and reasonable, but far from exceptional individuals at being affluent and comfortable islands in a sea of destitution, it was Guevara. He will endure as a symbol, not of revolution or guerrilla warfare, but of the extreme difficulty, if not the actual impossibility, of indifference.*

David and Christine's supporters say that the two reached a point in their comfortable lives in Canada when they could no longer remain indifferent to or even distant from the plight of Latin America's poor and oppressed. In 1989, full of noble intentions, they took the logical next step in their revolutionary education and waded — perhaps too readily and too naively — into "the sea of destitution."

"David and Christine are like Che Guevara. They are committed. They have principles," said José, as if reading my mind.

■

Born in Boston on April 21, 1959 while her father Keith was doing his specialist training in surgery, Christine Gwen Lamont developed a social conscience early in life. From her affluent home in Langley, B.C., where the family moved when she was six, Christine became concerned with the world's poor when she was nine years old and sponsored a foster child in India. Marilyn, her mother, recalled in an interview how she and her daughter organized tea parties to raise money for the little girl so far away.

"Ever since she was a little girl, Christine began to educate us about the world's less fortunate. It was a shock for us to find out that our little Canada was like a utopia compared to the rest of the world," said

Mrs. Lamont, who used to teach piano but now works full time in the campaign to liberate her daughter.

"We're talking about a girl who from a very young age was always involved in do-gooder causes," said Eric Robinson, a family friend of the Lamonts who heads the White Rock chapter of the Committee for Justice for Christine Lamont and David Spencer, an ad hoc national group that is petitioning the Canadian government to intervene in the pair's release.

Following his daughter's arrest and imprisonment, Dr. Lamont told a *Vancouver Sun* reporter: "We absolutely trust that what Christine was doing was for the betterment of her fellow man."

Christine and her brother Mark and sisters Heather and Beth were almost unanimously described as nice kids who had grown up in a close-knit family in a comfortable Langley neighbourhood.

But some paint a different picture of Christine. One of her friends says that she could at times be irresponsible and had no qualms about lying to her parents. Other friends say that Christine was being supported by her parents when she was attending university, but that she spent much of that time skipping classes and never completed her degree. Christine dropped out of her first year at the University of British Columbia and got a job with an import–export firm. When the firm folded, she enrolled at Simon Fraser Univeristy to study communications and political science. However, she did not finish her degree. When Christine was arrested in December 1989, Mrs. Lamont told a *Globe and Mail* reporter that she didn't know whether or not Christine had actually graduated from university. "We didn't go to a graduation ceremony," she said.

Cheque-books found after the Managua blast show that Christine received a comfortable allowance from her parents. Every two weeks leading up to her departure for Central America, she received $417.08 from a company called Lamont Holdings. At one point the allowance was raised to $422.

"Christine was really smart and sincere, but she always struck me as this poor rich kid," said a family friend.

It's little wonder then that Christine, who has been described by some of her friends as being overindulged by her parents, spent much of her formative years looking for a cause — something to do. But while in high school she spent her summers working at uninspiring jobs, such as bookkeeping for her father and selling jewellery at the Pacific National Exhibition.

SEE NO EVIL

Patrick Jordan, a Vancouver-based jewellery importer who employed Christine in 1985 and 1987 and who has known her and her sisters for fifteen years, said that when he first met Christine she did not strike him as very politically aware.

"When I first met her she really struck me as a bit of a space cadet. She was more interested in smoking a joint than anything else," he said. Jordan, who asked me to bring him crystal specimens from Brazil for our meeting in Vancouver, says he remembers that Christine had joined an EST workshop ("One of those seminars where you paid $400 so that you could get in touch with your feelings," he said) and was forever "harassing" him to join. "I guess her mission was to convert as many people as she could," said Jordan, who upon examining the Brazilian crystals I brought him, proposed that we team up in the jewellery business.

Christine appears to have been influenced by several 1980s fads. In addition to her interest in *Erhand Seminars Training*, her family noted in one letter that she had spent several years as a committed vegetarian "because of health theories about meat but also because she disapproved of the killing of animals for her own use."

But in 1987, after a ten-day trip to El Salvador as a participant in an educational seminar organized by Simon Fraser University, Christine seemed to find her mission in life. "After that, she started to care about every cause in the world. She became insufferable," said Patrick Jordan.

Mrs. Lamont agreed that the El Salvador trip at the height of the country's civil war had had a profound effect on her daughter, who returned to her family's 6,000-square-foot home in Langley feeling "terribly upset," describing the bodies she had seen lying in the street and the "inhuman" conditions in some of the hospitals in the poorest parts of the country.

As a result of the trip, Christine took up the cause of Latin America's oppressed. She helped to organize a Central American solidarity group at Simon Fraser, called the Central America Simon Fraser University Students' Association (CASFUSA), and spent a lot of her time organizing benefits, rallies, and seminars in support of the struggle for social justice in Central America, particularly in El Salvador.

Jorge Garcia, who headed up Simon Fraser University's Latin American Studies department at the time, recalled seeing Christine around campus. "She was never my student, but she was an active member of the student society," he said in an interview with the *Vancouver Sun*. "She'd studied some course in political science and she was aware of many things that were going on, and she exercised her student duties as she saw fit."

In 1989, Christine headed for Nicaragua, the first stop in her revolutionary mission to change the world. She wasn't alone. Christine had met David Robert Spencer during her conversion to the cult of Latin American left-wing politics. An earnest and committed activist, David was very much involved in Salvadoran solidarity groups.

"He struck me as very sincere, intelligent, and very sensitive," said Raul Gutierrez, a Salvadoran who met David at a fundraiser in Toronto in 1988. "When I met him he hadn't left Canada. He asked me about the poor and wanted to come to Central America to see what kind of conditions they lived under."

David's social conscience had been formed around the supper table in his family's modest working-class home in Moncton. Born in Nova Scotia on August 22, 1963, David grew up with two sisters in Moncton, listening to the stories of their father Bill Spencer, a retired Air Force cook, who had grown up poor during the Depression in the Maritimes.

"I received my political training from my father, who used to be a street kid, just as bad as the ones in Brazil," said David in our first conversation at the Penitenciária do Estado in São Paulo.

After graduating from high school in 1982, David enrolled in a general arts program at Mount Allison University, but after about a week on campus, he quit to begin a cross-Canada odyssey that would take him to Toronto, Winnipeg, and eventually Vancouver. His father, who is himself somewhat of an autodidact and a deeply intelligent man, described his son as a real nonconformist. Others have described him as "cocky and overconfident" and arrogant.

"If David had been born sooner, he would have been a hippie," said Mr. Spencer, adding that his son took all sorts of odd jobs to support himself and spent much of his free time in public libraries reading about Marxism.

Although David never really attended university, his approach to his politics is very academic. There is nothing knee-jerk about his opinions, and his arguments are logical and extremely well-informed. In our first meeting, we discussed a wide variety of issues that ranged from the Chiapas uprising in Mexico to the political situation in Angola and the educational system in Brazil. It's a measure of his acute curiosity that in a 1990 letter to his sister Judy, David requested that she send him

SEE NO EVIL

Patricia Smith Churchland's *Neuro Philosophy: Toward a Unified Understanding of the Mind* in addition to weighty texts on U.S. foreign policy and germ warfare testing.

"I find Chiapas very interesting," he told me in a four-hour interview that took place in the warden's office at the Penitenciária do Estado. "It's the first post–Cold War peasant uprising in Latin America, but unlike previous revolutions the rebels' demands were for a more democratic process in Mexico, not to take over the country."

When he's not working at menial tasks in the jail, David devotes his time to study and writing. He has already written a few opinion pieces on the Brazilian political situation and his time in jail for the *Ottawa Citizen*, and he says he took a Canadian correspondence course in journalism two years ago. "It was one of those courses that you find on matchbook covers," he laughed. "It wasn't very deep, but it helped pass the time." He said the course, which he eventually completed, became almost impossible to follow because it required that he analyse coverage in Canadian newspapers, to which he has only very limited access in São Paulo.

David says he listens to his shortwave radio every day to find out what is happening in the world, watches late-night Brazilian television ("You can learn a lot from a society by watching its late-night TV."), and interviews his Brazilian fellow prisoners to find out about life in the outback regions of the country. He subscribes to *The Economist*, which he says he reads for international news. He also reads *Newsweek* "for its lifestyle articles" and *Maclean's* for news on Canadian politics. I asked him why a committed leftist like himself would bother with *The Economist*, which is very conservative and supports issues, such as free trade, that are anathema to most leftists. David responded that he reads the magazine because it's written for the world's business elite and that the business elite needs good information upon which to base multi-million-dollar investments. It's true, he says, that he doesn't always agree with the magazine's point of view, but he finds the writing excellent. David confesses he has turned into a bit of an anglophile during his years in jail, listening to the BBC regularly on shortwave and immersing himself in British novels because he never really had the chance to read fiction when he was involved in politics in Canada.

In an interview in October 1994, David enthusiastically discussed Jorge Castañeda's *Utopia Unarmed*, which I had sent him in the mail. He told me he was so taken with the dense book that he finished it in a very short time, but that he didn't really agree with Castañeda's prescriptions for modernizing the Latin American left to make it more reformist and social-democratic.

David made his first foray into political activism in 1983 when he campaigned for the release of the Squamish Five, members of a small British Columbia–based anarchist group motivated by a concern over the dangers of nuclear weapons and pollution. Known as Direct Action, the group announced their concerns in 1982 by bombing a hydroelectric facility on Vancouver Island and later the Litton Systems Canada plant in Toronto. The Squamish Five were taken into custody by police in 1983 at a fake highway construction roadblock in B.C. Although there is little evidence to suggest that David was formally involved with the group, he campaigned vigorously for their release, so much so that RCMP agents saw fit to start a file on the twenty-year-old activist.

"It's true there are no criminal charges against David in Canada, but we do have criminal information," said a Canadian intelligence official who did not want to be identified. "The RCMP and later CSIS made note of David's actions so that they could be retrieved later. A lot of the stuff that they gather about demonstrations and protests never makes it into a file. For some reason someone was interested enough in him to find out who he was, where he came from, and why he was campaigning for the release of the Squamish Five."

David also joined the Coalition Against Bill C-157, formed in 1983, when the federal government, through that enabling legislation, was setting up CSIS.

Although the Lamont and Spencer families admit that there probably are CSIS files on both David and Christine, the information only serves political ends and is not to be trusted, they say. Marilyn Lamont said that officials in External Affairs made up their minds that her daughter and David were guilty as soon as they were arrested in Brazil, based on the information in the CSIS files. Mrs. Lamont also said that David and Christine's CSIS files only prove that they were victims of a right-wing conspiracy to discredit the left. "The decision was made on information obtained entirely from the Brazilian police and courts and on information contained in CSIS files which remain secret.... If you are involved in any left-wing activities, if you've signed an antigovernment or antinuclear petition, if you are active in union work, if you've attended a protest against the government or police, there will be a

CSIS file on you," Mrs. Lamont said in an interview with Kim Bolan printed in the *Vancouver Sun*.

Sometime in 1983, David's father received a phone call from his son, who was at the time heading out west, to tell him that he had made friends "with some people from Nicaragua." Mr. Spencer says he wasn't surprised to hear that David was devoting much of his time working in Central American solidarity groups in Vancouver.

"When I used to spout off about being born very poor, David would always get really angry and say that it wasn't fair that people should have a hard time in life because of birth," said Mr. Spencer. "His heart went out to those people [the Central Americans] and they had a great influence on him."

In addition to helping Christine organize fundraisers for the FMLN in El Salvador, David helped to polish the English translations of bulletins from Radio Farabundo Marti, an underground radio station in El Salvador. Mr. Spencer noted that his son couldn't speak Spanish at that point.

In Vancouver David took on odd jobs to support himself while he worked full time for the El Salvador Information Office, a resource centre that offered information on FMLN activities in El Salvador and news on human rights violations. He also contributed articles to *Conexiones*, a small bimonthly magazine that published news about Latin America. And he contributed to a weekly bulletin in the magazine *El Salvador On-Line*, which consisted of information culled from the radio broadcasts on Radio Farabundi Marti. Friends say that David spent a lot of time trying to convince the mainstream media to run stories on human rights abuses in El Salvador.

"The thing that always struck me about David was his extreme commitment," said Stephen Stewart, a Canadian activist who is on the editorial collective of *Conexiones*. "Whenever there was any fundraiser or event tied to Latin America, David would be there helping, handing out pamphlets."

Stewart, who met David in Vancouver in 1985, said that David lived near Commercial Drive but did not fall in with the trendy left crowd. "I used to laugh because here were all of these ultraradical people wearing black and probably turning up their noses at David, who was always carrying a briefcase. He was a well-dressed and well-combed young man, who was probably doing more for Latin America than any of them would ever do."

According to Stewart, who lives in Vancouver but travels frequently to Latin America, David still contributes the occasional piece about

Brazil to *Conexiones* and has even offered suggestions on new editorial directions for the magazine. "He felt that we were still focusing too much on Central America and should be concentrating more on South America, which David felt was of crucial global strategic importance," he said. Stewart lost touch with David when he left with Christine for Toronto in early 1988 to work for the branch of the El Salvador Information Office there. Christine got a job at the CN Tower to support herself and David. The two moved on briefly to Ottawa before leaving for Managua the following year.

David has been described by his friends, his family, and Canadian diplomats in Brazil as extremely committed to his political beliefs. But at the same time he is very critical of and under no illusions about the Latin American left. In one discussion, he readily criticized some of the left's activities in Cuba, El Salvador, Nicaragua, and Brazil. When I told him that I was interested in his case as it pertained to the militant left in Latin America, he gave me a puzzled look and said: "We mean nothing in the overall history of the Latin American left. Christine and I are just two drops of water in the bucket."

Christine, on the other hand, appears to be more of a doctrinaire leftist — some might even call her dogmatically politically correct — in her beliefs. Friends say that she is very intelligent but not as much of an independent thinker as David. "When they were in Latin America, Christine didn't make a move without consulting David first," said one of Christine's friends in Vancouver.

Whereas David is worldly and interested in a wide variety of topics, Christine seems to me to be more narrow in her frame of reference. For someone who now has quite a bit of experience in Latin America, she speaks in the same kind of dated generalities that characterize the world-view of many of her supporters in Canada.

In our first interview, Christine spent some four hours discussing the world as it affected her. Brazil was nothing more than "a xenophobic, hysterical place, riddled with corruption." She and David had known nothing about the kidnapping and had been used as pawns by São Paulo politicians to discredit the Brazilian left, she said. During another interview, she asked me not to write this book. "What purpose would it serve us?" she said.

But what she lacks in analytical ability, she makes up for in sheer persistence — some might call it stubbornness. Her friends say she is relentless, committed, and used to getting things done her way.

Canadian diplomatic officials say that these qualities have resulted in some friction between her and her Brazilian lawyers and the warden at the Penitenciária Feminina, where she is imprisoned.

In a 1990 letter to his sister Bev, David said that it was this subtle ability to get her way that endeared Christine to him when they were dating in Canada. Writing about a trip he and Christine made to the Pacific National Exhibition while they were still living in Vancouver, David says that she managed to convince him to ride the rollercoaster, something he'd had a deep-seated phobia about since he was a child. According to David, Christine had been threatening to do this for months, and although when the moment arrived he told her that stepping onto a rollercoaster would be like making a descent into hell, he reluctantly agreed. It was at that moment, wrote David, that he knew he had to be in love with Christine.

"Christine is subtle and persistent when it comes to getting her way," he wrote. "Looking back, it was the rollercoaster incident which convinced me I must be in love with Christine. It was the only thing approaching a logical explanation I could think of to explain how any woman could have gotten me on a rollercoaster without the aid of a firearm."

Even though they were familiar with Christine and David's resolve and commitment to Latin America's oppressed, many of their friends were shocked when they saw the lithe brunette and the earnest, bespectacled autodidact on their television screens on December 17, 1989, stepping gingerly through the gates of the suburban São Paulo house where terrorists had been holding one of Brazil's wealthiest men.

"I was sitting at the breakfast table, reading the newspaper.... When I opened the page and saw a picture of them, I was completley shocked," Brent Anderson, a former roommate and co-worker of David's at the El Salvador Information Office, told journalist Kim Bolan. "Just like everyone else in the Salvadoran community, I was totally shocked."

Patrick Jordan, the Vancouver jeweller who had employed Christine, was also amazed. He was later to find out that Christine and David had forged his signature on letters of introduction bearing his company's name to rent at least two safe houses in São Paulo. "I couldn't believe that she could have organized something as complicated as a kidnapping. I was blown away," he said. However, he later recalled that when Christine and David had returned to Canada for a visit with their families in the summer of 1989 before heading off again to Latin America, he was struck by some of Christine's odd requests. She was particularly interested in how to move money between different countries. When he asked her why she wanted to know, she replied vaguely that somebody had asked her to find out.

At least two people who knew Christine well in Canada mentioned to me that her case reminded them of John le Carré's *The Little Drummer Girl*. In the novel, le Carré delves into the mind of a middle-class British actress named Charlie and tries to examine why she becomes a terrorist. For le Carré, the process is mixed up with guilt, genuinely good intentions to help the world's oppressed, a frustration with the inadequacy of legitimate means to bring about social and political change, and a desire for adventure.

"Christine saw the so-called democratization of the Latin American countries as being ineffectual in producing social improvement. Her motivation visa vi [sic] Latin America has been to better the lot of the oppressed," wrote the Lamonts in a letter to Humphreys.

The same kind of frustration is noted in Charlie's desire to help the world's oppressed as a group of Israeli terrorists try to win her to their cause.

> *She had a picture of herself beating her puny, girl's fists uselessly against a huge wood door, while her strident voice battled with dangerously unconsidered slogans.... "We're fighting a different war, Mart — the real one. It's not power against power, East against West. It's the hungry against the pigs. Slaves against oppressors. You think you're free, don't you? That's because someone else is in chains. You eat, someone starves. You run, someone has to stand still. We have to change that whole thing."*

But you would be hard-pressed to find anyone in Vancouver who would use the word "terrorist" to describe Christine Lamont. "I know my sister," Heather Lamont told a *Toronto Star* reporter after Christine was arrested in Brazil. "She's a caring person. She's no terrorist."

Still, even her staunchest supporters are at a loss to explain what she was doing in Latin America in 1989 or how she and David got involved with the likes of Humberto Paz and with the kidnapping in Brazil.

"Let's look at some of the ethics of this," said Ronald Newton, a professor of Latin American studies at Simon Fraser University. In 1987 he taught a Latin American history course that Christine enrolled in but never completed. "When you are fighting for social justice and you have exhausted all legitimate, democratic means, then what do you do? In Latin America, you join the armed struggle. Some people might call that terrorism, but at what point does terrorism become absolutely necessary?"

Despite David's commitment to his political beliefs, his friends also hesitate to call him a terrorist. "My personal feeling is that there is a possibility that David could have been involved with a clandestine organization," said Stephen Stewart. "A lot of these groups are divided into cells and if you got involved that deeply you would probably know better not to ask any questions."

Moreover, many of Christine and David's supporters on the militant left in Canada and Latin America told me outright that they saw nothing wrong with kidnapping what they describe as a member of Brazil's "morally repugnant elite" and holding him in an underground cell for six days to raise money to finance the struggle for social justice in the region.

"You've got to attack the cause of social injustice," said a Canadian who had been active with the FMLN during the civil war in El Salvador. "David and Christine knew this from the start. They trusted their comrades 100 per cent. They knew that the causes of injustice were the forces of imperialism and wealth."

The Canadian, whom I will call Stan, did not want to be identified because he was sure that CSIS agents were watching him. We met in an abandoned warehouse in Toronto after he spent three days "checking me out" to find out if it would be safe to talk to me. He asked me several times if I was "wired" and agreed to talk only after making sure that I wasn't taping the conversation. "And by the way, if you write anything that discredits the movement, we'll get you."

I couldn't figure out if this was a self-aggrandizing bluff or an actual threat. Either way, it was more of the secret-society cult mentality of Latin America's militant left that is useless to question.

I asked Stan, who is a successful businessman, why he got involved in the FMLN, and why David and Christine, whom he obviously knew, would get themselves mixed up with terrorists. He admitted that he was at first drawn to the cause by an overwhelming desire for "fun" and adventure and a feeling that his life in Canada was extremely empty. "To the uninitiated, the secret world is of itself attractive. Simply by turning on its axis, it can draw the weakly anchored to its centre," writes le Carré in *The Little Drummer Girl*. Stan said that when he was working for the FMLN, he felt loved and needed.

SEE NO EVIL

Le Carré explores this sense of belonging as one of Charlie's main motivations for becoming a terrorist. "Do you think we do not understand that your politics are the externalisation of a search for dimensions and responses not supplied to you when you most needed them? We're your friends, Charlie. We're not mediocre, bored, apathetic, suburban, conformist. We want to share with you, to make use of you."

Stan said he volunteered to work for the rebels because he was deeply moved by their struggle and by the suffering of the people he befriended.

"You really learn to respect people who have nothing but a body full of bullet holes," he said, adding that he was particularly influenced by an FMLN fighter who had twelve bullet holes in his body and an unwavering passion for social justice. "When people like that become your friends, you'll do anything for them, without questioning what it is you are doing. I trusted the people I worked with 100 per cent."

Indeed, there are several cases of North Americans and Europeans, known as *internacionalistas*, volunteering to join the struggle in Central America and perhaps getting a little bit more than they bargained for. In 1990, a young American woman named Rebecca Tarver was found wounded in a rebel zone outside San Salvador. The military and U.S. officials suspected that Tarver, who had been shot in the head and leg, was a soldier for the FMLN.

"There is no question she was fighting with the guerrillas in a combat zone," a U.S. Senate aide told a reporter from the *Washington Times*. Tarver said that she was working as a freelance journalist for Salpress, an FMLN information agency based in Mexico, and was wounded in the crossfire between government troops and FMLN guerrillas. However, U.S. officials said Tarver was recruited by the FMLN in 1980 and known by the code name "Clara." Although she vigorously denied that she had engaged in any combat, U.S. and Salvadoran officials were convinced she was "deeply involved in FMLN activities."

A year earlier, another young American woman named Jennifer Jean Casolo had been detained by the Salvadoran military after they discovered a large cache of arms buried in her backyard. Casolo, who described herself as a church worker, spent eighteen days in prison for stockpiling arms for rebels but was later released by a military judge for lack of evidence and deported. Although police found 213 blocks of TNT, 103 Soviet 60-mm mortar shells, 405 electrical detonators, 20,000 bullets for AK-47 and M-16 assault rifles, and Dragonov sniper rifles —

a pretty large haul — Casolo denied knowing anything about the arms, which belonged to the FMLN. Although she maintained that someone must have buried them in her backyard, press reports noted that her backyard was enclosed by a ten-foot-high stone wall, and anyone burying arms there would have to bring them through her living room.

"Moreover, the arsenal was contained in sacks tied with twine. Was it only coincidence that the authorities discovered a letter addressed to 'Jeny' asking that she purchase 'another twenty sacks and a bag of twine?'" asked the *Arizona Republic*.

When she returned to the United States, Casolo was heralded as a heroine by the militant left and embarked on a country-wide speaking tour. She said that El Salvador's Marxist guerrillas, who at the time had been labelled terrorists by the Pentagon and the State Department, were "not a terrorist" force but were killing civilians in order to further the cause of "economic justice."

"If you were an *internacionalista* in El Salvador during the civil war, you learned to keep your mouth shut and not ask any questions," said a U.S. photographer who made her career covering the civil war in El Salvador. "If someone told you to take a box of stuff across a border, you just did it without question. Unfortunately, there are elements of the left in Central America that used people's naivete to further their political ends."

In a 1992 interview in *Saturday Night* magazine, Christine was to offer much the same explanation for why she did not question her housemates' activities in Brazil.

"The judge didn't take into consideration that we were working in solidarity, that we knew people who knew these people and you're not going to be investigating them. You're going to have confidence in them. You're not going to go down with a flashlight in the middle of the night and ask is that bookcase really a bookcase. Because you know what they are like. You know what their work is like, what their conception of justice is, that they're good people."

In fact, many people I spoke to in Latin America were certain that this was precisely what had happened to David and Christine. They had been taken in by these "good people."

"Poor kids," said Australian journalist Vivien Altman, who has covered events in El Salvador and Central America since the early 1980s. "It really looks like those two were horribly used."

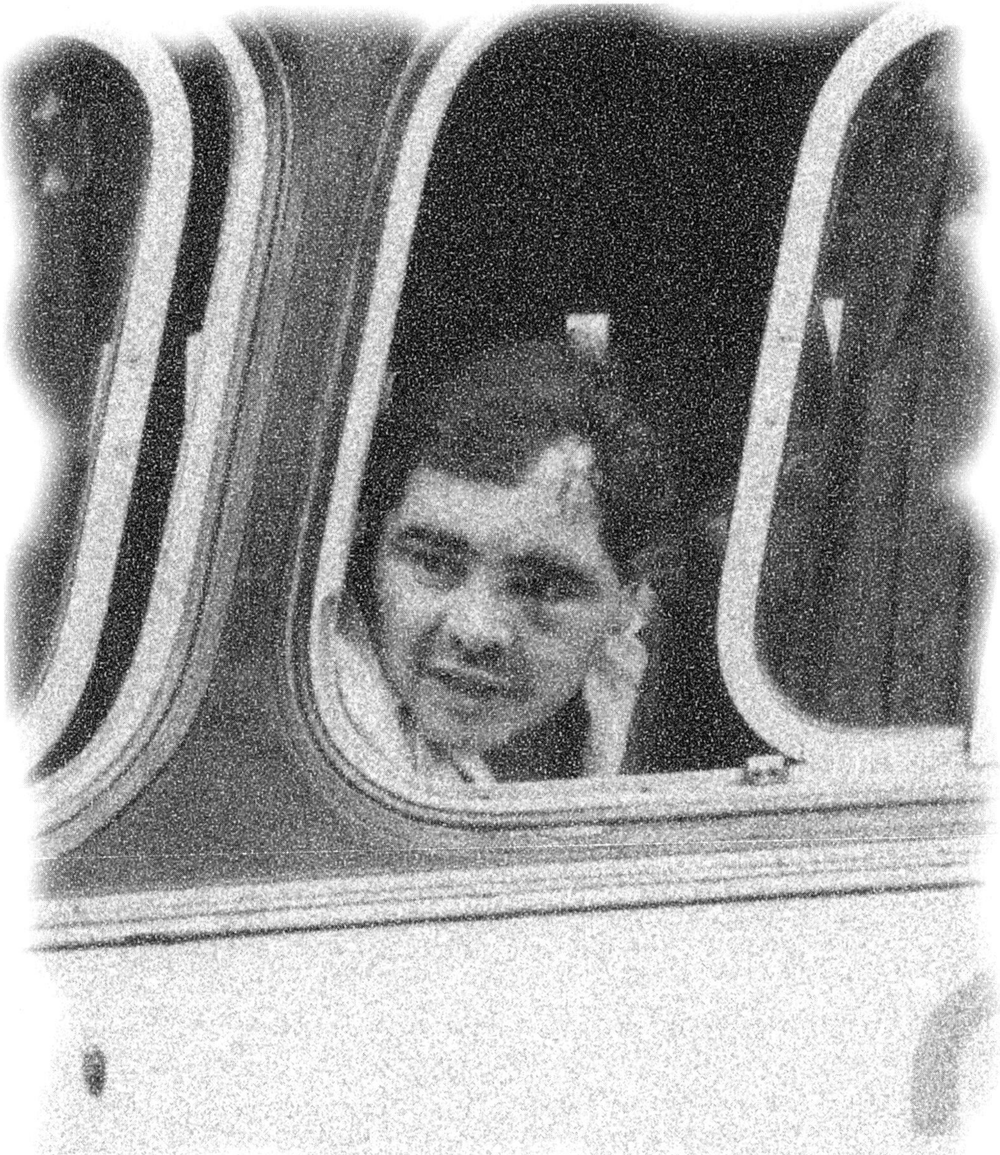

Three

Things fall apart; the centre cannot hold;
Mere anarchy is loosed upon the world,
The blood-dimmed tide is loosed and everywhere
The ceremony of innocence is drowned;
The best lack all conviction, while the worst
Are full of passionate intensity.
William Butler Yeats, "The Second Coming"

In "The Second Coming," Yeats was writing about the end of a cycle of history and the confusing beginning of a new one that was dominated by the Bolshevik Revolution in Russia and the rise of fascism elsewhere in Europe.

But his observations might well be applied to Latin America in the late 1980s, arguably the most pivotal period in its modern history. Latin American politics have always been labyrinthine, but they were particularly so in the late 1980s, and it is almost impossible to understand the actions of *internacionalistas* like David and Christine without setting them in the context of the time and place.

In November 1989, a month before Christine and David were to make headlines in Brazil, things fell apart for the left around the world. The fall of the Berlin Wall signalled the collapse of the left's "centre" — communism and the socialist bloc. The end of the Cold War had devastating effects for the armed left in Latin America. Not only did many militant groups lose financing from traditional support centres, such as the Soviet Union and Cuba, but many also lost the Marxist–Leninist grounding that had guided the majority of dissidents in the region. Although the conditions that had initially provoked armed struggle in many countries after the Second World War — social injustice, growing violence, huge disparities between rich and poor — remained pretty much unchanged in many places since the late 1950s, those on the militant left in Latin America found themselves disoriented and without an ideological axis.

"For the left, the fall of socialism in the Soviet Union and Eastern Europe represents the end of a stirring, effective, nearly century-old utopia," writes Jorge Castañeda in *Utopia Unarmed*.

> *Indeed, the very notion of an overall alternative to the status quo has been severely questioned. It is now practically impossible for the left to think outside the existing parameters of present-day Latin American reality. Moreover, the idea of revolution itself, central to Latin American radical thought for decades, has lost its meaning.*

Cuba, which since the 1959 revolution had been the guiding force for much of the Latin American left, had fallen on hard times. In the late 1980s, the Soviet Union, grappling with its own political and economic crises at home, had cut off much-needed foreign aid and subsidies to its Caribbean ally and last enclave of communism in the Western hemisphere. Life for ordinary people on the island became a daily grind with severe shortages of everything from gasoline to basic foodstuffs. Energy was strictly rationed, and the Castro regime urged Cubans to ride bicycles to work. More than ever, many Cubans were resorting to desperate means to get off the island and seek a better life in the United States. With such depressing living conditions, many Cubans found Fidel Castro's hardline brand of Marxism difficult to stomach.

"Were people just fleeing Cuba because of the shortages?" writes U.S. journalist Andres Oppenheimer, who spent nearly half a year in Cuba researching his 1992 book, *Castro's Final Hour.*

> *Judging from the statements of many middle-class rafters after their triumphant arrival in Miami, ideological fatigue had also been a major factor in their decision to flee. Ricardo Presas Grau, a young physician who fled on a tractor inner tube, told me he had felt asphyxiated by the regime's Communist propaganda. In light of the world collapse of Marxism, Cuba's official credo was harder than ever to swallow.*

Ironically, self-described freedom fighters Christine and David arrived to bring "democracy" and "social justice" to Latin America at a time when ideological fatigue was crippling the left throughout the region.

With the decline of the left, the biggest revolution sweeping Latin America in the late 1980s was neoliberal in scope. Chile, Mexico, and Argentina were at the forefront of the struggle to carry out an International Monetary Fund–sponsored plan to put their economic houses in order by creating freer markets, cracking down on runaway inflation, privatizing money-losing national industries and streamlining bloated and often corrupt public sectors.

According to Castañeda:

> *Free-market policies, wide-open trade and investment approaches, and total reliance on the private sector came to be seen as a foolproof recipe for economic success in Latin America. This belief was buttressed by the perception that these policies had worked in countries like the United States and Britain, and that they were also responsible for the Asian success stories. Therefore, the shift from state-sponsored, protected, inward-looking, and subsidized economic development to the "free-market" model was already under way in Latin America before the collapse of socialism. However, the collapse accelerated it and enhanced the attractiveness of the alternative....*

Mexico, an economic powerhouse, was poised to enter into a free trade agreement with the United States and Canada. Chile, whose economy underwent a sweeping overhaul under General Augusto Pinochet in the 1970s and 1980s with the guidance of University of

Chicago economist Milton Friedman, developed the fastest-growing economy in the region. For the first time in almost two decades, this new Latin American dynamo was throwing its borders wide open to foreign investment and offering the added bonus of political stability.

In Argentina, Peronist Carlos Saul Menem swept to victory in July 1989 and set about reforming the Argentine economy. With the aid of his Harvard-trained finance minister Domingo Cavallo, he cracked down on runaway inflation. The Cavallo Plan, a ground-breaking anti-inflation measure that saw the Argentine currency pegged one to one with the U.S. dollar, brought an end to hyperinflation in the country, which had been hovering near 80 per cent per month when Menem took office. Cavallo put tight curbs on federal spending and began an ambitious program of privatizing money-losing and inefficient state companies.

In Bolivia, Harvard economist and whiz kid Jeffrey Sachs, who was acting as an economic adviser to the Bolivian government, stemmed hyperinflation that had run at 24,700 per cent per year in 1985. In Peru, president Alberto Fujimori cracked down on terrorism and instituted a series of tough neoliberal reforms that have recently turned the country into one of the region's foreign investment hot spots. In 1994, Peru was one of South America's strongest-performing countries with economic growth topping 8 per cent.

Despite the macroeconomic success of these reforms in fuelling growth and attracting foreign investment, Latin America's traditional problems of poverty and corruption refused to go away. In 1990 delegates at a United Nations conference in Quito, Ecuador estimated that 62 per cent of — or 270 million — Latin Americans lived in a state of poverty. In some countries, the situation was growing steadily worse.

Even in the more prosperous countries of the region, poverty remained a black mark on an otherwise healthy macroeconomic picture. In Argentina, where the social safety net is tenuous at best, pensioners were staging protests on the steps of the finance ministry in downtown Buenos Aires, demanding an increase in their $150 U.S. monthly pensions in a country where a cup of coffee had shot up to as much as $4. Despite the protests of the pensioners, Domingo Cavallo refused to increase the pensions for fear of fuelling inflation. Federal money had to remain tight if the plan was actually going to work, he said.

Brazil, which has been slow off the mark to reform its economy, was suffering from a deep recession and hyperinflation when Fernando Affonso Collor de Mello was elected president in 1989. In the 1980s, thousands of migrants from the country's impoverished northeast, where the local oligarchies still control most of the land and therefore most of the wealth, were streaming into large urban centres in Brazil's industrialized south in search of work and a better standard of living. Most of the migrants ended up in the *favelas*, or shantytowns, which continue to grow at an alarming rate in Rio de Janeiro and São Paulo. The country's widening disparity between rich and poor earned it the nickname *Bel India*. Analysts say that while some Brazilians enjoy a standard of living similar to that in Belgium, more than one third of the population of 150 million live in India-like states of poverty.

Violence was increasing in the *favelas*, which have always been dominated by drug trafficking gangs. Residents increasingly found themselves caught in the crossfire between police and drug gangs and, on some nights, Rio and São Paulo turned into armed camps, with gang members lobbing grenades from hillside shantytowns and local police calling upon the assistance of the military to contain the violence.

Ranilton Lima, a photographer for O *Povo Na Rua*, a tabloid that documents Rio's most violent crimes, told me that it wasn't unusual for the newspaper to photograph fifty dead bodies on a particularly violent weekend in greater Rio de Janeiro. There were 6,293 homicides in Rio in 1993 alone, according to statistics from the city's Civil Police. Many of the dead were caught in gun battles between rival drug trafficking gangs.

Elected with so much hope in Brazil's first direct elections in nearly three decades, Collor faced a country on the verge of chaos when he took office in 1990. Inflation was running at more than 80 per cent per month and 35 million Brazilians lived below the official poverty line, which in Latin America's largest nation meant that they were not earning a minimum salary. At the time a minimum salary would have been roughly equivalent to $80 U.S. per month. Sixty-five per cent of the population had an income of one, or less than one, minimum wage, said Brazilian social scientist Helio Jaguaribe. In what was arguably Latin America's richest and most industrialized country, an estimated 20 million Brazilians were going hungry every day and 5 million school-aged children never saw the inside of a classroom. In 1993, Brazilian composer Caetano Veloso compared the poverty of many Brazilians to the situation in the poorest country in the Western hemisphere. In the song "Haiti," Veloso and fellow Brazilian composer Gilberto Gil surprised an entire nation with their damning declaration: *"Haiti é aqui.* Haiti is here. Nobody's a citizen here.... Think of Haiti. Pray for Haiti. This is Haiti."

The economic situation in Brazil was so bad that kidnappings of wealthy and even middle-class Brazilians started to increase at an alarming rate. In large urban centres, criminals, most of them tied to the drug trade, began kidnapping as a way of obtaining quick cash. When Collor launched a tough anti-inflation shock plan in March 1990, freezing bank deposits for eighteen months, small-time kidnappings went through the roof. Rio sociologist Alba Zaluar said that drug traffickers, many of whom buy drugs on consignment, were in need of quick cash after their bank accounts were frozen by what came to be known as the Collor Plan. Brazilian industrialists and owners of small businesses were kidnapped for ransoms that ranged between $1,000 and millions of dollars. In Rio de Janeiro alone, police investigated 39 kidnappings in 1989, 93 in 1990, 84 in 1991, and 146 in 1992.

Collor argued that the best way to crack down on violence and poverty in Brazil was to reform the economy and impose the same free-market reforms that were sweeping other large industrialized nations in the region. Unfortunately, many of his reforms were to become mired in corruption and political infighting. By the time he was impeached in September 1992 for his involvement in one of the biggest influence-peddling scandals in Brazilian history, many of the country's long-overdue economic reforms were on hold and inflation was edging up to more than 1 per cent per day. Brazil became known as Latin America's slow man, dragging down the economic output and growth of the entire region.

In addition to the free-market revolution that swept the Americas, the 1980s in Latin America saw many countries throw off repressive military regimes in favour of democracy. But democracy, which arrived with remarkably little bloodshed in many countries, came with a price. It was often a result of political arm-twisting and dangerous compromise.

In Chile, a country dominated for seventeen years by the brutal dictatorship of General Pinochet, a civilian leader was elected president following a plebiscite that effectively removed the general from office in 1988. Elections were called for the following year. However, while Patricio Aylwin, the country's new president, enjoyed a peaceful transition to power in 1990, the General insisted upon rewriting the constitution so that he could remain commander-in-chief of the armed forces until his retirement in 1997. He also made sure that his colleagues in the military, responsible for a myriad of human rights abuses and thousands of "disappearances" of leftists and other opponents of his dictatorship in the 1970s and 1980s, would receive nothing less than a blanket amnesty. In an interview just before his term came to an end in 1993, Aylwin remarked that leading the country with Pinochet lurking in the background was a little bit like ruling Spain under the watchful eye of General Francisco Franco. Although Aylwin enjoyed a relatively peaceful tenure, General Pinochet publicly rattled his sabre on more than a few occasions.

So, although the late 1980s heralded the arrival of modernity in Latin America, democracy remained fragile, and there was still little resembling a social contract between citizens and their governments anywhere in the region.

In the introduction to her book *The Heart that Bleeds: Latin America Now*, American journalist Alma Guillermoprieto analyses Latin America in this modern era:

> *The questions not yet answered in Latin America have to do with a coherent future vision, not only of how the hugely unequal sectors of Latin American society can all modernize themselves into the same century — or, in these times of catapulting technical change, into the same decade — but of how they can modernize each other into the same ethical standard and a rough consensus regarding what it is that a modern society owes its citizens and what those citizens owe each other.*

While many regimes certainly had all of the outward appearances of healthy democracy, fraud and corruption were still a problem at the polls. This was evident in the Mexican elections of 1989 that saw the ruling Partido Revolucionário Institucional (PRI) sweep to victory. When I covered the Paraguayan elections in 1993 and the Salvadoran elections the following year, the best that a host of international observers could say about them was "Well, yes there were a few instances of fraud and irregularities, but *for Latin America* these were very free and fair elections." In Paraguay, which was holding free elections for the first time in 142 years, there were several incidents of fraud in the countryside. In the first free elections following the end of the civil war in El Salvador, irregularities in voters' lists prevented thousands of people in the countryside — as many as 15 per cent of the electorate — from casting their ballots on election day.

In Argentina, Mexico, and Peru, democratically elected leaders started to behave like nineteenth-century *caudillos*, or strongmen. Argentina's Carlos Menem and Mexico's Carlos Salinas de Gortari began to rule by decree. Menem stacked the Argentine Supreme Court with his political allies and lobbied for an amendment to the constitution that would allow him to run for a second term.

In Nicaragua, the Sandinista party, which had ruled the country since its revolutionary victory in 1979, promised to hold free elections in 1990. The Sandinistas, who had become known more for their corruption and disastrous experiments in Marxist–Leninist economic planning than for their revolutionary zeal, had been steadily losing support throughout the 1980s. A decade-long civil war against the U.S.-backed Contra rebels helped drain the country's public coffers and contributed to the Sandinistas' unpopularity.

As soon as they took power in 1979, the Sandinistas began to seize property and businesses, arguing that they were mismanaged. As American journalist Glenn Garvin notes of those early years in his book *Everyone Had His Own Gringo: The CIA and the Contras*, "Finally, anything of 'public utility' was fair game. As a result, the production of beans fell by 25 per cent and cotton by 33 per cent in the first three years of Sandinista rule. The declines rippled through the rest of the economy too." However, that didn't stop the Sandinistas from doubling the government's military spending from prerevolution levels.

The party was also marked by undemocratic tendencies. In 1986, President Daniel Ortega told *The Economist*, "We are not going to be so naive as to accept a civic opposition, because that doesn't exist anymore." Two years earlier Nelba Blandon, the director of censorship in the Interior Ministry, had this to say about the opposition newspaper, *La Prensa*, in an interview with the *New York Times*: "They [*La Prensa*] accused us of suppressing freedom of expression. This was a lie and we could not let them publish it."

With so many changes sweeping Latin America in the 1980s, the left found itself in disarray. However, it was still largely identified as a positive force in the fight for social justice, even if its methods of armed revolt were outdated.

Mexican writer Carlos Fuentes suggested that perhaps the end of the Cold War would have a positive impact on a redefinition of the left in Latin America:

> *Free from the alienation of Soviet policy and Marxist dogma, the modern left in Latin America has before it the obligation of promoting and defending social justice in a continent where the absolute number of poor continues to grow, as income distribution continues to deteriorate; where salaries shrink, jobs disappear, food becomes scarce, public services decline, security forces become autonomous and repressive in the name of the war on drugs, malnutrition and infant mortality rise dramatically.*

In a pamphlet printed in 1990, Brazil's reform-minded president Fernando Henrique Cardoso stuck with a more traditional view. "The left means being against the existing social order, the right, in its favour," wrote the sociologist, who had been one of Latin America's leading leftist intellectuals in the 1970s and 1980s.

But despite this reformist, social-democratic current sweeping the Latin American left in the late 1980s, pockets of radicalism remained. On January 23, 1989, a group of young and inexperienced guerrillas launched an attack on the La Tablada military barracks outside of Buenos Aires, and thirty-two people were killed. The group said they were trying to prevent a military coup in Argentina.

In November 1989, just as the world's attention was focused on the dismantling of the Berlin Wall, one of the world's most potent symbols of communism, the FMLN launched its final offensive in El Salvador. On November 11, the FMLN attacked the presidential palace, the private residence of President Alfredo Cristiani, and various military installations in San Salvador. The rebels also took up positions in and around the University of Central America and occupied various suburbs in the capital. There were simultaneous attacks in San Francisco Gotera, San Miguel, Chalatenango, Santa Ana, and Usulutan as the FMLN announced its intention to establish popular governments in eight of El Salvador's fourteen provinces. The government responded by declaring a state of seige and launching full-scale aerial assaults on many of the sites where the guerrillas were entrenched. More than 2,000 people died in that first week of fighting. By November 19, the FMLN was calling on the U.S. to withdraw support for the Cristiani government and announcing its willingness to renew peace talks. Cristiani refused.

Further complicating the situation in the country was the November 16 murder of six Jesuit priests and two women servants at the University of Central America in San Salvador by a group of thirty Salvadoran soldiers.

On November 26, following the crash of a Nicaraguan-registered plane in eastern El Salvador, Cristiani suspended all relations with Nicaragua and accused it of supplying anti-aircraft missiles to the FMLN. The plane was found to have twenty-four Soviet SAM surface-to-air missiles on board.

■

Against this backdrop, as 1989 was drawing to a close, a ragtag group of mostly washed-out Latin American revolutionaries met in São Paulo to revive the fortunes of a declining and ill-defined Latin American movement. But instead of waving revolutionary banners or waging the guerrilla struggle in the bush, they engaged in a much more cowardly act: they kidnapped one of Brazil's wealthiest men, stuck him in an underground cell, and prepared to wait for the ransom money.

■

Among foreign reporters and diplomats in Latin America, Managua has become an unofficial yardstick by which many of us classify truly miserable places. If a place is worse than Managua it has to be pretty awful. If it's just slightly better than Managua, then it's still pretty awful, if slightly more bearable. Before embarking on my first trip to Port-au-Prince last year, I asked one of my colleagues what the Haitian capital was like.

"It's really bad," he said.

"Yes, but is it as bad as Managua?"

He thought about it for a moment and then said that few places are as bleak or as depressing as Managua. Indeed, it's something about the unfinished quality of this city — the fact that it has no real centre, but appears to be a collection of grimy, impoverished suburbs with no street names — that depressed me when I was there in 1994. There's still a war-weary feeling about the city, even though the civil war, which pitted the ruling Sandinistas against the Contra rebels, officially ended in 1990.

The decaying remains of buildings stuck in the middle of median strips overgrown with weeds are a legacy of the neglect of Violetta Chamorro's government, a decade of Sandinista mismanagement and war, and rampant corruption during the dictatorship of the Somoza family. The buildings are left over from an earthquake in 1972 that killed 18,000 people and destroyed most of downtown Managua. The Nicaraguan government collected donations from international aid agencies to clean up the city after the earthquake, but much of that money appears to have made it no further than Anastasio Somoza's pocket. "Somoza pocketed much of the foreign aid that flowed into Nicaragua afterward, while he bought up property at bargain-basement prices from stricken owners," writes Glenn Garvin. "While Somoza kept the cash, the National Guard looted relief supplies and then sold them on the black market."

Among the first things the Sandinistas did when they swept to victory in 1979 was to dissolve the bicameral national congress and replace the National Guard with the Sandinista People's Army. This proved an unpopular measure in some quarters, and by 1981, two hundred former members of the National Guard, some of them still regarded as loyal supporters of the Somozas, had started organizing against the Sandinistas in the northern part of the country, counting on financial and military support from the Honduran government. The Contras later relied on U.S. aid to wage the war against the Sandinista government.

In addition to having to deal with the beginnings of a nasty civil war, the Nicaraguan government found itself reeling from a U.S. decision to suspend all financial aid and its demand that Nicaragua be boycotted by other lending agencies as well. The situation, coupled with the Sandinistas' mismanagement of the economy, brought Nicaragua close to the point of collapse. By 1988, the fiscal deficit was 27 per cent of GDP and inflation was running at 36,000 per cent per year.

Despite the civil war and the disastrous economic climate, Nicaragua became a hub for all sorts of *internacionalistas*. Tomás Borge, who headed the Interior Ministry during the Sandinista regime, turned the country into a haven for Basque terrorists and Latin American militants, many of whom arrived in Nicaragua in the 1980s to regroup, train, and escape international authorities.

Although they were reviled by many ordinary Nicaraguans, *internacionalistas* were welcomed with open arms by the Sandinista regime throughout the 1980s. In *Holidays in Hell*, U.S. journalist P.J. O'Rourke writes about one of his experiences in a market in Managua in 1987:

> *A little later I got a rotten onion thrown at me. I wheeled round, but there was nothing to see except a crowd of impassive faces.*
> *"What was that about?" I asked the translator.*
> *"Oh," he said, "Somebody thought you were an internacionalista, one of those Americans or Europeans who come down here to help the Sandys."*

David and Christine travelled to Nicaragua in January 1989 just as Sandinista leader and Nicaraguan president Daniel Ortega was promising to hold free elections that would be overseen by international observers from the UN and the Organization of American States (OAS). The country was particularly bleak when the two arrived because Ortega was in the process of imposing austerity measures to revive the economy and cut inflation. Government expenditures, including military spending, were to be reduced by 44 per cent.

Christine and David told their parents they were doing "solidarity work" in the human rights field and wrote pleasant letters home about their experiences in the war-torn Central American country. Friends and family say they lived in the country from January to June 1989, and Marilyn Lamont recalls that Christine called her a few times from Managua, asking her to send chocolate, Zero soap, and, on at least one occasion, money for rent.

"Chris's most frequent request was for clicker erasers," wrote Mrs. Lamont in a letter to her Ottawa lobbyist David Humphreys in 1990.

In another letter, the Lamonts wrote that while in Managua, Christine and David were working as translators for Salpress, the publicity arm of El Salvador's FMLN guerrillas, and that Christine's purpose in travelling to the country was "specifically to attempt to bring this information [of political and military repression] to the attention of the Western World through the media. She did this because she thought that if people were made aware of the injustices, that they would in fact be stopped."

Although Christine was carrying credentials for alternative media in Toronto, such as *NOW* magazine and radio station CKLN, she and David were virtually unknown among journalists in the alternative media. Foreign journalists who have covered the situation in Nicaragua since the early 1980s had no recollection of David and Christine. Moreover, friends in Canada said the two had a very rudimentary knowledge of Spanish, and many said that they were surprised to find out the two were working as translators in Managua.

"It was a real surprise to us when we saw that they had press credentials from *NOW*," said Michael Hollett, editor of *NOW*. "They are not known in the alternative news community. We were really, really surprised with this whole thing."

Felipe Vargas, a Salvadoran who worked as the Managua-based bureau chief for Salpress from 1987 to 1989, said he doesn't remember David or Christine working for the news organization in Managua.

"If they worked with Salpress I would certainly have known them," said Vargas, who is affiliated with the FPL, a faction of the FMLN, and teaches journalism in San Salvador. "I feel very sorry for them, but they didn't work with me." He added that "lots of people" said they had credentials for Salpress, but that they didn't necessarily work for the news organization.

Vargas is a well-known figure in the Salvadoran community in Canada. When he was in exile in Vancouver from 1981 to 1985, he was active in Salvadoran solidarity groups. Kim Bolan, the Vancouver journalist, who knows both Vargas and Christine and David, originally told me that Vargas did indeed know the couple in Canada. But when I spoke to her later, she said that she had talked to Vargas and that she had made a mistake. "Felipe Vargas told me he'd never seen them before in his life," she said.

So what were Christine and David doing in Managua? Nobody seems to know. Christine and David refuse to speak about that period except to say that they were involved in "human rights work." The return address on the letters they sent home to Canada, a post-office box in a neighbourhood known as "Carretera Sur, Km. 2.5 near Monte Tabor," was registered to a Salvadoran with ties to the FMLN. The Monte Tabor neighbourhood — if a collection of scattered mansions and fairly prosperous country homes overlooking the city of Managua can be called a neighbourhood — is home to many foreigners and wealthy Nicaraguans. Tucked into rolling green hills and fragrant forests on the outskirts of Managua, the area is a far cry from the congested, grimy, and impoverished centre of the city.

In 1994, equipped with a few photographs of Christine and David, I set out with two Nicaraguan journalists on a sweltering March afternoon to try to find their old house or anyone who might still remember them after five years. Roberto Orozco, a journalist who works for *La Prensa*, agreed to accompany me to the area because it had been the site of one of the largest bunkers that the FMLN handed over to the Nicaraguan government in 1993. The bunker had been dug out of the basement of a modest wooden house and had contained a cache of arms belonging to a Guatemalan guerrilla group. Still intact albeit stripped of arms, it turned out to be no more than 600 metres away from the house that Christine and David allegedly occupied.

It was hard work tracking down clues because the area is large and rambling, with some of the houses tucked away from view, off rough dirt roads. Many of those we spoke to said that they recognized the people in the photos, but that the area had been so full of *internacionalistas* five years earlier that it was difficult to make a positive identification. "They look like some of the people who used to buy ice from me, but I can't tell you anything more. I have no idea where they lived," said vendor Francisca Hernandez, who operates a small general store in a tin shack that also doubles as her home, just off the main highway in Monte Tabor.

Argentina Briceño, who lives and works as a housekeeper in the neighbourhood, said she remembered the two Canadians. She recognized the photo of David right away and after a few moments' hesitation even remembered his first name. They were the nice *canadienses*, who couldn't speak much Spanish but would give her a ride in their Toyota jeep every time they passed by. Mrs. Briceño said that the two had lived in a small red and white chalet a few metres up from her house five years before. She remembered that the year was 1989 because at the time she was in the final months of pregnancy with her first child.

"I remember them very well. They said they worked in *ayuda internacional* [international aid], but I'm not sure what that was," said Mrs. Briceño. She added that her two former neighbours had transported building materials, such as wood and tools, in the back of their jeep, which would always return mud splattered at the end of the day. "They said they worked with the poor in the mountain zones. Maybe they were building houses for the poor," said Mrs. Briceño. But they left quite suddenly in the middle of the year. "They were so nice, always asking about my health. I hope you find them."

The little red and white house shares a sizeable lot with a larger house. It looks like a doll's house with its neatly painted shutters and rows of flowers off the front porch. Inside, the place smells of mould and is covered in dust. Cobwebs cling to the wooden ceiling rafters. In the front room, there are cabinets of dusty books, most of them philosophical texts and Sandinista propaganda pamphlets in Spanish. From the tiny kitchen window you can see part of the city of Managua, spread out beyond green and brown hills.

Whether or not David and Christine actually lived here is impossible to ascertain. The area described as "Carretera Sur, Km 2.5 near Monte Tabor" is quite large, comprising at least 2.5 square kilometres, off the southern highway in the vicinity of Monte Tabor Church. In Managua, there are no street names, just vague directions for places.

Moreover, there are no rental records to speak of. Gioconda Belli, a Nicaraguan writer who used to work for the Sandinistas, bought the house "sometime in 1989," but says the foreign couple living there was gone by the time she took possession of the property.

It is also impossible to say with any certainty just what Christine and David were doing in Central America at the time or how they could afford to buy or even rent a jeep on the monthly allowance that Christine was receiving from her parents. Interpol, the international policing organization based in Lyons, says that the two were training at guerrilla camps in Nicaragua and possibly in Cuba. "They received specialized training in terrorism while they lived in Managua," said Romeu Tuma, Jr., a São Paulo police officer and vice-president of Interpol for Latin America. His father used to direct the regional office of the organization. "They learned how to use weapons and were trained in intelligence gathering. Christine received emergency medical training."

The Lamonts say the theory that their daughter was participating in some kind of terrorist summer camp in Nicaragua or Cuba is not only unsubstantiated but ludicrous. "This must have been the place where Marilyn could phone and say, 'Could I speak to Chris Lamont, please,' and get her on the line in a few minutes," Dr. Lamont wrote in a letter in 1990.

David and Christine deny that they were doing any of this in Nicaragua. "It's all a really sick fiction," Christine told me. But neither will elaborate on what they were doing in Nicaragua for six months in 1989.

Although David and Christine had devoted much of their time up to this point to solidarity work for the FMLN in El Salvador, they say they stayed exclusively in Nicaragua and did not visit the war-torn country. Since the FMLN was receiving aid from the Sandinistas and there was a large Salvadoran community in Managua, it would seem strange if at some point David and Christine did not cross over to El Salvador via Honduras. Such a trip, probably through rebel-controlled territory on the border with Honduras, would not have been difficult to organize through their FMLN contacts in Managua or Tegucigalpa.

David's father is certain that his son did not visit El Salvador during this period. "I would really be surprised if David went to El Salvador because it was essentially going behind enemy lines," said Bill Spencer, adding that David called his family once a month from Managua. "We talked about that when he called and I told him to stay away from El Salvador."

On the occasions that I spoke with David and Christine in São Paulo, they both made a point of emphasizing that they had not been to El Salvador in 1989. However, a *Miami Herald* reporter claims that David and Christine travelled first to El Salvador in early 1989 to do social and human rights work before settling in Nicaragua. Futhermore, the Nicaraguan police report on the bunker explosion in Managua states that two receipts from souvenir shops in San Salvador in Christine's name were found in the bunker. The report notes that Nicaraguan police asked their Salvadoran colleagues to verify the authenticity of the receipts and the response was positive.

Christine and David returned to Canada in mid-1989 for a three-week visit. While they were in Vancouver, David's mother died suddenly and David went to Moncton for the funeral. "I'm thankful she died then and wasn't around to witness the stuff of the last five years," said Bill Spencer. "It would have killed her."

David and Christine headed back to Latin America in late June. According to a 1992 article by journalists Kim Bolan and Augusta Dwyer in *Saturday Night*, to finance their trip, they sold the car that Christine's parents had given to her.

And this time they had taken a precaution that was later to cast suspicion on them. It was suggested to them by someone they had worked with in the Latin American refugee community. They took along a pair of extra passports in the names of Vancouver acquaintances who had never been involved in solidarity work — with pictures of Christine and David substituted for the real ones. Such passports just might get them out of a tight situation; in El Salvador, especially, the practice was fairly common among human-rights activists, even members of the press, in order to elude Salvadoran surveillance forces and death squads.

David and Christine acquired passports from two Vancouver friends, Lisa Lynn Walker and Paul Joseph Mendes. They told the CBC's *Fifth Estate* in 1992 that they were human rights workers and that everyone knows that human rights workers in Latin America need to travel on false passports to ensure their own safety.

"It's true we were breaking the law, but we were protecting ourselves," said Christine.

According to David and Christine's account in the *Saturday Night* article, while in Nicaragua, David was given the name of an Argentine leftist named Humberto Paz, who was recommended "as a good contact for human rights information" in Buenos Aires. Following a rather circuitous route that took them to Mexico, Panama, and Brazil, they ended up in Argentina in August 1989. David said he looked up Paz, who was at the time organizing a new "multinational political organization... that was going to organize across borders in support of the poor. The group was left wing and many of its members had suffered through political troubles in the past, so it was clandestine...."

According to Christine and David, Paz asked them to rent a house in São Paulo. In October 1989, they settled on one in a middle-class neighbourhood, and before they knew it members of Paz's organization arrived from Buenos Aires to share the rent: Paz's brother Horacio, a Brazilian named Raimundo Costa Freire, and a Chilean named Hector Collante Tapia became their house-mates. Christine and David said they spent their days at Portuguese classes, shopping, and sightseeing in South America's largest and most congested city. Sometimes, after classes, they would try to visit the city's *favelas* to practise their Portuguese and find out about the conditions of the poor, most of whom lived in the filthy and overcrowded shantytowns on the outskirts of this city of 17 million people.

Humberto Paz also arrived in São Paulo at about that time and asked David to put up money for some building supplies for the house because Tapia was going to make a wooden wardrobe with shelves. The construction reportedly lasted for more than a month, but David and Christine say that they knew nothing about it because they left the house each day at 7:00 a.m. for their Portuguese classes and returned late in the evening.

■

According to subsequent testimony at the trial, on Monday, December 11, 1989, Humberto Paz and two other men kidnapped Abilio Diniz as he was driving to work in the morning. At 8:10 Diniz set off for work as usual, but as he approached a quiet intersection in the upscale Jardim Europa neighbourhood where he lived, he was cut off by a Caravan station wagon, painted white with a red cross to make it look like an ambulance. Diniz said he immediately grabbed his gun, got out of his car, and "assumed the shooting position" but was, momentarily distracted by a group of people driving a white Opala sedan. Before he could react, he was hit hard in the back of the head, possibly with the butt of a revolver. During the trip to their hide-out the kidnappers abandoned the Caravan near Diniz's house and bundled the supermarket magnate into a coffin, which was transported in a white Volkswagen Kombi minivan. Diniz said he lost consciousness as soon as he was struck on the back of his head, and the next thing he knew, he was lying in a dark, windowless cell.

Humberto Paz, the leader of the group, took part in the preparation and execution of the kidnapping. On December 11, he dressed up in the uniform of a Military Police officer. He was assisted by Chilean kidnappers Sergio Martin Olivares Urtubia and Ulisses Fernando Gallardo Acevedo, who were reportedly also in the Caravan. The three men bundled Diniz into it and then transferred him to the Kombi, which was waiting down the street and reportedly being driven by David. Diniz, unconscious until his arrival at the Praça Hachiro Miyazaki cell, was tied up and transported in a coffin in the Kombi to escape police detection.

Paz and the others took Diniz to the house on Praça Hachiro

SEE NO EVIL

Miyazaki, where he was held for the next six days in an underground cell that some of the group members had spent at least a month preparing, according to São Paulo police accounts. David and Christine say they continued with their daily routine and didn't notice anything out of the ordinary.

While Diniz was being held in the underground cell, a few members of the kidnap group sent a ransom note to his family, demanding $30 million U.S. A special division of the São Paulo Civil Police, known as Delegacia Anti-Sequestro (Anti-Kidnapping Division), moved heaven and earth to find him. Luck was on their side. When they discovered the abandoned Caravan near Diniz's house, they stripped the car and found a business card from a repair garage, Auto Eletrico Mecanica e Borracharia São Jorge, on Rua da Consolação in downtown São Paulo. They speculated that the card had slipped through the windshield ventilator.

"Their big mistake in the operation was getting mad at the mechanic who couldn't finish the repairs to the Caravan on time," said Officer Waldomiro Bueno Filho. He added that when the van needed repairs just before the kidnapping, the kidnappers were so angry with the mechanic for not keeping his promise to deliver the vehicle on time that they threw his business card at the dashboard. Bueno said that the mechanic's delay forced the kidnappers to put off the kidnapping for at least three days. It was originally planned for Friday, December 8, he said.

On December 12, a mechanic at the garage found the phone number that Pedro Lembach, one of the members of the kidnapping gang, had left when he brought the Caravan in four days earlier. This led police to a flat on Aureliano Coutinho, rented by Ulisses Fernando Gallardo Acevedo under the false name Pedro Segundo Solar Venegas. The police staked out the building and finally apprehended Acevedo, who assaulted Roberto Kawai, the police officer conducting the investigation. After a thorough search of the Aureliano Coutinho flat, police found a light bill for an apartment on Rua Charles Darwin in the Higienopolis neighbourhood, where they found "a large quantity of office material" that they suspected was used to make false identification documents.

The police then staked out the Charles Darwin flat and on December 13 captured Humberto Paz and Chileans Maria Emilia Badilla, Sergio Martin Olivares Urtubia, and Pedro Lembach. Police apprehended Paz and Badilla as the two were making their way to a Fiat parked outside the building. Badilla was carrying a ransom note addressed to Silvio Bresser Pereira, a close Diniz family friend who was acting as the family's chief negotiator in the kidnapping.

The five captured gang members were tortured by police to find out where Diniz was being held. Maria Emilia, aged forty-three at the time, later told the trial judge that she had been stripped naked, beaten on the head, and had electric shocks applied to her mouth, breasts, and vagina. She also said that she had salt poured down her throat, followed by large quantities of hot water. Five years later, she was reportedly still being treated for a lung infection.

At the trial, Sergio also described his torture in graphic detail:

They stripped me, threw me to the ground, then threw water over me and attached electric cables to my feet and my genitals and started to give me electric shocks. They kept asking me the same question, "Where's the house?" I couldn't answer because I didn't know what they were talking about. . . . They tied me to a wooden pole that they passed between my legs and arms and kept giving me electric shocks. This continued for a time, I can't be certain how long because I fainted.

One of the police officers who conducted the torture sessions said he was "impressed" by the resilience of the kidnappers, who at first refused to crack under pressure. "This cop told me that he couldn't believe how hardened these guys were. He couldn't believe that they didn't break down. He said he thought he was going to lose it," said Tony Pereira, an RCMP officer who was stationed in Brazil at the time and followed the São Paulo Civil Police investigation of the case.

At his cluttered office in the Department of Special Criminal Investigations in São Paulo, Officer Bueno told me that the police had no other option but to torture the five kidnappers. The police had learned that the other kidnappers, who were guarding Diniz at the house, had orders to kill their hostage if their plan went awry. In twenty-six years on the police force Bueno, a tall, mild-mannered officer with a pleasant disposition and a boyish face, has investigated forty-seven kidnappings.

"We had to make a choice," said Bueno, pausing to answer his telephones, which seemed to be constantly ringing during our three-hour interview. "It was either their lives or the life of Abílio Diniz."

Bueno offered me a sugar-free raspberry candy from an elegant tin. He had been nervously popping the red candy throughout the interview. Every time he paused to put a fresh one in his mouth, he became contemplative and fixed me with an expectant stare. Two of his four telephones were ringing off the hook again, but this time he made no move to answer them.

"Given the situation," he said, "what would you have done?"

■

Christine and David say that they didn't think anything was amiss until December 16 at about 5:00 a.m. when Humberto Paz rang the front doorbell of the house. How Humberto came to be there was part of an elaborate sequence of events.

After nearly three days of torture, Paz broke down and told police where the group was hiding Diniz. In the early morning of December 16, police surrounded the Praça Hachiro Miyazaki house. Paz, who accompanied the police team, convinced the two young and inexperienced police officers assigned to guard him that it would be better if he entered the house alone since his colleagues would probably be armed and there could be shooting. Handcuffed at the time, Paz awkwardly gave the doorbell three quick rings — the code that the kidnappers used with each other to indicate trouble. The two police officers testified that then David Spencer and Hector Tapia, who were heavily armed, opened the door, grabbed the police officers and pulled Paz inside. The police officers were eventually let go, but once inside, Paz didn't come out for thirty-six hours. The other kidnappers sawed his handcuffs apart, but were not able to take them off his wrists, and when Paz eventually surrendered, he was photographed still wearing them.

As Christine and David tell it, the bleary-eyed and startled members of the group were shocked to find two hundred police surrounding the house. In addition to Christine and David, Brazilian Raimundo Roselio Costa Freire, Hector Collante Tapia, and Humberto's brother Horacio were in the house when Humberto showed up at dawn.

For the next nerve-racking thirty-six hours police attempted to negotiate with Paz. They took their positions around the house and cut off the electricity to pressure the kidnappers into surrendering. At this point the kidnappers were forced to take Diniz out of his tiny cell to prevent him from suffocating because the underground room was ventilated twenty-four hours a day with the aid of the electrically powered stove exhaust in the ground-floor kitchen. According to Christine and David, they were completely unaware of Diniz's presence in the house until he was brought up from his cell, his wrists handcuffed behind his back and his feet tied up with a piece of rope. He was forced to lie down on the floor of the front room of the house, although later he was untied and allowed to sit in a chair.

Christine and David said that they did not surrender to police at that point because they were afraid they might be shot if they left the house.

The mood inside the house was tense and each member of the group, including Christine and David, reportedly carried weapons. They all pitched in frantically to build makeshift barricades by tearing apart the beds and leaning mattresses and dresser drawers against the windows. In the upstairs bathroom, they burned "a large quantity" of documents. Bueno and Kawai's video of the house shows a smoke-blackened toilet covered with ashes and charred remnants of documents scattered throughout the room. Bueno suspects that the group may have burned as much as one hundred kilograms of incriminating documents during the stand-off.

"They all went about with heavier weapons or at times with lighter weapons, except for Susana [Christine], whom I saw with a light weapon... and Modesto [David] also had a lighter weapon," said Diniz under cross-examination at the trial (the kidnappers called each other by aliases, at least in front of Diniz). From Diniz's testimony, the São Paulo trial court judge concluded that "It was clear that they all prepared, loaded, and carried weapons in the house during those thirty-six hours of negotiations."

David later told *The Fifth Estate* that he had carried a gun solely for defence purposes during the stand-off. "I will defend my life any way I can possibly do it and defend the life of the people I love, in this case Christine."

At some point during the stand-off, Humberto Paz lost his nerve, fired a few shots into the backyard, where a police officer was trying to scale a wall, and provoked a police response. A bullet came through a window and grazed Paz in the forehead. Diniz and members of the group, who had a small stash of surgical instruments and other medical supplies, helped to dress the wound.

None of the kidnappers trusted the São Paulo police. Everyone, including Diniz, was under the impression that if the police managed to break into the house they would all be killed, and Diniz's death would be blamed on the group. Paz now called for the presence of foreign diplomats and Cardinal Paulo Evaristo Arns, the leading human rights spokesman, to negotiate their surrender.

During his ordeal, Diniz says he sympathized with the kidnappers and was moved when Paz told him he had been tortured several times since becoming a political activist at the age of nineteen. Paz then tried to show Diniz his scars from his torture at the hands of the São Paulo police.

"I think kidnapping is barbarous, it's a terrorist act," said Diniz at a press conference after his release. "But I think torture is even more barbarous. Juan Carlos [Humberto Paz] said that he had been tortured three times. I had to insist that he not show me the parts of his body that had been affected. In a moment of great anger, I might be able to kill someone but I'd never be able to torture them. I promised them that if they gave themselves up, they wouldn't be tortured, but judged according to the law."

Diniz even offered to pay for the kidnappers' legal defence, a gesture that was later refused by the lawyers for the defence, who said they felt uncomfortable receiving money from the victim to pay for the defence of the accused. More cynical observers said that Diniz never had any intention of paying the kidnappers' legal fees. But, as with so many of the details of the case, we may never know the truth. Diniz has refused to talk about the kidnapping and will neither confirm nor deny that he ever paid any legal bills.

Most of the negotiations with police and diplomats took place through the slats of the open second-floor bathroom window as kidnappers held a gun to Diniz's head. Although Paz had first demanded an armoured car and an airplane as two of the conditions for the group's surrender, he eventually settled for Cardinal Arns's assurances that they would receive a fair trial and protection from any more torture. Cardinal Arns also said that he would see to it that the group secured the best human rights lawyers in São Paulo, and he called Belisario dos Santos and Marco Antônio Nahum, who were counsellors for the archdiocese of São Paulo. Both the lawyers and Cardinal Arns accompanied the kidnappers to the police station and stayed with them throughout their first night there to make sure there would be no further torture.

"The great fear these men had was basically that they would be tortured," said Diniz in his first public statement after he was released. "And between torture and death, they preferred death."

David later told *The Fifth Estate* about the horrible feelings of fear he experienced during the seige. "I had nightmares, in fact, many months after it happened. Not of the house itself, but of the feeling in the house of being surrounded, of being chased, of being cornered and then shot. It was like the most terrifying moment in a horror movie when you're waiting for the killer to jump out of the closet. That moment lasted for more than forty hours."

The nightmare ended when Paz finally decided to release Diniz, partly in return for Diniz's offer to pay for the group's defence and the promise of a fair trial. Following the accord with Cardinal Arns, the kidnappers held a meeting at which they all decided they would surrender with dignity. According to Diniz, all of them decided to take a bath and put on their best clothes, and before they left one of the kidnappers opened a bottle of wine to make a toast. Diniz said he didn't drink because he hadn't had any food and was not feeling well. "At that moment I understood that they were going to leave that house with a great deal of pride," Diniz told the *Jornal do Brasil*. "They made a point of walking out with their weapons raised in the air so that they could be photographed and filmed. I walked out last, thanking God that everything had ended so well for all of us."

Then came the scene that was to be played so often: the kidnappers, led by Christine and David, came out of the house in single file into the glare of lights from TV cameras. Along with Cardinal Arns and the diplomats, they took their places in a waiting police bus. Only then did a dazed Diniz stagger out of the gates of the driveway into the glare of the camera lights and into the arms of his distraught family members.

■

Christine and David, who claim they were completely disoriented during the whole ordeal, were charged with extortion by kidnapping, a crime that carries a sentence of eight to fifteen years in Brazil. (Additional charges of resisting arrest and forming a gang for criminal intent were ultimately ignored by the first judge — though not by the appeals court.) They were counselled by Nahum and dos Santos, their lawyers, not to say anything about the kidnapping. Nahum and dos Santos, who accompanied the kidnappers to the police station at Cardinal Arns's request, became Christine and David's lawyers by default. Perhaps due to the confusion of the situation, Christine, David, and their parents were pleased to retain two lawyers with such a good track record in human rights issues. At the time neither Christine and David nor their families gave much thought to their legal defence. Nahum and dos Santos defended the ten kidnappers as a unit, which immediately identified the two Canadians in the eyes of the Brazilian press as members of a gang of international terrorists.

But in the confusion of the kidnapping and the arrest, nobody seemed to be thinking very clearly. Christine and David were counting on the fact that they had no previous criminal record and looked like good, clean-cut Canadian kids. Trim and neatly dressed, they were in sharp contrast to their bedraggled, overweight, and scruffy Latin American counterparts, who really did look like terrorists. Who would ever believe that two nice Canadians were involved in terrorist activities? Surely, everyone would understand that they were unwitting dupes. This defence — if it ever was supposed to be a formal defence — would backfire in Brazil, where millions of viewers had seen David and Christine lead the others out of the house where one of the country's most prominent citizens had been caged like an animal.

"The day we walked out of the house we were guilty in the eyes of the Brazilian media and, of course, the Brazilian media has an incredible impact on Brazilian society, so we were guilty in the eyes of the Brazilian society," David told *The Fifth Estate*.

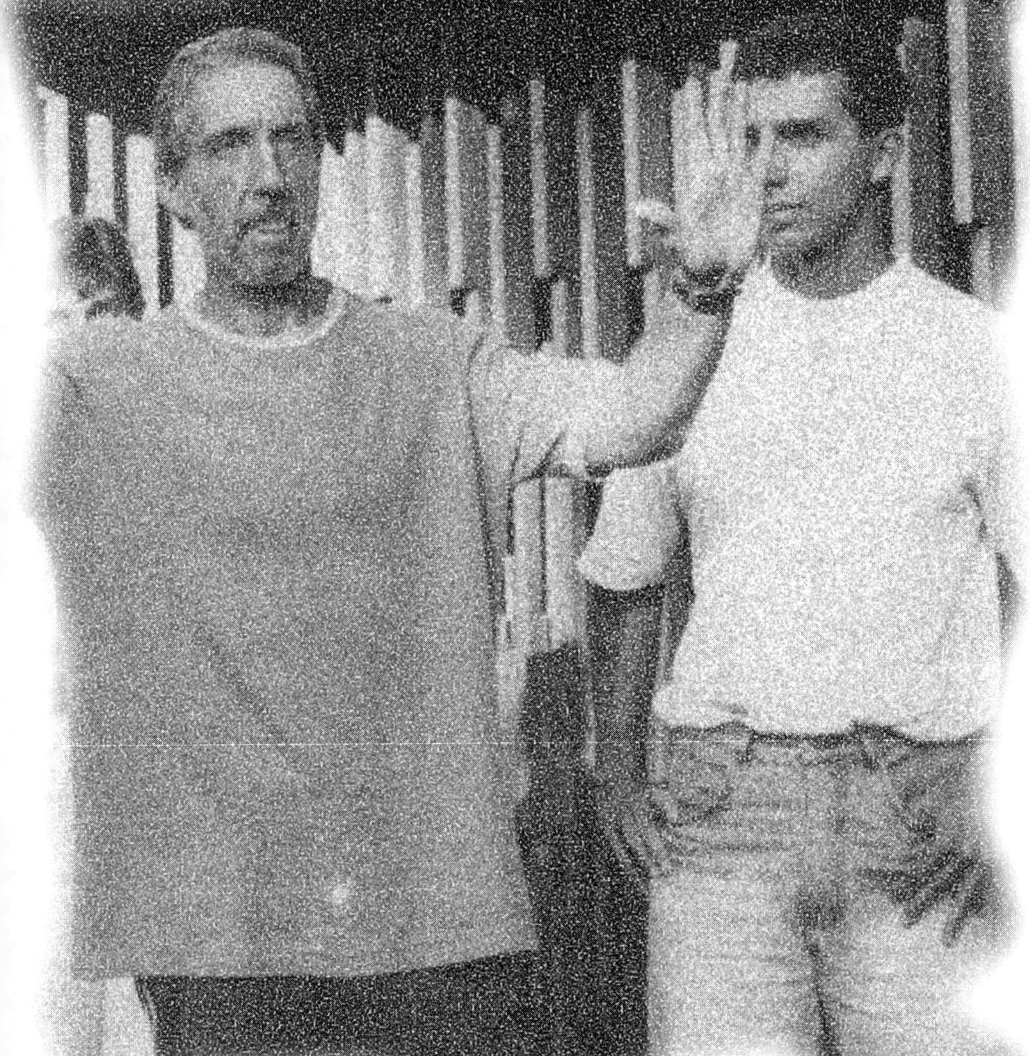

Four

The rules of conduct were printed on a sheet of white paper in neat block letters in Portuguese and stuck onto one of the styrofoam-padded walls of the underground cell.

No screaming.
No knocking on the walls.
Please observe the lights. When they go off, you sleep.
When you see a light flashing, get up, face a corner of the room, and sit on the floor.

These straightforward commandments guided Abílio Diniz's life for the six days he spent in his cell.

Diniz said that when he arrived at the house he was blindfolded, stripped of all of his clothes, and forced into the cell, where he lost all sense of time. His kidnappers gave him an old pair of blue Adidas training pants and a grey pyjama top. They played repetitive northeastern Brazilian music at a high volume "to depress me and get me under their control," Diniz told a reporter from the *Jornal do Brasil* after his release. For the first two-and-a-half days he was given nothing to eat, and the only communication between him and his kidnappers was through hand-scrawled notes passed under the door. Diniz, a devout Catholic who goes to church every Sunday, later recalled that for the first two days of his confinement he was so tense that he couldn't even bring himself to pray.

The cell itself, a plywood cubicle described as "a tank" during the trial, was 1.5 metres by 3 metres and padded in styrofoam so that no sound could escape. "It was sound deadening. The victim could yell all he wanted. Nobody would have heard him," said Officer Bueno, who conducted a thorough examination of the house after the surrender of the kidnappers.

Equipped with a sophisticated ventilation system hooked up to the stove exhaust in the kitchen, the cell was almost always kept dark and only contained a thin foam mattress and a portable toilet. It was accessible through a cupboard with a false bottom, located in an enclosed patio in the backyard. The door that separated the cell from the adjoining guard post was several centimetres thick. Cables and wires, neatly strung from the guard post into the cell, allowed whoever was on duty to control the light and sound in the cell. Raimundo Costa Freire, the only Brazilian in the kidnap gang and the only one who could speak fluent Portuguese at the time, was charged with guarding Diniz, although the trial documents suggest that others who lived in the house also took shifts. The guard on duty took care of Diniz's personal needs and also had to subscribe to a rigid set of rules that were posted on the wall of the guard cubicle in Portuguese and Spanish. Among other things, whoever was on duty couldn't look at their watch in Diniz's presence and was not allowed to speak to the victim. When dealing directly with the prisoner, the guard also had to wear a crude cloth mask which resembled something that might have been worn by a medieval executioner.

"The work here was obviously done by a professional. This is a fine piece of craftsmanship. It wasn't built overnight," said Bueno of the cell in the videotape he and colleague Roberto Kawai made right after the kidnapping.

"There's no way someone who was living here could not have known there was someone being held captive because the [stove] exhaust was on twenty-four hours a day," Bueno told me. When I said that David and Christine claimed that they didn't know Diniz was in the cell until he was brought up into the house, Bueno said this was impossible since no one had made any effort to switch off the exhaust, which would have caused Diniz to suffocate. "Tell me you're not going to inquire why your exhaust is on twenty-four hours a day? Nobody turned it off because they knew it served a very important purpose."

The construction of the cell convinced police that a great deal of planning had gone into the entire kidnapping operation, which they described as a very professional job.

■

Abílio dos Santos Diniz, executive vice-president of the largest supermarket chain in Brazil in 1989, was afraid he would be kidnapped sooner or later. A sudden wave of kidnappings of wealthy industrialists in Brazil had so alarmed him that he took a course in firearms offered by São Paulo's Military Police. Although he did not travel with bodyguards like other wealthy Brazilians, he always carried a gun in his Mercedes Benz.

Ironically, a week before he was kidnapped, Diniz, a trim fifty-three years old and an accomplished sportsman, gave an interview to Brazil's *Playboy* magazine in which he spoke about how secure he felt in São Paulo.

"I know that nothing's going to happen to me. I'm in good health, a good driver, and I am very careful," he said.

But Diniz's nightmare began a few days later. At the trial, the defence lawyers argued that Diniz was kidnapped because he was a member of the "oppressive" elite and should be held responsible for many of the ills besetting Brazilian society. Essentially, the defence argued he deserved to be kidnapped and held for ransom. The defence lawyers hoped to have the crime of kidnapping judged as a political act, which is tried at the federal court level in Brazil and carries a far more lenient sentence.

"From the socio-economic standpoint of the accused, the Latin American people live in the midst of the real Third World," said the defence lawyers in their written submission to the court. They continued:

> *Here, for lack of food, infant mortality rates are among the highest level in the world. Slums proliferate. Illiteracy is growing. There is misery on an alarming scale and the great majority of the people live in*

a state of hopelessness. In sharp contrast to this macabre scene is the image of the victim, Mr. Abílio dos Santos Diniz, a man whose almost daily promotion in the media presents him as one of the most powerful people in the nation.... The daily newspapers say he owns two Mercedes Benz cars... and a yacht that would have been the envy of the late Onassis, that he has assets of about U.S. $180-million.... In addition to these material assets, he is said to have an athletic body because he swims every day at lunch hour and jogs in the evening. Despite this public posture, which is at the very least unusual, he never uses personal security. Such behaviour characterizes Mr. Abílio dos Santos Diniz beyond all doubt as a propitiatory victim.

It's true that, as the scion of one of Brazil's most powerful families, Diniz was not the most popular person in the country. One Brazilian newspaper even called him "public enemy number one" because he allowed his stores to increase prices in violation of government price freezes during the *Plano Cruzado*, an economic shock plan that came into effect in 1986. In 1989, his company ended the year with a $65 million U.S. profit and occupied ninth place in a ranking of Brazil's five hundred biggest and most powerful private companies, according to the Brazilian business magazine *Exame*. Diniz, who inherited the supermarket chain Pão de Açucar from his father Valentim, a Portuguese immigrant, was overseeing 548 stores and 33,500 employees at the time of the kidnapping. As the oldest son, Abílio Diniz practically ran the company, which his father had founded with a single neighbourhood bakery in São Paulo in 1948. But despite his success, there were signs that things could go awry. One of the biggest problems was in the Diniz family itself. Abílio's management of the $2 billion U.S. company was sparking a family feud between him and his brother Alcides.

More recently, in June 1994, during the *Plano Real*, another economic plan aimed at combatting inflation, Aloízio Mercadante, vice-presidential candidate for the Marxist Worker's Party and its principal economic adviser, said that his party was studying a way to sue Diniz "for crimes against the people's economy." Diniz was accused of grossly inflating prices on the eve of the economic plan to make a quick profit. He later said that his comments about raising prices were distorted by the Brazilian press.

Diniz may not be an angel, but in his concluding remarks at the kidnapping trial in 1990, Judge Roberto Caldeira Barioni noted that "Abílio Diniz is not 'guilty' of being a millionaire, nor can he be recriminated for going about without security, being a person very well known throughout the country as executive vice-president of a powerful conglomerate of enterprises. Abílio Diniz had and still has, like all of us, the right to go about without security and not be molested."

Indeed, Diniz just doesn't quite fit the mould of a morally repugnant member of the elite. Despite his hard-nosed business sense, he broke ranks with the São Paulo business elite in 1988 by voting for the Worker's Party mayoral candidate, Luiza Erundina, who won the elections. Diniz refused to support Paulo Maluf, the favourite among business leaders in São Paulo for the mayoral post, because he said Maluf was not as forward thinking as Erundina.

The day after his release, it was back to business for Diniz, who held a two-hour press conference about his ordeal at the executive offices of Pão de Açucar. Sporting a dark blue business suit, a haggard Diniz addressed the country's journalists as if he were conducting a board meeting. When a journalist asked if he was afraid of being kidnapped again, Diniz replied succinctly, "I haven't yet done a proper accounting of that issue; I haven't weighed the profits or the losses. I plan to put together a life plan, but I'm not thinking about this at the moment. I want to relax a bit."

Two days after his release, two hundred of his family and friends celebrated a mass at the São Pedro church in Morumbi, an upscale residential neighbourhood in São Paulo. But Diniz would do anything but relax. In the following year his empire would take a beating. In 1990, Pão de Açucar was forced to close dozens of stores all over Brazil when the French supermarket chain Carrefour aggressively entered the Brazilian market. The company also suffered when the country's new president, Fernando Affonso Collor de Mello, instituted a disastrous economic shock plan to tame inflation. The hardline economic austerity measures, known as the *Plano Collor*, froze personal bank deposits for eighteen months and plunged the country into chaos. Diniz was forced to scale back operations drastically as his family fought among themselves for control of the company. That year, Pão de Açucar suffered a $32 million U.S. loss.

Although he immediately reverted to his public image of hard-nosed executive and weekend sportsman, Diniz remains a haunted man. After his initial press conference just before Christmas in 1989, police revealed that the kidnappers had planned to kill Diniz if Humberto Paz hadn't returned to the house to help with negotiations. "If Juan [Humberto] didn't return to the house by Saturday morning, it was a sign to the others that he had been captured by the police. The group's instructions were to kill the businessman, abandon the house, and burn all of their documents," said Gilberto Alves da Cunha, director of the Anti-Kidnapping Division of the São Paulo Civil Police.

Perhaps for this reason, Diniz has refused to speak about the kidnapping or any of the members of the group. "The people who were arrested for this kidnapping in Brazil were also participating in other kidnappings abroad," he said. "The brains behind these kidnappings lives outside of Brazil and the police are certain that they only got the tip of the iceberg when they arrested these people, who are only ten members of a much larger gang."

Indeed, São Paulo police suspect that as many as twenty-four people may have made up the entire kidnapping gang. During their investigation into the case, police found a dossier on Diniz listing all of his financial assets and personal habits. Known as "Operation Carmelo" by the gang, the kidnapping appears to have been preceded by several months of careful planning. The kidnappers apparently kept daily tabs on the supermarket magnate, noting his personal habits. Their file on Diniz is extremely detailed and says that he is "stubborn, reserved and not very nice." It also notes that his family is divided over his management of Pão de Açucar. Police say that the kidnappers observed Diniz for at least two months before they made a move. According to police reports, the file, along with the financial records of the Diniz kidnapping, was found under the false bottom of a night-table drawer in the bedroom used by David and Christine in the house.

In addition to the file on Diniz, police found files on other Brazilian executives, among them Horácio Sabino Coimbra, founder of the Grupo Cacique, a coffee exporting company. The file on Coimbra includes financial as well as personal information. Files on Brazilian television personality Sílvio Santos, politician Paulo Maluf, and entrepreneur José Ermírio de Morais were also found in other safe houses used by the group.

To this day, police suspect that many members of the gang who participated in the Diniz kidnapping and are still at large live in Brazil and are helping to pay their jailed comrades' legal expenses.

It's little wonder, then, that Diniz will no longer speak about his ordeal. In one of the last public statements that he was to make about the kidnapping in 1989, he said that he remained "very nervous."

∎

Judge: "Would you ask her if she knows what she has been accused of?"

Interpreter: "She says she has an idea, but would like to know exactly what it is."

Judge: "First, she's being accused of being associated with a group of terrorists and kidnapping the victim, Abílio Diniz, and also of resisting arrest. Does she admit to these crimes?"

Interpreter: "No, she does not."

Both Christine Lamont and David Spencer wouldn't admit to much of anything during their first trial in São Paulo. Although David pleaded guilty to the charge of resisting arrest, he pleaded innocent to the other two charges of forming a gang for criminal intent and kidnapping for extortion. Christine pleaded innocent to all three charges.

All the defendants in the case were considered dangerous international terrorists, and the trial, which began on January 5, 1990, was held under very tight security. Police wielding machine-guns guarded the courtroom. Outside, armoured cars, guard dogs, and police in bulletproof vests patrolled the streets as sharpshooters pointed their weapons from nearby rooftops. Every day of the trial, the accused were transported from prison in a ten-vehicle convoy. The eight male defendants arrived in an armoured personnel carrier and the two women in a police van.

During the trial Christine and David's version of events went like this: they said they were tourists and interested in human rights work. They had travelled to Latin America in early July 1989, met Humberto Paz in Buenos Aires in August, and agreed to rent a house in São Paulo to share with him and some of his friends. David later told *The Fifth*

Estate that Humberto asked him to rent the house because as a Canadian it would be much easier for him to do so in Brazil. As they have maintained to this day, David and Christine said they had no idea there was a cache of arms in the house or an executive being held in an underground cell until the morning of the stand-off when the police surrounded the house and Diniz was released from his cell.

The strategy of the defence lawyers was to differentiate the level of participation of each of the members of the group. While Paz may have planned and executed the kidnapping, others, such as David and Christine, had relatively minor roles, argued lawyers Belisário dos Santos and Marco Antônio Nahum in their written defence.

However, the São Paulo police and the trial judge, Roberto Caldeira Barioni, painted a very different picture.

According to the trial transcripts, David and Christine left Canada in June and travelled to Mexico, then Panama on July 1, where they got a Brazilian visa stamped in their false passports on July 4, 1989. On July 5, they arrived in Brazil and travelled to Argentina, where they did indeed meet Paz.

Christine had said that she was travelling on her false passport because she had lost her real passport when she was in Argentina, but as Judge Barioni pointed out, "Had this been true, her passport would have been issued by the Canadian Embassy in Buenos Aires. But that document shows Vancouver as the issuing office. Like David, she had already left Canada under a false name."

When questioned by Judge Barioni about why he was using a false passport, David "dithered a fair amount in explaining.... He finally said he did it because, among 'other reasons,' he had debts in Canada." However, a credit check conducted by a *Toronto Star* reporter in 1993 found that David had no debts in Canada.

Christine and David said they travelled to Brazil, then spent six weeks in Argentina, returning to Brazil in October to rent the house on Praça Hachiro Miyazaki. However, they omitted to say that they had rented another house in São Paulo in mid-August.

Under cross-examination, David said that he and Christine had been living in an apartment hotel near the city centre before renting the house on Praça Hachiro Miyazaki. But São Paulo police told a different story. Posing as gem merchants, "Lisa" and "Paul" rented a house on Rua Francisco Pugliese in suburban São Paulo on August 17, 1989 and used a forged letter of reference from Patrick Jordan's jewellery import company in Vancouver as a rental guarantee. The letter identified David under the alias Paul Joseph Gomes Mendes; stated that he was a buyer for Sartoricraft, Jordan's old company; and guaranteed all of his expenses.

The rental agreement was signed by both "Lisa" and "Paul" and the two paid six months' rent in advance in U.S. dollars. David would tell *The Fifth Estate* that as a North American it was far easier for him to rent a house in Brazil, but this is far from the case. Renting any accommodation in Brazil is a bureaucratic nightmare. Most landlords require a Brazilian *fiador*, or guarantor, who will agree to pay rent if the tenant defaults. This applies for both Brazilians and foreigners. However, most middle-class Brazilians who are in a position to sign such an agreement are not likely to do so for a foreigner, since they must surrender all sorts of income tax information. In Brazil, an estimated 50 per cent of the population does not file a tax return.

When I moved to Brazil in 1991, I looked at forty-four apartments in Rio de Janeiro over a two-week period before finding someone who would rent to a foreigner without a *fiador*. When I finally found a place, however, I was forced, like David and Christine, to pay a minimum deposit of at least three months' rent up front — in U.S. dollars. In Brazil, U.S. dollar contracts were technically illegal, but common for foreign tenants, especially when inflation was as high as 80 per cent per month and the local currency was devalued daily. For foreigners, a dollar contract was often the only way to enter into a rental agreement without a guarantor.

While in the Francisco Pugliese house, David and Christine set about doing construction work. The front of the house was altered so that passers-by could not discern what was happening in the garage, and the windows of the house were barred with strips of wood. David told his neighbours that he was "into" handicrafts.

At the trial, one of their neighbours, Raquel Aparecida dos Santos Tanaka, said "the couple gave the impression that they feared they [the neighbours] would snoop inside the house." She had told police that she suspected the couple were involved in narcotics trafficking because of the care they took to ensure that no one could glimpse the interior of the garage from the street. For instance, after the locksmith had installed an iron gate, a gap of five centimetres was left on one of the sides. David ordered the locksmith to close the gap.

Despite all of the work the two did on the house, they moved out after only two-and-a-half months. Dos Santos said she found this strange because she knew that they had made a down payment for six months, but "Lisa" told her that "her mother was ill in Holland, with cancer" and that she and "Paul" would have to leave right away. Dos Santos remembers finding the statement awfully odd because a few days before, "Lisa" had mentioned that she was awaiting the arrival of another six people who would be living in the house.

Judge Barioni concluded that Christine and David must have left the house on Francisco Pugliese in October because a police officer lived right across the street and "there was constant police vehicle traffic by the premises." He added that they had appeared to have been preparing the house to receive the kidnap victim.

The two then rented the house on Praça Hachiro Miyazaki. David claimed that they moved there on the first of October, which is not consistent with evidence that they did not leave the Francisco Pugliese house until the end of that month. The lease was signed under David's alias only, although he testified that Christine had rented the second house with him.

David bought building materials that would ultimately be used in the construction of the cell. In his cross-examination, he said that he left the materials — wood and cement — in the backyard and never saw them again. He repeated the story that one of his housemates, Hector Ramon Collante Tapia, was going to build shelves. David said that the construction of the shelves took only a weekend to complete and he had no idea that Tapia was also building an underground cubicle. "David asserted that he did not know about the underground cubicle. However, Tapia stated that he spent nearly a month building it, and Humberto Paz confirmed this. It is not possible, therefore, that David did not know about the 'tank,'" said Judge Barioni. He added that Christine had "also lied" about the underground cell. The judge agreed with Officer Bueno that it was impossible for them not to have known that a person had been kidnapped and was being held prisoner in the cell.

David and Christine also lied when they said that they constantly travelled together. Police found that Christine had travelled separately from David in November. She entered Argentina on November 29 and left on December 2, 1989. David went to Uruguay on November 21 and left on November 24, 1989. However, there was another entry for

David into Brazil on November 21, 1989, which was never explained. The two have never addressed what they were doing on these trips. Police in São Paulo say that all of the contacts among the kidnappers were made in Montevideo, Uruguay. At different points in 1989, all of the kidnappers went through Montevideo, where police believe they planned the Diniz kidnapping. Like Nicaragua under Sandinista rule, Uruguay had become a kind of safe-haven for international terrorists in the southern cone of the continent, according to intelligence officials. The country had a long tradition of giving asylum to left-wing militants, in particular Spanish radicals during and after the Spanish Civil War. Today the country has the biggest population of Basques in South America. Many ETA members, fleeing the Spanish authorities, have taken up residence in Uruguay.

In addition to renting the house and buying building materials, David also helped with some of the other logistics of the kidnapping. For instance, although David claimed that he had never seen the white Caravan that was used in the kidnapping, witness Cesar dos Reis Simplício identified him as accompanying one of the kidnappers, Pedro Lembach, the first time the latter took the vehicle to the service shop for repairs. David later countered this statement, saying in a letter home to his family that under cross-examination a witness for the prosecution identified him as having a moustache and speaking perfect Spanish.

The trial judge found that Christine and David knew at least four other members of the gang — Humberto Paz; his brother Horácio; Raimundo Costa Freire, who guarded Diniz; and Hector Collante Tapia, who constructed the cell. Although Christine said that she seldom spoke to the other people who were living in the house, David said he cooked dinner for the group. Under cross-examination, he admitted he sometimes cooked dinner for as many as twenty people, but when asked why there were so many people coming and going, he simply replied, "Nobody told me and I didn't ask."

Furthermore, Officer Bueno maintained that David was in charge of the group's logistics and actually drove the Kombi minivan during the kidnapping. (David and Christine had bought the minivan on first arriving in Brazil. Under cross-examination the Canadians said they had planned to use the vehicle to travel through the country, perhaps as far as the Amazon region.)

"We know David drove the vehicle because his driving habits sparked a lot of attention," Bueno told me. "The neighbours said they saw him driving back with the others on the day of the kidnapping. David drove like a Canadian, signalling for left turns and turning on his flashers when he stopped the car in front of the house. Nobody in Brazil drives like that." Indeed, Brazilian drivers are among the most reckless in the world and rarely signal for a turn, much less use their flashers when they have stopped.

Although police say that David organized the logistical and financial end of the kidnapping, Humberto Paz was the self-confessed brains behind the operation. When asked by the trial judge about his role in the kidnapping, Paz replied with an air of triumph, "I took Abílio Diniz." The judge was clearly impressed with the statement: "I have not forgotten the phrase exactly as it was uttered... as if, in a war, he had captured an enemy citadel."

Humberto implicated his brother Horácio and Raimundo Costa Freire, but tried to clear all of the other defendants. Judge Barioni, however, did not find Humberto's testimony credible. "Apart from implicating his brother Horácio, whom Humberto obviously knew was going to confess, and Raimundo, this defendant tried to clear all the other defendants. He refused to say who the other participants were, besides himself and his brother, who operated at the time of the kidnapping." Judge Barioni also noted that all three "confessed in court to their participation in the crime," but he concluded that "at least five people took part in the act."

Both David and Christine were extremely vague about their movements on the day of the kidnapping, December 11, 1989. David said that he thought they were home; Christine said that she couldn't remember, but that she might have spent the day checking out courses in Portuguese, shopping, or sightseeing.

Throughout the trial, David and Christine contradicted each other and their co-defendants several times. For instance, David testified that he had bought the Kombi minivan for touring through Brazil, but Judge Barioni noted that "He did not make a single trip through Brazil." David also said that he lent the Kombi to Christine and the others, but in her testimony Christine testified that only David drove it.

Christine said that she rarely spoke to her other housemates and that there were only two other occupants of the house. However, David contradicted this when he stated that he often cooked for up to twenty people. Both said that they only knew Horácio Paz and Tapia, but under cross-examination David admitted that he had talked to Humberto Paz in Argentina about renting the house. When Judge Barioni asked David when Humberto had arrived in São Paulo, David said that he didn't know, but later he admitted that he had talked to him the day before he rented the house.

After stating that she knew only Horácio and Hector, Christine later also identified Humberto, whom she said she knew only as "Juan," from a photograph. She said he was the person with whom David had talked in Buenos Aires about sharing living expenses in São Paulo. However, she also said that she didn't meet him before the police brought him to the house on December 16. But when the judge asked her if she had ever heard of a person named Humberto Paz or Leonardo Rozas, one of many aliases used by Paz, she replied that she knew that "David had a meeting with Juan." The statement suggested that she knew his alias in addition to his real name.

Judge Barioni concluded that much of David and Christine's testimony was nothing more than lies. "David's version is completely unacceptable....His statements are contradictory and vague. He impressed me as more cynical than Humberto.... The impression is very strong that David left Canada with a clearly defined objective: to commit a kidnapping for a million-dollar ransom. He came here knowing exactly what to do. He carried a fair amount of money: he bought a minivan, probably used to carry Abílio; he paid six months' rent for a good house in the Butantã neighbourhood, in dollars, and did some construction work there; he paid three months' rent on the house on Praça Hachiro Miyazaki; he travelled at least twice to Uruguay and Argentina; finally, he lived here for several months, maintaining a level of expenses that is not for any 'tourist.' He was fully aware of what he was doing."

Although he acknowledged that Christine had many good character references, "is a very good and lovable person" and from a good family, the judge said that "her guilt is inescapable," even though she might not have been aware of the kidnapping plot in its entirety.

"Christine believes she is being tried for the simple fact that she was in the house where the victim was held, something which, it is claimed, she learned about only when the police arrived with Humberto," said Judge Barioni. "Her version is plausible; it fits with the type of organization that existed and also with the discipline shown by its members. After all, each of them only knew part of the plan. I do not believe, however, that she was unaware that a person had been kidnapped and was incarcerated there."

The trial judge and other observers concluded that the kidnap group was divided into cells so that one part of the group did not know what the others were doing. This structure, which is common to many terrorist organizations, is set up partly for protection of information. In the Diniz case, police say that it is certainly possible that one or more cells within the group didn't know they were participating in a kidnapping. However, police also return again and again to the fact that it would have been impossible for the group members who were living in the Praça Hachiro Miyazaki house not to know that a kidnapping had taken place since the construction of the cell had taken at least a month to complete and the cell was ventilated twenty-four hours a day for six days with the noisy exhaust from the stove in the kitchen.

In Brazil, few people sympathized with Christine's protestations of innocence. For many the proof of her guilt rested with the Globo footage of her leading the other kidnappers out of the São Paulo house. "It is a pity that perjury does not exist under Brazilian law. This lady left the house wielding a gun, she helped rent the house and then lied, saying the firearm was to defend herself from the police," said Luiz Antônio Fleury Filho, who was at the time the secretary of security for São Paulo state.

With so much evidence stacked up against the ten kidnappers, the main strategy of defence lawyers Nahum and dos Santos was to argue that the Diniz kidnapping was politically motivated. Not only would this defence ensure that the ten be turned into political martyrs who acted without criminal intent, but if successfully argued the case would be referred to the Federal Court of Justice of São Paulo and the National Security Law would be applied. If found guilty of a political crime, the defendants would receive far lighter sentences. They believed that their argument was strengthened by the fact that few of the defendants had a previous criminal record.

In order for a crime to be considered political in Brazil it must violate the National Security Law, which covers crimes that endanger Brazil's territorial integrity and national sovereignty, the democratic system, or the heads of the various branches of government.

All of the accused appeared to be militant leftists and all of them spoke about participating in a pan-Latin American political group that would work to further the interests of the poor. The $30 million U.S. in ransom that they had hoped to obtain from the Diniz kidnapping would have gone to finance the new political organization and help the region's impoverished. But despite their stated good intentions, their political aims were extremely vague. For instance, Chilean Maria Emília Badilla spoke of finding "new alternatives for Latin America." Her compatriot Sergio Martin Urtubia said that the group would analyse "the political situation in which the Latin American countries find themselves." David was equally vague about the motives of the group during his cross-examination.

"He would like to say that the responsibility and decision to collaborate and help the organization [sic] he felt a need to do something when he saw the conditions of the poor living in Latin America," said David's Portuguese-language interpreter. "Coming from a Canadian city and seeing here the kids begging in the streets, the position people find themselves in, he felt he needed to help."

All of the accused, including David and Christine, had been involved in militant political organizations before the Diniz kidnapping. But for such hard-line militants, their utopian vision of working for the poor was simplistic and vague, leading Barioni to conclude that their actions in kidnapping Diniz had no political weight behind them.

The judge concluded that although the kidnappers were sincere when they spoke of social justice, the political organization they claimed to represent did not really exist. "[The] defendants also spoke, generically, of social injustice, destitution, unemployment.... All said that the organization was still under discussion, in formation, had not yet taken shape, which, let us agree, isn't much." Judge Barioni also made the point that in order to work for social justice in Brazil, a democratic country, "there is... no need whatever to act in a clandestine way in order to preach the most radical reforms." There could be no clearer evidence of this than the 1989 elections, which had pitted a militant Marxist presidential candidate against a neoliberal reformer.

Furthermore, Judge Barioni argued, the group's actions did not pose a threat to national security in Brazil. "Now I do not see how a political organization or movement whose objectives are to find alternatives for the southern cone countries, that wishes to resolve the political problems of the Latin American countries in general, can place in 'danger of injury' or cause injury to, the representative and democratic system in effect in our country. Nor put the federation at risk or endanger the state of law."

During the trial, Diniz's kidnapping was described as a mercenary crime, its main objective to raise money. Diniz himself said that he felt his kidnapping was nothing more than "a normal business deal" for the kidnappers. And right after the stand-off, Humberto Paz told Cardinal Arns on the bus that took him to the police station that the group did it "for money."

In a public statement made after he was released, Diniz said that although they spoke of "social inequality," his kidnappers' motives were not so altruistic or high-minded. "Their idea was to make money," he said. "I don't think... I can deduce connections with any national or international political faction."

The evidence gathered by police after the stand-off seemed to suggest that the ten kidnappers were part of a well-organized Latin American Marxist terrorist group that raised money for its activities by kidnapping Latin American business leaders. Police suspect that two other women who played key roles in the Diniz kidnapping are still at large along with twelve other men and women who provided minor support services for the group. Interpol has claimed that all of the kidnappers, including David and Christine, had passed through Nicaragua at different times to receive specialized training in guerrilla warfare. Brazilian Federal Police agents said David and Christine knew a Chilean member of the group, Sérgio Martín Olivares Urtubia, in Canada. Olivares, who had been a member of socialist groups in Chile, had been admitted to Canada as a political refugee and settled in Winnipeg in the late 1970s.

Police had discovered a sizeable cache of arms at the six safe houses used by the kidnappers in São Paulo. The police video made after the stand-off shows several semi-automatic weapons, and Uzi and Beretta submachine-guns, piles of boxes of shells and bullets, all found at the Praça Hachiro Miyazaki house alone. São Paulo police noted that the weapons were imported and could not be obtained in Brazil, even on the black market. "That's war stuff. That's not stuff you find on the street," remarked RCMP officer Tony Pereira. A police video made after the stand-off shows radio transmission equipment, surgical scissors, and dozens of boxes of antibiotics and painkillers.

Brian Jenkins, a consultant with Kroll Associates, a private investigation firm that specializes in terrorism, was also impressed with the kidnappers' weapons. "The weapons used in this kidnapping suggest that there is a bigger connection here," said Jenkins, who investigated the

Diniz case. Diniz himself, who was forced during much of the thirty-six-hour stand-off to lie on the floor of the front room, said he saw a large quantity of arms in the room.

Based on this evidence, Judge Barioni concluded that there was enough proof to suggest that the group had worked as "an armed band for the commission of criminal acts." Judge Barioni, a respected member of the São Paulo legal profession, stuck to his convictions despite the fact that he reportedly received death threats by telephone throughout the trial. Police believe the callers were members of the Diniz kidnap group who were still at large. Spooked by the threats, which continued after the trial, Judge Barioni requested a transfer to another judicial division.

In his judgement, Judge Barioni wrote: "Abílio Diniz was impressed, after thirty-six hours of contact in which he not only conversed, but also observed 'with surprise the strict discipline they all showed, and at no time was there the slightest dispute among them'.... And, Abílio went on, 'They honoured the night shifts, so long as the physical conditions permitted, with the greatest strictness and showed impeccable discipline'.... As Abílio commented, this was true teamwork. Each member performed a specific task without the knowledge of another. They also had a reasonable level of education and knowledge and probably some military or paramilitary training."

Hours after the stand-off the police had already linked the group to the July 1989 kidnapping of Brazilian media guru Luiz Salles, who had been held in a basement cell similar to Diniz's for sixty-five days and $2.5 million U.S. in ransom, and the 1986 kidnapping of banker Antonio Beltran Martinez, who was held for forty-two days for an estimated $4 million U.S. in ransom. In both cases, police had been looking for a group made up of radical leftists from several different countries. Maria Emília Badilla was later identified as the woman who delivered the ransom notes to the Beltran Martinez family. Salles later identified the apartment on Rua Charles Darwin, where Maria Emília was picked up by police in the Diniz case, as the place where he was taken just before he was released by the kidnappers. Moreover, police noted that the kidnappings followed the same pattern as that of Diniz's. Both Salles and Beltran Martinez were caught off guard as they were leaving their homes for work. In all three cases, the victims said they were dealing with kidnappers who were Spanish-speaking Latin Americans.

According to police reports, the group that kidnapped Diniz was made up of five Chileans, two Argentines, a Brazilian, and the two Canadians. The roly-poly Brazilian member of the group, Raimundo Rosélio Costa Freire, then twenty-four years old and the only one who smiled for the Brazilian press and raised his arms in victory when he was escorted out of the kidnap hideout, had been involved in fringe leftist groups in Brazil's impoverished northeast, where he was born. Costa Freire, described by São Paulo police as "a militant Trotskyite" when he attended the State University of Ceara, did not have a previous criminal record. According to trial transcripts, he worked on the preparations for the kidnapping, helping to paint the "ambulance," and during Diniz's imprisonment, he was responsible for taking care of his personal needs and much of the guard duty.

The Chileans — Pedro Alejandro Fernandez Lembach, Sérgio Martín Olivares Urtubia, Ulisses Fernando Gallardo Acevedo, Maria Emília Honoria Marchi Badilla, and Hector Ramon Collante Tapia — were all said to have strong ties to Chile's Movement of the Revolutionary Left (MIR). Founded in Chile in 1965 by Pascal Allende, nephew of Marxist president Salvador Allende, who was overthrown in a military coup in 1973, the group sought to put an end to the Chilean ruling class through armed struggle. The movement was particularly popular among left-wing university students and professionals. However, after the 1973 coup, it was practically wiped out when many of its leaders fled to Cuba, but many radical splinter groups emerged.

Even though the official MIR was functioning as a legitimate political party in Chile when the Diniz kidnapping occurred, many of its more militant members were still operating underground. In an interview from Santiago after the kidnapping, the MIR's coordinator, Patrício Rivas, said the group had no ties to the Chilean kidnappers of Abílio Diniz. But Rivas was talking about the official arm of the MIR, not the underground movement.

Interpol also linked several of the Chilean kidnappers to the ultraradical armed wing of the Chilean Communist Party, the Manuel Rodriguez Patriotic Front (FPMR), which was involved in the 1986 assassination attempt against General Pinochet. The FPMR, named after a Chilean independence hero, has Maoist tendencies. Members of this group have directed armed attacks against U.S.-related property and targets, such as Mormon churches and former officers in the military government.

Most of the Chilean members of the Diniz kidnap group had been involved with the MIR during the Pinochet regime in Chile. All had certain skills that contributed to the smooth operations of the kidnap group. Some had professional training in electronics, engineering, and carpentry that enabled them to construct Diniz's cell quickly and efficiently. Years of fighting an underground war against the Pinochet regime had also honed their terrorist skills. One member was an expert at making explosives and another at forging documents. Police say they were all extremely disciplined and handled weapons, including submachine-guns, with great ease.

Olivares, then thirty-eight and an electrician by profession, was accused by Chilean authorities of participating in a number of assaults and bombings in Chile. A member of the MIR-affiliated Organización de Resistencia Armada (ORA) since 1974, he had robbed banks to help finance the armed struggle and the Chilean Socialist Party. Expelled from Chile on May 4, 1978, he had gone, as we have seen, to live in exile in Winnipeg. Interpol said that he shared a house with David there at some point before returning to Chile in September 1988. However, David claimed to have met him for the first time at the São Paulo police station.

Interpol suspects that Olivares was somehow involved in the 1987 kidnapping of Chilean army colonel Manuel Carreno, who was held from September 1 to December 3, when his family paid $75,000 U.S. in ransom, which was used to buy medicine and food for impoverished shantytown dwellers in the Chilean capital.

São Paulo police say that Olivares participated in the abduction of Diniz on December 11 and helped design and construct the lighting and sound system that linked Diniz's cell to the guard post.

Pedro Lembach, then thirty-nine, belonged to one of the MIR's most militant factions. In 1980, he was sentenced to ten years in jail for illegally possessing firearms. Two years later, Chilean authorities sentenced him to twenty-three years for making explosives and forming a paramilitary group. He was eventually freed and went into exile in England in 1987. In the Diniz kidnapping, Lembach also helped grab the victim and bundle him into the "ambulance," and he was the person who had gone to the auto repair shop to get the kidnap vehicle fixed. Police say that it was Lembach who provided police with the biggest clue to the Diniz kidnapping when he left the mechanic's card in the car.

Ulisses Fernando Gallardo Acevedo, then thirty-six, had spent most of his militant career working with MIR splinter groups, including the radical Movimiento de Pobladores Revolucionário (MPR). He participated in several robberies and was arrested in 1980 and sentenced to fifteen years in jail. After an unsuccessful appeal the following year, his sentence was increased to eighteen years. He escaped police custody and left the country and was unable to return to Chile until 1988, when the Chilean government allowed all exiles to return. Acevedo also helped in the logistics of the Diniz kidnapping.

Badilla, then forty-three, is an engineer and is credited with designing Diniz's cell. In Chile, she was involved with a number of militant movements until she was arrested in 1974 for her participation in "subversive acts." Sentenced to ten years in jail, she was released in December 1984 and later went into exile in Argentina but returned to Chile in 1988. The mother of two children, Badilla arrived in Brazil in late 1989 with no less than thirteen identity documents with six different names.

Unlike his compatriots, Hector Ramon Tapia, then twenty-five, had no past involvement with Chilean leftist groups and no previous criminal record. A carpenter by trade, he supervised the construction of Diniz's cell. In his interrogation by São Paulo police, he said that he was hired by Humberto Paz while he was in Argentina in August 1989 to build what he thought would be a wine cellar in a São Paulo house.

Argentine militant Humberto Eduardo Paz, then thirty-four, was the leader of the group. According to court documents, Paz "hired" his brother Horácio, Hector, and David and planned much of the kidnapping. He entered Brazil with ten forged identity documents. Horácio Enrique Paz, then thirty-nine, led the actual kidnapping.

Like the Chileans, the Argentine members of the group also had ties to left-wing militant organizations in their home country. Born in an impoverished household in a Buenos Aires suburb, the Paz brothers were active in Argentina's radical Movimiento Todos por la Patria or the All for the Homeland Movement (MTP), an urban guerrilla organization that often posed as a human rights group. In January 1989, the MTP launched the disastrous attack on the La Tablada military barracks outside Buenos Aires in which thirty-two people died.

Argentine police say the La Tablada attack was organized by one of Latin America's most wanted terrorists, Enrique Gorriarán Merlo. Gorriarán, also known as El Pelado (the bald one) has been active since the 1970s either as a military strategist or as a contributor to some of Latin America's biggest revolutionary movements. In the 1970s, his group in Argentina, the People's Revolutionary Army (ERP), donated money to the MIR, and in the early 1980s it organized two of the FMLN's most spectacular and successful commando operations. Gorriarán also organized a raid that resulted in the destruction of nearly 70 per cent of El Salvador's Air Force in April 1981 and the blowing up of the country's most important bridge. He has been at large for several years, but Interpol has recently spotted him in São Paulo and Porto Alegre, in southern Brazil. Many suspect him of masterminding some of Latin America's biggest kidnappings, including that of Abílio Diniz.

For years, militant left-wing movements in the southern cone countries of Argentina, Chile, Paraguay, Uruguay, and Brazil worked together, planning joint paramilitary operations and sharing weapons. Argentine police investigating the La Tablada massacre said that arms for the attack may have been partly financed by the ransom collected in the Beltran Martinez kidnapping in November 1986. Interpol also suspects that the money from the Beltran Martinez kidnapping went to help the militant Chilean group, the FPMR, organize the assassination attempt against General Augusto Pinochet in 1986.

■

After four months and numerous witnesses, Judge Barioni handed down his decision on May 2, 1990. All ten group members were found guilty.

Unable to refute the circumstantial evidence against them, Christine and David cast themselves in the roles of victims of harsh Third World justice. They tried to argue that their detention by police was arbitrary because they were not informed of the charges against them. In a much later submission to Barbara McDougall, Secretary of State for External Affairs in 1992, Edward Morgan and Jeremy de Melo, Christine and David's Canadian attorneys, argued that there were several irregularities in the case that warranted intercession on the part of the Canadian government. They said that David and Christine were held without charge until January 4, the day before the trial started, and that upon being served with citations by a court official "Christine and David were informed that they had ten minutes to read them."

However, Judge Barioni found that since both Christine and David were "taken in the act," the charges against them were not a surprise and therefore not invalid.

Christine and David further argued that they didn't have enough time to consult with their lawyers before the trial and that the citation was in Portuguese, a language neither could speak at the time. "No interpreter or translation of the citation was provided to them. Accordingly, they were unable to adequately prepare a defence or to instruct counsel," said Morgan and de Melo. David and Christine argued that Brazilian law enforcement officials did not inform them in detail of the charges against them and that their lawyers had only three days from the time they formally heard the charges until they would have to present their case.

Judge Barioni, on the other hand, said that the charges were not a surprise to the defence and that they had indeed been properly laid. Canadian consular officials in São Paulo stressed that the two "had highly qualified counsel from the time of their arrest."

Although David was later to comment to *The Fifth Estate* that the Brazilian media negatively influenced his case, that he was presumed guilty as soon as he walked out of the gates of the driveway on Praça Hachiro Miyazaki, the judge was very careful not to be swayed by media coverage of the case during the trial. Both the defence and the prosecution presented their written arguments to the judge, who interrogated all of the accused and the witnesses. In his judgement, Judge Barioni wrote:

> *The prosecution has asked that the accused be given the maximum penalty [twenty years], arguing that the crimes they perpetrated are execrable and revolting and also that the penalty should serve as an example to others. I cannot accede to that request, both because the law does not cover it and because it would violate my conscience, a fundamental asset which I need to live in peace. A judge cannot allow himself to be pressured by emotions from without or from within.*

Nor could the judge hand down the same sentences to all of the members of the group, who each had participated in the kidnapping to varying degrees. As the leader of the group, Humberto Paz was sentenced to fifteen years. Horácio Paz and Raimundo Costa Freire, who "played a prominent role in the crime but... less important than that of

Humberto," received twelve years each. David was sentenced to ten years for his "important role in the preparations of the kidnapping." The rest, including Christine, were sentenced to the minimum sentence — eight years each. Humberto, Horácio, Raimundo, David, and Ulisses were ordered to begin serving their sentences under "the closed system," whereas Christine and the others might eventually eligible for a semi-open regime whereby she could leave her prison on weekends.

In addition to the jail terms, David was fined $8,500 and Christine $1,800. The others were also fined, depending upon their level of participation in the crime as determined by the trial judge.

Morgan and de Melo later tried to argue that the case against David and Christine should be challenged by Canada because under the Brazilian legal system they were presumed guilty right away. "Brazilian criminal law contemplates guilt by association and an effective reversal of the burden of proof.... Guilt was determined by the trial judge based primarily on the circumstances of their association with the several co-accused," said Morgan and de Melo.

However, Barbara McDougall responded: "Although Mr. Spencer and Ms. Lamont's association with the others was considered as part of the circumstantial evidence, it was only part of the broader picture of their involvement. The Brazilian investigative system may not formally presume innocence, but there was certainly evidence in this case to support their conviction.... I should reiterate the fact that while the Brazilian legal and judicial system differs from that in Canada, this does not diminish its legitimacy and all persons in Brazil are subject to it."

Defence lawyer Nahum said he would appeal the sentences and convictions of the defendants, including those of David and Christine, who maintained that they were innocent and the victims of a corrupt justice system.

But few people had any sympathy for them in Brazil. "Justice is justice," said Diniz in the only public statement he would make about the original sentences.

In desperation, perhaps, the two Canadians now concentrated their efforts 8,000 kilometres away from Brazil. Christine appealed to her parents, who through dogged persistence and hard work would manage to turn the case into the most contentious diplomatic issue between Canada and Brazil, and who, later, had to watch helplessly as it degenerated into a national embarrassment.

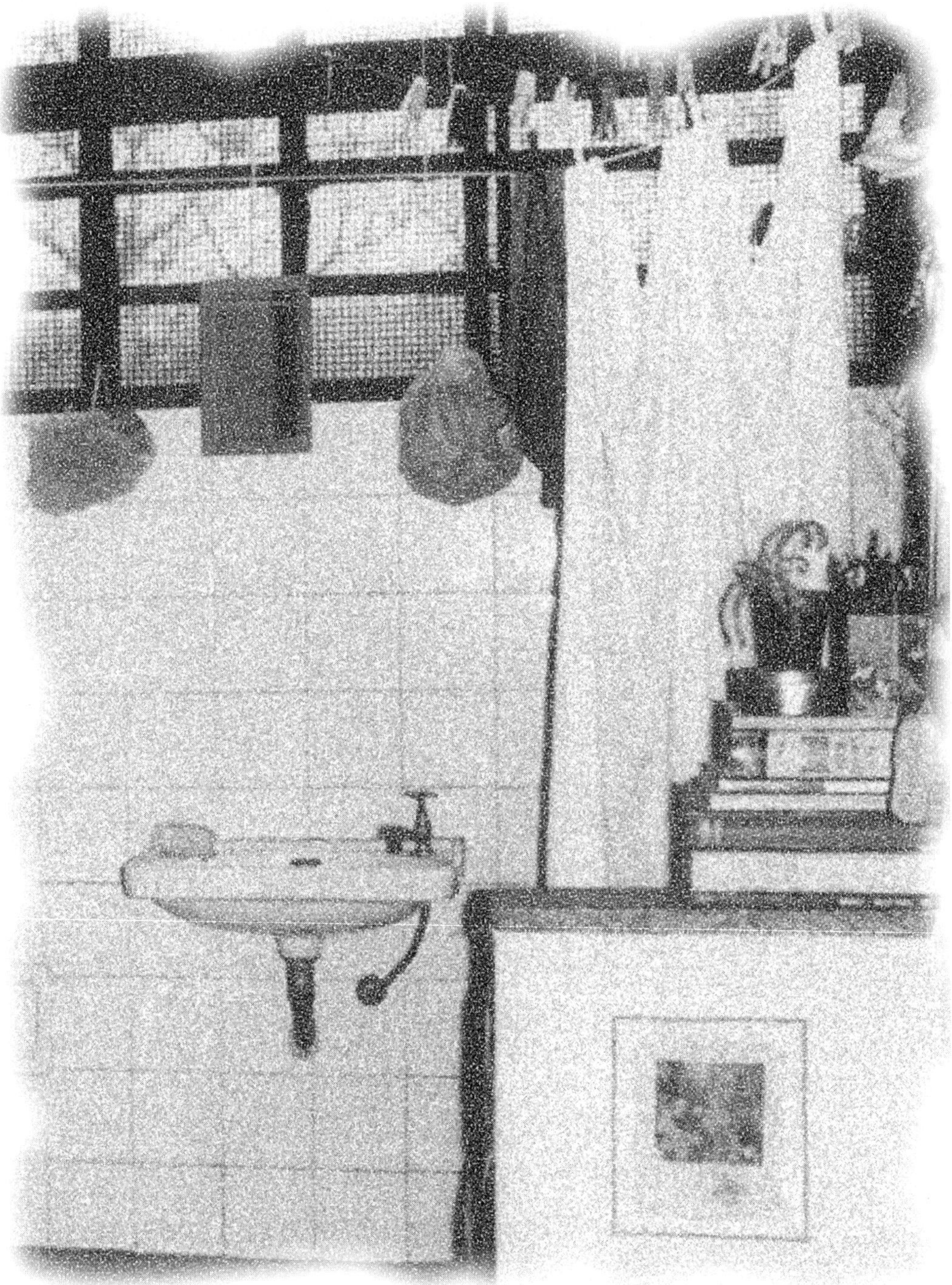

Five

Among the items that Christine Lamont requested from her parents during her first few months in jail were cigarettes, chocolate, and her favourite book, *The Little Prince,* by Antoine de Saint-Exupery. The book, which chronicles an adult's journey to the simpler world of childhood to discover the true meaning of life, would serve as a metaphor of Christine's ordeal — principally the frustrating task of trying to explain to the "grown-ups" of the world that she and David were innocent victims of warped Third World justice.

In the first part of the book, the narrator draws a picture of a boa constrictor swallowing an elephant whole. To the unenlightened adult world, the drawing looks like nothing more than a hat, but to the clear-sighted eyes of children, the drawing is much more complex.

> *My drawing was not a picture of a hat. It was a picture of a boa constrictor digesting an elephant. But since the grown-ups were not able to understand it, I made another drawing: I drew the inside of the boa*

constrictor, so that the grown-ups could see it clearly. They always need to have things explained.

The narrator, a pilot, tries to live in isolation from the adult world. He develops a kind of secret society and divides people into two categories: the special, imaginative, and open-minded inhabitants of the Earth — those who, like himself, understand the complex, true meaning of life — and everyone else, who, well, just doesn't get it.

Christine's world is divided in much the same way. She and her supporters would have you believe they understand the real issues in this case. For them, no amount of circumstantial evidence is sufficient to cast doubt on her and David, who have maintained their innocence throughout their ordeal. They know it's a boa constrictor swallowing an elephant whole.

Then there's everyone else — the skeptics in the media, the Canadian and Brazilian governments. They're not really capable of understanding complexity, Christine and her supporters would argue. Like most of the unseen adults in *The Little Prince*, they are the enemy because they "always need to have things explained." To them, it's just a hat.

So, is it just a hat or is it a boa constrictor swallowing an elephant whole? Are they terrorists or are they freedom fighters and victims of a corrupt Third World system of justice?

"Grownups never understand anything by themselves, and it is tiresome for children to be always and forever explaining things to them," writes Antoine de Saint-Exupéry. David, Christine, their supporters, and to a large extent the Canadian media all took it upon themselves to explain not only the convicted kidnappers' actions, but Latin American politics, international terrorism, and Brazilian justice to the skeptical grown-ups of the world. Unfortunately, all of these were subjects they knew little about.

■

Somebody has gone through a file of photocopied press clippings, methodically collected from newspapers across Canada and Brazil, and marked in clean block letters the words NOT TRUE beside several offending paragraphs. In some cases, the handwriting is scrawled and more urgent: "Is the wording intentionally misleading in the headline or is it an error?" asks the writer, making comments in the left-hand margin of a story from February 1990 headlined "Money motivated kidnapping, Brazilian archbishop testifies." In another story, beside a paragraph that reads in part: "Canadian police believe Lamont and Spencer met Olivares in Canada before Olivares returned to Chile in 1988," the same person has emphatically written "NOT TRUE — they met at the police station in São Paulo."

Armed with a pencil and yellow scratch pad, Marilyn Lamont has doggedly analysed, annotated, and filed every article written about her daughter since Christine was arrested in 1989. She has studied her daughter's case; written copious letters to Canadian politicians, legal experts, and lobbyists; collected thousands of names on petitions; organized candle-light vigils in Vancouver, and travelled several times to Brazil in the single-minded pursuit of getting her daughter out of jail. The slight, white-haired piano instructor from Langley has turned her basement into the headquarters of a national campaign to free Christine and David. Convinced that Christine is innocent, she works around the clock to convince everyone else.

"She has literally set up a headquarters in her basement. She has a fax machine, a copy machine, and a word processor. And she works full-time at the campaign to get Christine back," said the family's Ottawa lobbyist in an interview with the *Miami Herald*.

Although I had spoken to her several times on the telephone from Brazil, I met Marilyn Lamont for the first time in Vancouver in April 1994. She and her husband, Dr. Keith Lamont, struck me as personable and very decent. Despite our rather tense interview, the Lamonts insisted upon driving me through a rainstorm to my next appointment and showed me snaps of their new grandson, Luke, who had been named after Dom Luciano Mendes de Almeida, president of the National Council of Brazilian Bishops, in honour of his work on behalf of Christine and David.

The Lamonts are completely devoted to their daughter. As one journalist remarked, "Christine Lamont's mom and dad are the kind of parents anyone in trouble overseas would love to have. They are convinced beyond a doubt that their. . . daughter is innocent. No amount of evidence can change their minds."

SEE NO EVIL

Although they've spent an estimated $500,000 on the campaign to free their daughter, they do not strike me as extremely wealthy. True, they have a 6,000-square-foot ranch-style home in Langley with an in-ground pool in the backyard, but they say the expenses over the last several years have not been easy for them. "We've spent more than we could afford," said Dr. Lamont, who was forced to put off early retirement because the family needed to raise more money for the lobbying effort. When I met them, I had the impression that they were passionately concerned about their daughter and would spend anything it took to get her out of jail.

In fact, they are so genuinely committed to their daughter that I almost felt guilty asking them difficult questions about the case. During our interview, Mrs. Lamont eagerly asked me questions about Brazilian politicians and studiously noted down everything I said — names, phone numbers, book titles — in that urgent handwriting on the yellow scratch pad that she fished out of her purse. She has the same subtle, persuasive quality that David noted in her daughter, but you get the impression that she can be strongly persisitent when it comes to reaching her goals. As one *Vancouver Sun* columnist noted about Marilyn Lamont, "There is steel under her soft voice."

Indeed, the Lamonts are so good at persuasion that in June 1992, they convinced one of Christine's old professors to sign an affidavit attesting that it was common for human rights workers to obtain false passports "to protect their safety." Ronald Newton, professor of history and Latin American studies at Simon Fraser University, also swore that "the act of obtaining a false passport is not necessarily an indication of criminal intent but can be equally consistent with the desire to protect one's safety."

All of the legitimate human rights workers I spoke to, including representatives of Amnesty International, disagree with this assessment.

Regardless of what they think about the case, just about everyone feels sorry for the Lamonts. Their faith in their daughter's innocence is infectious, and people who know nothing about the details except for what they've heard from the Lamonts start passionate letter-writing campaigns to their local MPs, urging them to work to free Christine and David. Mrs. Lamont says she still receives letters in the mail with contributions (some as little as $2) from concerned Canadians who want to help in the campaign to free Christine and David.

"A lot of mothers feel for Marilyn Lamont," said Anne Robinson, a retired nurse who helps organize the White Rock, B.C. chapter of the Committee for Justice for Christine Lamont and David Spencer.

Despite their good-natured disposition, the Lamonts are bitter, and by their own admission, they have become very cynical about the Brazilian legal system and their own government over the last few years. Mrs. Lamont pursed her lips and tried to remain calm when she described one of her last visits to Brazil, on Christine's thirty-fifth birthday in April 1994. "Can you believe it, they wouldn't let us have a cake?" she said, forcing a smile. "We saw Chris for an hour and fifteen minutes every day, and on her birthday we were allowed two extra minutes."

They admit they had no idea what they were getting themselves into when they became involved in the campaign to free Christine and David. They've learned the hard way about the bureaucratic hassles of getting anything done in Brazil. "We now know that you can't do anything during Christmas, Carnival, or Easter or shortly thereafter, because people spend an awfully long time recovering from each of these holidays," joked Dr. Lamont, who once tried to knock on official Brazilian doors in February just before Carnival, the pre-Lenten festival that paralyses the country for more than a week.

The Lamonts had hoped that by presenting themselves as good, hardworking, and decent Canadians, they might convince Brazilian authorities to release Christine and David. The strategy worked up to a point and won the family several supporters, some of them influential, in Brazil. In his written citation, Judge Barioni said about Christine: "Finally I obtained an excellent impression of her parents. All these circumstances will be taken into account in sentencing."

Through their church contacts in Vancouver and São Paulo, the Lamonts also managed to win the support of Paulo Evaristo Arns, the archbishop of São Paulo who was one of the chief negotiators in Diniz's release. "I developed a profound conviction about the innocence of Chistine and her companion David. . . . My conviction crystallized even further after meeting Christine's family and listening to her life story and that of her companion." Cardinal Arns would prove a useful contact despite the fact that he knew nothing about the case. The Lamonts would dust him off from time to time when they felt he could be useful as a "credible" authority from official Brazil. It was through the good cardinal's offices that the Lamonts were able to press their case with high-level officials. Cardinal Arns, who is said to be a very good friend of the recently elected president Fernando Henrique Cardoso, is now being called upon to lobby the Brazilian president for Christine and David's expulsion.

When they took their first trip to Brazil right after Christine and David had been arrested, the Lamonts managed to get an audience with Judge Barioni just before the trial began in January 1990. According to them, Judge Barioni confessed that he was under a great deal of political pressure to convict all ten of the accused. Later, the Lamonts tried to convince the Canadian public that Judge Barioni was being pressured by big political and business interests in São Paulo to make Christine and David pay for a crime that they really had nothing to do with. They questioned his impartiality and even suggested he was not fit to preside at the trial. The Lamonts were to confide to friends afterwards that what they really should have done was somehow try to bribe Judge Barioni at their first meeting. At the time, however, they admitted to being "too naive" in terms of understanding how the Brazilian legal system "really works."

However, legal observers say that Judge Barioni's judgement in the case was restrained and surprisingly unpolitical. While he did in the end find everyone guilty of participating in the Diniz kidnapping, he did not convict David and Christine of the other two charges of resisting arrest and forming a gang for criminal intent. In fact, as noted earlier, he differentiated the level of participation of all of those involved in the kidnapping and made a point of saying, in his summary, that he would not turn the case into a political victory for the prosecution team, who were demanding that each member receive the maximum twenty-year sentence for the crime of kidnapping for extortion. As it turned out, none of the kidnappers, not even the ringleader, Humberto Paz, received the maximum sentence for the crime. Most of the group, including Christine, received the eight-year minimum sentence. "A judge cannot allow himself to be pressured by emotions from without or from within. In addition to independence, a judge is required to conduct himself calmly," Judge Barioni said. Brazilian appeal court judges would not be as principled or as lenient.

SEE NO EVIL

■

Despite consultations with Canadian consular officials, the Lamonts were completely out of their depth when it came to dealing with Brazil, a foreign country they soon found out was not like their safe, ordered, and uptight Canada.

They began to concentrate their efforts on familiar ground and turn the case into a political issue in Ottawa. In February 1990, the Lamonts hired lobbyist David Humphreys, a former Ottawa bureau chief for *The Globe and Mail*, who helped them arrange meetings with senior officials in the Department of External Affairs. In addition to Cardinal Arns, Canadian diplomats in Brasilia and São Paulo were enlisted to set up meetings with high-ranking Brazilian officials, including former justice minister Jarbas Passarinho, to get Christine and David out of jail. The media campaign to free David and Christine was so expertly handled in Ottawa by Humphreys that Jeff Sallot, a *Globe and Mail* reporter, referred to it as "a well-oiled publicity machine that keeps two convicted Canadian kidnappers before the public eye."

Under Humphreys' direction, the case leap-frogged from being a simple consular affair to a full-fledged political issue in Canada. Humphreys, an old friend of Joe Clark, who was Secretary of State for External Affairs at the time of the kidnapping, used his Ottawa connections well in the early days.

As soon as the case was imbued with political overtones, ambitious Canadian diplomatic officials in Brazil, perhaps eyeing an easy promotion, jumped on the bandwagon to work on Christine and David's behalf. When the Lamonts made their first trip to Brazil following Christine and David's arrest, they were not only picked up at the airport by Canadian consular officials, they were invited to stay at the official Canadian residence in São Paulo. Sources say that Canadian consular officials were only too eager to help them by suggesting lobbying tactics to employ with External Affairs in Ottawa.

Under political pressure in Ottawa, Canadian consular officials spent an inordinate amount of time on this case. Consul General Bill Ross personally went to visit Christine and David in jail and even attended part of the trial, though such duties are usually reserved for lower-echelon consular officials. But as one External Affairs official pointed out to me, "there is no firm rule for consular cases." Whenever Christine or

David complained about the slightest problem, the Canadian consulate dispatched an official to the prisons to investigate. In fact, whenever new diplomats were appointed to Brazil, it became a sort of rite of passage for them to present their credentials not only to the Brazilian president but also to David and Christine. The Lamonts' campaign turned them into Canadian celebrities in Brazil, and a stop at the two jails in São Paulo became de rigueur agenda items for Canadian parliamentarians and church leaders visiting the Latin American country.

"We have a number of foreign prisoners in this jail, but no other foreign government representatives have spent so much time with a prisoner as the Canadians," said Carmen dos Santos, the warden at the Penitenciária Feminina, where Christine is serving her sentence. "You think the Argentine or Chilean or Bolivian consuls general ever come to visit the other prisoners here? The Canadians are incredible. They're always here."

At one point, things got so out of hand that David was calling the consul general at home whenever he had a problem in jail. The extraordinary amount of attention that was being paid to Christine and David became so embarrassing that consular officials began to worry that it would start to look bad to Ottawa. At the same time that David and Christine were arrested in Brazil, another Canadian woman was arrested on a drug charge in Corumbá, a jungle city near the Bolivian border in western Brazil, but no effort was made to visit her until someone at the consulate pointed out that Christine and David were getting too much attention.

"They sent a Brazilian consular official employed by the Canadian government to visit the poor girl in jail. You see, she wasn't as politically important as Lamont and Spencer were, so she wasn't worth the taxpayers' money," said a consular official, formerly stationed in Brazil, who did not want to be identified. "There was nothing sensible about the way Canada handled this case."

■

Following the first trial, the Lamonts and David Humphreys suggested to the Canadian media that Christine and David were the victims of grave injustices. "This has brought a change to all our lives. We will never be the same. It has certainly heightened our awareness of the injustices in the world," Marilyn Lamont told the press.

In addition to disputing every piece of evidence that the São Paulo Civil Police gathered against the two, the Lamonts also convinced themselves that Christine and David were being pushed to the centre of a huge plot to discredit the left in Brazil.

The belief that the Diniz kidnapping was used by Brazilian right-wing elements to discredit the left came out of a confused state of events, which was further distorted by the Canadian press. While it is true that a few members of the São Paulo Civil Police tried to link the kidnappers with the Brazilian Worker's Party (PT), there is no evidence to suggest that this was some kind of well-organized conspiracy. The PT, a ten-year-old Marxist party that for the first time in its history was running a presidential candidate in national elections, clearly suffered as a result of other political and media conspiracies, but the Diniz kidnapping wasn't one of them.

Following the stand-off, somebody put a PT campaign sticker on the bus that transported the kidnappers to the police station, and several days later, on December 27, 1989, police held a press conference to show the weapons seized in the six safe houses used by the kidnappers. At the press conference, all sorts of PT election paraphernalia — posters, T-shirts — appeared in front of the weapons. The police said they had seized the material in one of the vehicles used by the kidnap gang, but repeatedly assured journalists that there was no PT involvement with the kidnapping. A reporter for *Veja* magazine found it strange that "the PT presidential campaign posters were placed in front of the other articles on display, making them more noticeable than the machine guns and the cartridges."

Despite this odd bit of theatre by the São Paulo police, it is ludicrous to think that they could have used the kidnapping to discredit Luis Inácio Lula da Silva, the burly PT presidential candidate and former metalworker from São Paulo, on the eve of national elections, the fact is that the Brazilian press was subject to a blackout on the case from the day of the kidnapping, December 11, to the day the stand-off began in front of the Praça Hachiro Miyazaki house on December 16, 1989. Balloting in the second and final round of Brazil's federal elections took place the following day. Furthermore, the polls closed at 5:00 p.m., just as the kidnappers surrendered and began to file out of the house. The blackout, which is not unusual when dealing with high-profile kidnappings in the country, was imposed by the nation's law enforcement authorities to protect Diniz and his family and to allow the police to conduct their investigation without media interference.

Nevertheless, PT militants still say that the Diniz kidnapping was partly responsible for their loss at the polls in 1989. "The kidnapping had grave consequences for us. Of course, it wasn't the only cause of our loss, but it was still very important," Eduardo Suplicy, Brazil's only PT senator, told me.

As if adopting the PT party line, *Saturday Night* magazine erroneously reported more than two years after the elections that the kidnapping had had a "dramatic effect" on the PT's chances at the polls. The *Saturday Night* story implies that Lula was somehow the favourite candidate in the elections, but it fails to provide the results of the first round of voting a month earlier, which put Collor in the lead with 28.52 per cent of the vote and Lula in second place with 16.08 per cent. In Brazil, a presidential candidate must win 50 per cent of all valid votes plus one to win.

On December 16, the day before the run-off vote, opinion polls from independent polling firms Vox Populi and the Brazilian Institute of Public Opinion indicated a Collor victory. Collor, a young, dashing politician, was leading with 51.5 per cent of the popular vote. Lula, a former union leader from the country's impoverished northeast, had 48.5 per cent. If anything tipped the balance in Collor's favour it was a last-minute smear campaign against his rival. A few days before the election, newspapers reported that Lula had tried to force an old girlfriend to have an abortion. Miriam Cordeiro, who reportedly was paid by the Collor camp to denounce Lula publicly, said that Lula had tried to force her to have an abortion when she was pregnant with their daughter Lurian, who at the time of the elections was fifteen years old. Lula refused to reply to the allegations, which were broadcast on national television by Collor's National Reconstruction Party (PRN); his fate was sealed even before the press blackout on the Diniz kidnap was lifted on December 16. The day before the elections, when Lula went to a soccer game at Morumbi Stadium in São Paulo, he was booed and cursed by hundreds of soccer fans.

"The collisions of the last week of campaigning left no doubt: Collor would be the new president of the republic," said an article in O *Estado de São Paulo* in January 1990. The piece makes no mention of the Diniz kidnapping or what influence it may or may not have had on the elections.

In fact, most of the reports in the mainstream Brazilian press link Lula's defeat directly to the abortion incident. None mention the Diniz kidnapping. "The polls had been showing for more than a week before the election that Lula would lose," said prominent Brazilian journalist Boris Casoy. "The Diniz kidnapping was nothing more than a little *bruit* during the campaign. Perhaps some members of the São Paulo Civil Police did use it to try to discredit the PT, but if it was a conspiracy, it was a badly orchestrated conspiracy that had absolutely no effect on the outcome of the election."

Yet the authors of the *Saturday Night* article would write that the country's news media linked the Diniz kidnapping with the PT:

> *Newspapers all over the country carried headlines stressing the connection and even accusing the PT of direct involvement. "It had a very great emotional impact on the voting because the whole freeing of Abílio Diniz took place during the process of opening the polls," said Senator Suplicy. So instead of being about the elections, the television coverage was about the kidnapping, with the connotation that the PT had kidnapped Diniz.*

A few months after the conviction of the ten kidnappers PT Senator Eduardo Suplicy called a press conference to announce an investigation into the use of torture by São Paulo police in the case and the smear campaign that he felt São Paulo politicians had mounted against the PT over the case. However, that year Luiz Antonio Fleury Filho, then secretary of security for São Paulo state, decided to run for governor. Ever the political opportunist, Fleury, who needed PT support to win the election, managed to convince the party hierarchy that he was responsible for dissuading the police from associating the Diniz kidnapping with the PT. As a result, Senator Suplicy's efforts were put on the back burner. Using the Diniz kidnapping in his political platform as a glowing example of the efficacy of the state's security forces, Fleury was elected governor on November 25, 1990. Nelson Guimarães, who had presided at the negotiations for surrender and investigated the case as the director of the Anti-Kidnapping Division of the São Paulo Civil Police, was promoted to head the São Paulo Police's Homicide Division. After Fleury's election, Senator Suplicy noted that the enquiry into PT involvement in the Diniz kidnapping had been shelved without explanation.

"Brazil has gotten what it wanted out of us," said Christine in her interview with *The Fifth Estate*. "They have Fleury as governor, the courts have got a really tough image, and the police have finally pulled off something without killing anybody. They look good, and Brazil has no motive for keeping us here."

When I interviewed him last year in 1994, Senator Suplicy still seemed very nervous about the entire issue of PT involvement in the kidnapping, categorically denying that the party had anything to do with it. However, a rental agreement for one of the São Paulo safehouses used by the kidnappers lists a PT party militant as the guarantor. José Antônio Leonel Vieira, a priest with strong links to the PT, signed a lease declaring that he would be responsible for the rent of the apartment on Rua Aureliano Coutinho if the tenant Pedro Segundo Solar Venegas could not pay. (Solar Venegas was the alias used by Ulisses Gallardo Acevedo, and the apartment in question was the address given to the mechanics who repaired the Caravan used in the Diniz kidnapping.) In a church bulletin published in January 1990, Father Vieira admitted that he signed the contract, but said that he did not know the tenant was planning a kidnapping. According to the church bulletin, *Igreja Hoje*, Acevedo was a leftist political exile from Chile who approached PT militants for help to settle in São Paulo. Strangely, most of the Canadian media ignored this little bit of evidence linking the PT, even indirectly, to the kidnapping. The *Saturday Night* article emphasized the planted PT paraphernalia:

> *Partway through the torture session, the police called a press conference to display [Ulisses] Gallardo and another member of the group wearing T-shirts with the logo of Brazil's largest left-wing political party, the Workers' Party or Partido dos Trabalhadores (PT). The reporters noticed the discrepancy between the men's filthy and beaten condition and the T-shirts which looked as though they had just been taken out of their plastic wrappings. Yet the story quickly hit the nation's newspapers that the Workers' Party was somehow involved in kidnapping Abílio Diniz.*

The torture of the five kidnappers happened between December 14 and 16, before the press blackout had been lifted. No stories about the Diniz affair appeared until election day, December 17, 1989. Of those that did appear that day, none mentioned the T-shirt incident. Although much of the Brazilian press corps was aware by December 16 that some members of the Civil Police were trying to link the kidnapping to the PT party, there was no significant press coverage of this until months after the election, and Rui Falcão, a high-ranking PT militant and state deputy for the party in São Paulo, admitted to me that there was no formal coverage of the incident before election day in 1989. However, he added that the word on the street at polling booths across the country was that the PT was associated with violence in the Diniz affair. "We lost those elections because Fleury tried to link us to the kidnapping. On election day, the media were alluding to the fact that we were somehow involved. It spread by word of mouth across the country." Falcão could not explain how a rumour spread "by word of mouth" could have possibly travelled across a country of 150 million in the space of a few hours before the polls closed. Yet this view is shared by most supporters of the PT, including Cardinal Arns, who has publicly stated that the PT lost the election because of the Diniz kidnapping.

But a Canadian who was in Brazil at the time of the kidnapping and the election was surprised by the conspiracy theories. In a 1991 letter to the *Vancouver Sun*, N.D. Schubert of New Westminster, B.C. wrote:

> *I was in Brazil during the 1989 presidential elections and the kidnapping and question the accuracy of a number of Cardinal Arns' statements, especially that police propaganda cost Luis Inácio Lula da Silva's PT the election. Election day newspaper reports clearly identified the kidnappers as Chilean members of the ultra left-wing MIR, and television coverage was limited to normal news flashes rather than "broadcast live for 36 hours to all Brazilian voters." Further, alleged police attempts to place PT posters on the prison bus would have occurred after the polls had closed on Dec. 17, and attempts by José Sarney and Luiz Antônio Fleury Filho to link the PT with the kidnappers was [sic] recognized by most Brazilians as election propaganda.*

According to the report, Brazilian president José Sarney sent an urgent telex to São Paulo governor Orestes Quércia on December 16, the day the stand-off began, instructing him to treat the case as a common crime "without political connotations." He reportedly warned Quércia not to associate the kidnappers with the PT or to let the case interfere with the elections. "I don't want this to get in the way of the electoral process," wrote Mr. Sarney, who was not a fan of either of the two presidential candidates, Fernando Collor or Luis Inácio Lula da Silva. According to the *Folha* report, Fleury told this story to the defence lawyers, but officially denies the existence of the President's telex. Still, even assuming this story is true, it suggests that high-level politicians in Brazil had little interest in turning the kidnapping into a political weapon against the PT on the eve of national elections. If anything, the telex shows a last minute effort to protect the party and allow Brazil's first direct elections in nearly three decades to proceed unfettered.

But in Canada everything that smacked of conspiracy against Christine and David, and was presented as gospel truth by the media, came from their parents, under the direction of David Humphreys.

From the very beginning, the Lamonts set about picking apart the Brazilian legal arguments against Christine and David by pointing out the "errors, inconsistencies, allegations, and lies" spread by the Brazilian media. In doing so, they sought to demonize Brazil, to demonize all of Latin America for that matter.

In one of their first letters to Humphreys, the Lamonts themselves exaggerate what little knowledge they have of the political situation in Brazil. The Brazilian media, they argue, is "still run much as it was during the military dictatorship" and "was fed unsubstantiated and wild theories as factual evidence."

There is certainly a case to be made that the Brazilian media, in particular the giant Globo television network, have a tendency to sensationalize and even manipulate the news. During the 1989 presidential campaign, for instance, Collor, a relatively unknown former governor from the impoverished Brazilian northeast, swept to victory largely because of Globo television. The network, the fourth largest in the world, was criticized for always showing Collor in a positive light during the election campaign. Globo actively worked against Luis Inácio Lula da Silva, portraying him as an inarticulate union organizer not fit to be president. In a country where fully one-third of the population cannot read or write, television is a very powerful medium. Globo's estimated nightly television audience is more than 50 million viewers.

But despite instances of media manipulation by Globo, there is by no means a conspiracy of the media in Brazil on any given issue. The country's six major dailies — O *Estado de São Paulo*, O *Globo*, *Jornal do Brasil*, *Folha de São Paulo*, O *Dia*, *Gazeta Mercantil* — hold varying opinions on a wide range of issues. *Veja*, the country's foremost newsmagazine, is one of the world's most sophisticated weekly sources of information and analysis of national and international events. Last year in Rio de Janeiro, members of the Freedom Forum, a private U.S. media think-tank devoted to promoting freedom of the press, called the Brazilian press one of the best in the world.

This is not to deny that corruption does exist, as it does in just about every facet of Brazilian life, but for the most part and compared to their Latin American counterparts, the Brazilian media are independent and responsible. For instance, during the 1989 presidential campaign, *Folha de São Paulo*, Brazil's largest and most outspoken daily, was running articles on Collor's corrupt administration as governor of the state of Alagoas. The newspaper was also the first to allude to Collor's sinister business partnership with Paulo Cesar Farias, his former campaign treasurer who ended up running one of Latin America's largest influence peddling rackets, which eventually led to the downfall of the Collor government. When Collor was impeached in 1992, the Brazilian press — *Veja* and the *Folha de São Paulo* in particular — were commended by foreign observers and journalists for acting with diligence and courage in their investigation of the scandal that toppled the federal government.

Contrary to what the Lamonts want to believe, the Brazilian press is not run as it was during the military period. It was largely thanks to a free press in Brazil that David and Christine and the other kidnappers were not killed during the police stand-off. Under the blazing media lights, it became impossible for the São Paulo police, notorious for violent human rights abuses, to shoot their way into the house in order to liberate Diniz. It is worth remembering that the kidnappers themselves asked for human rights activists, diplomats, and the Brazilian media to be present at the negotiations for their surrender. And following Diniz's release, the Brazilian media investigated the charges that five of the kidnappers had been tortured by São Paulo police. This is not the type of reporting that one would associate with Latin American military regimes.

But the media, in Brazil and in Canada, became both a tool and a punching bag for the Lamonts. If an article questioned Christine and David's involvement in the kidnapping, it was acting against their interests and therefore needed to be discredited. The entire journalistic establishment in Brazil, was discredited in one fell swoop by the Lamonts, whose aim has never been to get at the truth of what happened in the kidnapping, but simply to get Christine and David out of jail.

The Lamonts did not necessarily lie about the case; but they chose to omit salient points. For instance, neither they nor much of the Canadian press ever mentioned that Christine and David had rented not one but two houses in São Paulo, using forged letters and false documents. In what were arguably the two most influential reports to appear in the Canadian media in the early days of the case, the rental of the first house on Rua Francisco Pugliese is never mentioned. In both the *Saturday Night* article, published more than two years after the kidnapping, and the first *Fifth Estate* documentary, which aired at about the same time, there is no mention of the first house or the fact that witnesses testified that David and Christine did extensive work altering the premises, ostensibly to hide what was going on inside.

In fact, the *Fifth Estate* producers go overboard in their attempt to portray Christine and David as innocent, idealistic Canadians who had no idea that Diniz was being held in an underground cell in their house. Victor Malarek spends an awful lot of time in the backyard of the house on Praça Hachiro Miyazaki explaining to his viewers just how it is possible that two intelligent people could live there and not know that their housemates were building a cell over the course of a month or that a man was imprisoned in the cell for several days. Christine and David's supporters were so pleased with this journalistic account of the case that the *Fifth Estate* documentary was used as propaganda material whenever they held vigils for the jailed pair in Vancouver.

But had Malarek interviewed the main investigators in the case or the RCMP, he would have learned that Diniz's cell was ventilated twenty-four hours a day with the aid of the noisy stove exhaust in the kitchen on the ground floor of the house.

Furthermore, the police officers who investigated the Diniz case said that traces of sand and debris from the construction of the cell were found on David's clothes.

Through the lens of the Canadian media, Christine and David's purpose for being in Latin America in the first place took on a weighty, almost messianic significance. In the Brazilian media, they were portrayed alternately as dumb Canadian tourists or ruthless international terrorists. In those first Canadian media reports they were human rights workers involved in "dangerous" work in Latin America. The implication is usually that they are freedom fighters, working to improve the lot of the poor and oppressed. Malarek calls the Praça Hachiro Miyazaki house "a way station for Latin American refugees." Just where those refugees were coming from, Malarek never makes clear.

He notes that Christine and David are heroes, appointed by the Divine. "Guilty in the governor's eyes, but Christine and David have God on their side," says Malarek, referring to Cardinal Arns's comments about the innocence of the pair.

With God and the Canadian media on their side, David and Christine could do no wrong. Throughout Canada, they were depicted as heroic freedom fighters stuck in appallingly dirty and overcrowded prisons. "In effect, who are the real terrorists, Lamont and Spencer who had a vision of bringing justice to the poor and mistreated, or their accusers?" asked Bill Warden in an opinion piece published in the *Calgary Herald* as recently as September 1993. In another column on the pair earlier that year, Greg Weston of the *Ottawa Citizen* wrote that Christine and David were "condemned to a miserable existence in a Brazilian hell-hole."

Much of the news about Christine and David's courage and appalling prison conditions in São Paulo came from articles published by reporter Kim Bolan in the *Vancouver Sun*. Bolan, who said she knew both David and Christine from their days as Salvadoran solidarity workers in Vancouver, almost single-handedly turned their case into a cause celebre in Canada.

In an article entitled "No 'hugs and kisses' in letters from woman's nightmare cell," Bolan wrote a vivid account of Christine's agony in São Paulo — without having visited the jail. "She sleeps on a thin mattress on a cement block, with a tiny slit of a window too high to allow an outside view. Her toilet is a hole in the corner and her bland meals are slipped through a bolted slot in a heavy door. . . . This is the picture Lamont paints of her bleak existence in letters to her family and discussions with her lawyer."

Bolan goes on to describe how there is no heat in the jail "as the fall air begins to chill São Paulo, a city of 17 million, 800 metres above sea level." Bolan fails to note that few people in São Paulo, or Brazil for that matter, have heat. The article also details how Christine's letters to her family are regularly censored by prison authorities. In one letter several lines are blacked out, including the closing "hugs and kisses," notes Bolan.

And just in case the reader was wondering about the guilt or innocence of Christine and David, Bolan's writing style leaves little doubt in anyone's mind: "And they [the Lamont family] hope she will soon be able to walk free in the natural sunlight that filters briefly into her darkened world."

Bolan eventually visited Christine and David to research the article that appeared in *Saturday Night* in April 1992. In "Almost Innocents Abroad," Bolan and co-writer Augusta Dwyer describe Christine's bleak existence, although they themselves are hard-pressed to make it sound so bleak. "High up in the far wall, a small square of open window lets in daylight if not the sky," they say of Christine's cell in the first paragraph.

The cell in question is actually very well lit and just over six metres square, in accordance with UN requirements. It includes a tiny bathroom, complete with toilet and shower, is clean and painted white. The bathroom is located in the back of the cell, on a raised concrete platform away from the area where Christine has a bed and a small desk unit with shelves.

Christine has stuck Inuit postcards on the walls next to photos of David and her family in handmade paper borders painted in water colours. A jar of Estée Lauder hand cream and dozens of books and magazines are neatly stacked on a row of shelves above the desk. A basket of fruit sits next to the bed, which is covered in a cream-coloured crocheted bedspread. Colourful origami birds are suspended with bits of string from the book shelves. There are two potted plants resting on the columns that separate the bathroom from the rest of the cell. Piles of yarn, still in their plastic wrapping, are stacked against the wall near the bed along with a few volumes of *Vogue Knitting*. According to

SEE NO EVIL

Canadian diplomats, Christine is an accomplished knitter and passes a lot of her time making sweaters for her family.

There is a common room in Christine's pavilion, where prisoners take their meals and can watch television. The grounds are covered with trees and flowers, and for a maximum-security prison it's difficult to tell the inmates from the staff. In fact, the setting is much like a spartan university residence, except that the prisoners' cell doors are bolted from the outside at night.

While it is true that most prisoners in Brazil do live under terrible conditions, foreigners and university-educated Brazilians always get special treatment. As foreigners in Brazilian jails, David and Christine have it a lot better than just about any other prisoners, except maybe drug traffickers, many of whom have cellular phones and food delivered from some of the country's finest restaurants. Christine receives very expensive private medical and dental care, apparently paid for by her parents, and David has a colour TV and shortwave radio —items which are not permitted in many Brazilian jail cells.

It's a measure of just how well they have been treated from the beginning of their incarceration that neither was ever sent to a holding cell to await the outcome of their first trial, which is the normal practice in Brazil. The Casa da Detenção, the main holding cell unit, in São Paulo's Carandiru prison complex, is a filthy and overcrowded jail where riots are frequent and prisoners are often forced to share cells with several other inmates. According to São Paulo prison authorities, neither Christine nor David was ever forced to go to a holding cell or share their space with another prisoner. Christine has been in the same cell since her incarceration in 1989, and David has been in the same jail since his incarceration.

This is a far cry from the situation experienced by the majority of Brazil's prisoners, who are forced into often unhygienic, overcrowded conditions with no security. Over the last two years in São Paulo state alone, the number of prisoners has increased by 75 per cent. Investigators attribute the rise in the prison population to an inefficient judicial system that keeps many in jail awaiting trial for years at a time. A 1992 federal government enquiry on the state of the country's prisons found that in some jails in São Paulo, conditions were so overcrowded that prisoners were forced to live on the patios without a roof over their heads. A prison census completed in May 1993 found that overcrowding and "chaotic conditions" in the country's prisons resulted in an average of two rebellions per day. Brazilian prisons have 52,000 spaces for prisoners, but more than 126,000 occupants, many of whom are awaiting trial. Only 2 per cent of the prison population in Brazil can afford to hire a lawyer.

On October 2, 1992, one of Latin America's worst prison riots in history broke out at the Casa da Detenção in São Paulo. Military police were sent in to contain the uprising, but ended up gunning down 111 prisoners instead. Naked, blood-smeared bodies were piled up in the corridors and in the prison barber shop. In a fax to then Brazilian justice minister Maurício Correa, the International Penitentiary Foundation in Switzerland called it "the anatomy of the worst bloodbath in a single prison recorded in the last twenty years."

"We saw a reproduction of scenes from the Nazi extermination camps," Paulo Sérgio Pinheiro, a São Paulo sociologist specializing in violence and crime, told *Veja*. The massacre, which happened just before Brazilians were to go to the polls for country-wide municipal elections, was kept under wraps by São Paulo governor Fleury until after polls had closed on Saturday, October 3. Fleury did not want the massacre to adversely influence the voting for Aloísio Nunes Ferreira, his PMDB party candidate in the São Paulo mayoral race. Fleury's efforts were in vain, however. His candidate lost, and as often happens in Brazil, none of the authorities responsible for the prison massacre was ever brought to justice. Fleury, who had motivated his police forces so diligently during the Diniz affair three years earlier when he was secretary of state for security, did nothing to punish such gross violations of human rights by his own paramilitary police force, São Paulo's Polícia Militar henceforth became known as the deadliest police force in the world. Brazilians across the country watched the images on their television screens of the bloody massacre and hysterical family members gathered outside of the Casa da Detenção, waiting for news of who had died in the jail.

A few months later, in a surreal scene worthy of a Luis Buñuel film, the Military Police high command, responding to pressure from human rights groups around the world, announced that it would put together a series of music and art appreciation classes to teach its officers to be less violent. When I went to visit São Paulo Military Police headquarters about a year after the massacre, I was amused to find these hardened "killer cops," as they came to be known in the Brazilian media, doing t'ai chi exercises on the soccer field.

"Policing is a very tense job and so we must teach these men to relax. In Japan, for instance, policemen do flower arranging," said Major José Sílvio Turini, who administers the relaxation program at São Paulo's military police academy. "Our objective is to take a human being and make him more human." As we were speaking, a group of shock troops and regular patrolmen were crouching, feline-like, on the soccer-field.

"Now, breathe deeply and pretend you're a cat," whispered Roque Severino, the Argentine t'ai chi master whose job is to teach hardened military police to channel their aggressive energies through the Chinese martial arts exercise.

Although the Carandiru massacre occurred more than 100 metres and several reinforced concrete walls away from David's prison, the horrible images of blood-soaked naked bodies lying in the prison corridors at the Casa da Detenção were immediately used by David and Christine's supporters in Canada in their campaign. The suggestion in many of the Canadian media reports was that the massacre had happened in Christine and David's cell-block. *The Fifth Estate* put together another documentary on the two Canadians, using footage and still photos from the riot to illustrate what prison conditions are like in Brazil. Malarek interviewed a teary-eyed Mr. Spencer, holding a Brazilian press clipping showing piles of naked bodies, with numbers painted on the legs and arms. "I want him back," said Bill Spencer of his son. "But I don't want him back in a body bag."

Never mind that David and Christine were nowhere near the riot. The conditions at the Casa da Detenção, where more than one-third of the inmates are reportedly infected with the HIV virus, are nothing like the privileged prison enclaves in which David and Christine are incarcerated. Walter Hoffgen, the warden at the Penitenciária do Estado where David is imprisoned, said that in his seven years at the jail, there has been only one violent death. He also noted that out of a total population of 1,500 prisoners, only ten had the HIV virus that causes AIDS, and all of them were in the prison hospital. As horrific as the Carandiru massacre was, it really had nothing to do with David and Christine. However, the Lamont and Spencer families used the incident to condemn External Affairs for not doing more to protect David and Christine. "If the federal government doesn't act to get them out of there, they should be held responsible if anything happens to Christine and David," Christine's sister Heather told a reporter from the *Vancouver Sun*. "This incident proves that [External Affairs] cannot respond to a situation that puts Christine and David in extreme danger. How are they going to help? By bringing them home in body bags?"

A few weeks after the Carandiru massacre, Marilyn Lamont also criticized External Affairs for not acting to protect David and Christine. Mrs. Lamont pointed to another prison riot in São Paulo, noting "this just shows that External Affairs cannot act in any preventative measure whatsoever. . . . Does Barbara McDougall not realize there's not a safe prison in Brazil?" Mrs. Lamont told Kim Bolan, she omitted to mention that this second riot occurred at the Febem Juvenile Detention Centre, more than ten kilometres away from the prisons where Christine and David were being held.

These days, everytime a prison disturbance occurs in Brazil, Ottawa is on the phone to Brasília to find out if Christine and David are safe. In 1993, a riot broke out in Fortaleza, a city nearly 3,000 kilometres away from São Paulo. Officials in Ottawa called the Canadian Embassy in Brasília to investigate so that they could issue a statement to the Canadian media stating that David and Christine were safe.

Where did the majority of Canadian journalists covering the Lamont/Spencer case get their information about prison conditions? Obviously not from Brazil. Carmen dos Santos, the warden at the Penitenciária Feminina in São Paulo, says that she has received several Canadian journalists in the last five years to interview Christine, but that she found it strange that none of them asked her questions about prison conditions and few showed any interest in seeing the jail facilities or even Christine's cell.

"The Canadian journalists who have come through only ever want to speak to Christine. They don't ask us any questions," says dos Santos, who has worked in the São Paulo correctional system for twenty-three years, nine of them at the Penitenciária Feminina.

When I visited the jail for the first time in May 1994, I saw Christine's expense record, which lists her monthly expenses in prison. With the money she earns from menial tasks, Christine regularly buys chocolate, soft toilet paper, and up to eighty packs of cigarettes per month. Christine receives regular cash infusions from her parents, which are sent through her lawyers. In 1992, she spent more than $300

U.S. on a dentist's visit. Her dentist and physician are among the finest in São Paulo and make private house calls to the prison to treat Christine and fellow inmate and convicted kidnapper, Maria Emília Badilla. Although AIDS is a big problem in the Brazilian penitentiary system as a whole, dos Santos assured me that in her prison, there was only one woman suffering from the disease out of a total population of 323 female inmates.

"The Lamonts themselves were given a tour of the prison and Dr. Lamont was allowed to examine our facilities," said dos Santos. "He said that Christine's [private] doctor is as good as those in Canada."

But the Lamonts have persisted in dreaming up nightmare scenarios about their daughter, at one point suggesting that she was at risk of getting AIDS and that she had been exposed to tuberculosis. In April 1992, Liberal MP George Rideout, who represents Moncton, told the House of Commons that Christine risked exposure to the AIDS virus because she was working in an infirmary with "low health-care standards" that had caused her parents "to worry about her exposure to the AIDS virus." He added that the Canadian government should intervene to get her out of Brazil as quickly as possible.

In December 1992, the Lamonts began a campaign suggesting that Christine was very sick and had to undergo blood and urine tests because of a swelling in her joints. The *Vancouver Sun* reported that she was being checked for the HIV virus. "She doesn't think it's possible [she has HIV], but you know what conditions are like," Mrs. Lamont told Kim Bolan in an interview from São Paulo, where she was visiting her daughter. She added that she was upset that the Canadian consulate in São Paulo didn't contact the family until three days after Christine had been examined by one of its physicians. But a spokesman for External Affairs said that Christine's condition was not serious and that Canadian consular officials had indeed contacted Christine's Brazilian lawyers a day after she underwent the medical examinations. Nonetheless, in a particularly alarmist opening paragraph, Bolan wrote on December 14, 1992:

Blood tests done on Christine Lamont indicate she doesn't have lupus or several other conditions, but have still not ruled out hepatitis, tuberculosis or HIV, her father said Sunday. And Dr. Keith Lamont said he and his wife, Marilyn, are considering calling in a specialist to examine their daughter, who is serving a 28-year sentence in a Brazilian jail cell. The Langley couple are in Brazil to see Christine Lamont after learning a week ago that she had severe swelling in her ankles and other joints that could be symptoms of a serious illness.

Bolan and just about every other Canadian journalist who covered the story of Christine's declining health failed to mention that she had been exposed to tuberculosis as a child, and for that reason would normally test positive on a tuberculosis skin test.

While this incident might have won them sympathy in Canada, it backfired against the Lamonts in Brazil. Carmen dos Santos, who is earnest, hard working and takes her job very seriously, told me that she was so angry with the Lamonts for spreading the rumours about Christine's health that she made a decision in December 1992 not to allow the parents to visit again and to cut off all of Christine's special privileges, such as visitation rights. "We always respected the family and did everything we could to help them, and then they go around and start spreading vicious lies about sanitary conditions here. Well, I just lost my patience because the women are treated better here than many people on the outside," said dos Santos during one of our interviews. It took a grovelling letter of apology from Marilyn Lamont and several entreaties from the Canadian consulate in São Paulo before the Lamonts were allowed to visit their daughter again.

In addition to alarmist articles on unsanitary prison conditions for Christine and David, the Canadian media invented all sorts of other nightmare scenarios. In articles with headlines such as "A Cry from Brazil," and "Bleak Prison Life Bars Lovers' Plan to Marry, Raise Family: Reporter Bridges Loneliness for Jailed Canadians," life for Christine and David seemed heart-wrenchingly bleak. "Breakfast is a tiny beaker of black, sugary coffee and a piece of bread. Seven days a week, lunch and dinner are rice and beans," wrote Bolan in 1991.

However, upon inspecting the prison kitchen and perusing the menus, which change daily, I was surprised to find just how varied and nutritional the meals are. For instance, on Wednesday, May 11, 1994, lunch consisted of beans, rice, fried eggs, stewed squash, lettuce, and a banana and orange for dessert. Dinner on Friday, May 13, 1994 consisted of watercress salad, spinach pasta in an oil and garlic sauce, and beans. On the following day, lunch consisted of rice, beans, beef stew with potatoes, salad, and fruit. Breakfast was the only meal that I found lacking. In most cases it was coffee, milk, and bread with margarine.

Even Mrs. Lamont has been forced to concede that Christine's prison conditions are "reasonable by Brazilian standards," yet when any reference is made to prison conditions in Brazil, the Lamonts and their supporters mechanically cite Amnesty International reports and articles in the mainstream media that, like the Carandiru massacre, have little to do with Christine and David's quotidian reality. For instance, the Lamonts cited an April 9, 1990 article from *Time* magazine about overcrowded prison conditions in Brazil to further their cause. The article described the barbaric practice of the "death lottery" at the Santo André prison in São Paulo, in which inmates kill fellow prisoners to protest overcrowded and filthy conditions. The Santo André prison is nineteen kilometres away from David and Christine's jails.

During their children's first few months in prison, the Lamonts and Bill Spencer made much out of the fact that Christine and David were serving out their sentences in solitary confinement. Mr. Spencer, for instance, told me that David spent fifteen months in solitary confinement. But contrary to unsubstantiated Canadian media reports at the time, David and Christine did not spend their first several months in dark, damp, and gloomy cells, twenty-four hours a day. Technically, they never spent any time at all in solitary confinement, according to São Paulo prison authorities and Canadian diplomats.

When I asked Walter Hoffgen, the warden at the Penitenciária do Estado why David had spent so long in solitary confinement, he smiled and said that it was a lie. David spent his first fifteen months in "a provisional situation," waiting to be registered. "We cannot accept prisoners here who have not been definitively condemned," he said, adding that the only restriction on David during those first months was that he couldn't hold a prison job like most of the other inmates. Although David was convicted at the conclusion of the five-month trial in 1990, Brazilian prison bureaucrats were slow to officially register David and the other members of the gang. "It's against the law to maintain people locked up for twenty-four hours a day in Brazil," he said. Most prisoners in São Paulo usually spend this "provisional" period, awaiting the outcome of their trial, in a holding cell at the Casa da Detenção.

But according to the Lamonts, David and Christine did spend twenty-four hours a day alone in their cells, sleeping on concrete blocks and flimsy mattresses. Indeed, Christine and David's letters home from this period suggest that conditions were extremely difficult in those early days, but not quite as horrible as their supporters in Canada made them out to be. In a letter to her family, Christine describes her first month in jail:

> *I wake up and start scratching all my new mosquito bites. I watch the well-fed insects floating around for a while, which will mostly all disappear for the day within an hour or so. I review how the night before went — how many times I woke up, what nightmares do I remember, etc. (I am still having a lot of nightmares, hardly a night goes by without at least one, but practically no nice dreams). Half an hour later, I get up, wash and get dressed, and make the bed. Soon after, coffee comes. It's brought by two or three of the other prisoners who work in the kitchen. I have a plastic coffee cup which I hand out the trap door, they fill it and hand it back with sweetened coffee.*

In a letter to David Humphreys updating him on Christine's prison conditions in August 1991, the Lamonts say that Christine's sanitary conditions "continue to deteriorate." This means that Christine has to clean toilets without rubber gloves and there is no soap to wash the floors at the prison. As part of her rehabilitation work, Christine pasted fabric samples into catalogues, but the Lamonts noted that she is allergic to the fabric or dyes and "breaks out into blisters and has other allergic reactions for which she is given no medication or preventative measures." The Lamonts also said that Christine was subjected to "inappropriate" questions about her sex life from a male psychiatrist at the jail, and that she was at one point guarded in a dark and grimy room by "a large male guard." According to her letters and information obtained by her parents on several visits, notes a contemporary article in the *Vancouver Sun*, the women's prison is a dingy building with several burly male guards and a male psychiatrist "who gives pelvic examinations to women complaining of depression." Although the guard made no sexual advances, the Lamonts cleverly used the incident to suggest that something could have happened.

The Lamonts also used this same kind of suggestive technique to imply that because five of the kidnappers had been tortured by police prior to the surrender, David and Christine would surely have been tortured as well if Cardinal Arns and Canadian diplomat Paul Pichette hadn't accompanied them to the police station. However, because David and Christine are Canadian citizens, not Latin Americans like the others in the gang, and also because there would have been little reason to torture anyone after the surrender, there is no reason to believe that the two would have been tortured. However repulsive the act, torture was used on the five kidnappers for a specific purpose: to enable police to discover where Diniz was being held.

"There was no need to torture anyone after the stand-off," said Tony Pereira, the RCMP officer stationed in Brazil at the time of the kidnapping. "There was no danger that Lamont and Spencer were going to be tortured. Brazil would have had a lot to lose by torturing two Canadians."

In their first two years in jail, Christine and David's day-to-day problems seemed relatively minor. In a letter to his sister Judy, dated March 2, 1990, David reported that he had heard from his lawyers that Christine was allowed to receive fresh fruit once a week and had a radio. In letters home to her parents, Christine wrote of contact with other prisoners, in particular Maria Emília Badilla.

David's letters home from that period offer only cursory descriptions of his life in jail. They are mostly taken up with analysing the Brazilian political situation and the progress of his own case. However, the Lamonts said he was subject to "a certain amount of psychological violence," being wakened in the middle of the night "to the screams of a prisoner being beaten with metal pipes." However, Canadian consular officials, who made regular visits to the two in jail, agreed that David and Christine were never in danger of being tortured.

As David noted in a letter to his father, their prison conditions were not as gloomy as the Canadian media and the Lamonts portrayed them to be:

I think being in prison is harder on the families than it is on the prisoner. The person in jail knows what it's like whereas the families can only imagine — and often your imagination can paint a much gloomi-

er picture than things really are. I'm not trying to say this is Disneyland down here (that would be somewhat exaggerating the point!) but I do hope the Lamonts were able to convey what my situation is like, i.e. the majority of the guards are easy enough to get along with, the prisoners are friendly and I'm in good spirits and health. (Though they probably reported I'm underweight, but as you know I've always been underweight — I don't understand it, I eat like a pig and my most strenuous activity has to do with washing clothes — but I still don't gain weight — chalk it up to metabolism is the only thing I can think of!)

Indeed, in a letter home to her family Christine described the guards and fellow prisoners as extremely friendly and helpful.

It may surprise you to know that neither the guards nor the other prisoners could be characterized as hard or mean or tough. Well, maybe tough, but on the whole very, very helpful. (For example — despite having no cigarettes of 'my own' for nine days I have never yet been completely out. . . and if they don't have any themselves, sometimes half a day after I ask, some will get sent in which they've borrowed from someone else).

Incidentally, this exchange occurred while Christine was supposedly in "solitary confinement" and cut off from all of her fellow prisoners. As for David's solitary confinement in a dark cell without ever seeing the sun, in several letters home from that early period he speaks of being let out daily to take the sun. And both David and Christine received regular visits from consular staff and their lawyers. In a letter to his father, David said he was glad that the Lamonts had visited him and had met the "rest of the gang" of kidnappers, with whom he seemed to be in contact at the time. Despite David's solitary confinement, the Lamonts were able to give him a box of Smarties and peanut butter when they visited in mid-1990.

In those early days, about the most difficult thing that happened to David was that he ended up reading Leo Tolstoy's *Anna Karenina* three times and spent a few weeks without cigarettes. "For more than 3 weeks I've desperately been trying to buy cigarettes. Still no luck — it's a bureaucratic fiasco."

SEE NO EVIL

David and Christine's first few months were also complicated by having to write letters to each other in Portuguese so that they could be read by the prison censors. At the time, both had a rudimentary knowledge of Spanish and could only speak a few words in Portuguese, according to one of their lawyers, Marco Antônio Nahum.

Perhaps in an attempt to illustrate the cruelty of the Brazilian prison system, Mr. Spencer told me that one of the worst things that happened to his son during one of his first Christmases in jail was that he received some hard mixed candy by parcel post from the Lamonts. By the time the package made it to David, however, "all of the peppermints had been removed" by the prison authorities.

■

Sometime after her second Christmas in jail, Christine's letters home changed radically in tone and substance. Instead of recounting in detail her days in jail, Christine started to speak of "tactics" and "strategy" and "a diplomatic approach" in an effort to get out of Brazil. The new line of action reflected a frustration with the efforts of their lawyers and the plodding nature of the Brazilian legal system.

"If we don't want to be here for years to come, there are some things in which we had better take the initiative," she wrote in a letter to her parents on December 29, 1990. "I say 'we' but I really mean 'you' — our families, friends and our contacts, and the organizations and networks we can count on for support."

Much of the early lobbying effort was directed by Christine and David themselves from their jail cells. In their correspondence to their families in Canada, Christine and David demonstrate a good understanding of the Brazilian political and legal systems.

For instance, in January 1991, Christine suggested that her parents try to lobby Cardinal Arns, Diniz himself, and Brazilian president Collor to seek an expulsion order that would allow them to go back to Canada as free citizens. Christine suggested that her parents ask Diniz, who has a great deal of influence, to set up a meeting with Collor on their behalf. Christine wrote that Diniz's brother Alcides was "best friends" with Collor and could be useful in setting up a meeting to discuss their expulsion. Christine's observations of Brazilian political machinations are perceptive. In her description of Collor, she noted:

He's a very egocentric man, unpredictable and maybe a little bit crazy. With any other government it might be just as well to talk to the Foreign Minister or whatever but not in this one. He is the man you would want to see. He runs a kind of one-man show in this country. With his government at least, he's not what you'd call much of a "team-player" — we hope he's different with his friends.

In their letters home from this period, Christine and David suggest who would be worthwhile to lobby not only in Brazil, but also in Canada. In a letter to the Lamonts, written when he had been in jail for three months, David suggested a letter-writing campaign to start the lobbying effort in Canada:

I've been thinking between our families and friends there are quite a few people scattered all over Canada who would be willing to help us get home. For people who express an interest there are two things that cross my mind they could do. First their names could be filed away in case there comes a time in the future when a letter-writing campaign is necessary. And secondly, I think it would be good if people contacted their MPs and Joe Clark to ask about our situation and more importantly what's happening re: getting letters to Christine and me.... He's [Clark] fairly well connected and I think it would be worthwhile if you contacted him and told him about the "contacting MPs idea" i.e. he could probably get quite a few people writing letters.

Six months later, the Lamonts sent a letter to Joe Clark, then Secretary of State for External Affairs and David Humphreys' friend from Alberta. On October 12, the Lamonts, Humphreys, David's father, and his sister Judith were sitting in an Ottawa office speaking to Canadian government officials about the case. At the meeting, the Lamonts didn't waste any time. They clearly stated that they wanted the Canadian government to ask for the expulsion of Christine and David, which would require the Canadian prime minister to ask the Brazilian president to expel the prisoners, who would then be allowed to go free in Canada. Canadian government officials at the meeting said they had never heard of Canada making such a request of a foreign government, but would have their legal advisors review the procedure.

Encouraged by this response, Humphreys drafted a letter on October 15 to Nahum in São Paulo, asking him to send a letter to External Affairs officials, providing more information on how an expulsion would work in Brazil. Nahum was also asked to stress certain points in his letter: "Repeat this point: Without interference from Canada an expulsion will only be possible after completion of the full sentence in Brazil. The Brazilians will let the prisoner rot in jail if the home country of the prisoner does not show active interest."

Humphreys ended the letter by asking the Brazilian lawyer if the Lamonts should try to lobby the new Canadian ambassador, Bill Clarke, who had just been appointed to Brasília. The letter outlines the lobbying strategy in Canada and the plodding nature of Canadian bureaucracy:

> *The professional bureaucrats are cautious and guarded in their comments. This is typical in Canada. Our impression is that our goal is attainable, but we will have to keep pushing. . . . We will be working to build up our case here. For example, the bureaucrats were worried about the political impact involving other Canadians imprisoned abroad. They say there are about 500. We will determine how many are drug-related etc., and that will help our case.*

By November 13, Nahum had sent a response to Humphreys, who in turn sent it on to Terry Hobart, special assistant (consular affairs) to the Secretary of State for External Affairs.

A federal cabinet reshuffle in April 1991 left Barbara McDougall in charge of External Affairs, and almost overnight Canadian government officials became less cooperative, according to Humphreys.

Nevertheless, the lobbying effort took off with a vengeance when Christine and David's sentences were increased to twenty-eight years when an appeal was finally heard in December 1991. The appellate court judge in São Paulo found them guilty of all three original charges (resisting arrest, forming a gang for criminal intent and extortion through kidnapping). "The facts are incontrovertible. . . the accused being arrested in flagrante delicto," noted Judge Jarbas Mazzoni in his written judgement. "There is not the least doubt that the accused David Robert Spencer and Christine Gwen Lamont were shareholders who contributed greatly to the accomplishment of the crime of kidnapping. To them is due the leasing of the real estate utilized by the group, including that which served to imprison the victim and in which they came to be arrested."

Unlike the trial court judge, Judge Mazzoni refused to differentiate the level of culpability of the ten accused. He gave all the same sentences regardless of their level of participation in the crime. All received twenty years for extortion through kidnapping, six years for forming a gang for criminal intent, and two years for resisting arrest.

When I spoke to Nahum on December 2, 1991, the day the São Paulo appeal court decision came down, he told me he was bitterly upset because the sentence was nothing more than a political decision. The judge was trying to turn the ten kidnappers into an example for the country, he said, to show that Brazil was going to get tough on kidnapping, a crime that continued to terrorize the upper classes in the country. For this reason, the maximum penalty was applied and the appellate court judge, like Judge Barioni, refused to recommend that the crime be considered a political act, which would be judged at the federal court level and carry a lighter sentence.

"The crime of extortion by means of kidnapping. . . inspired by the ancient use in war of demanding a price for the rescue of prisoners, presently constitutes a motive for constant alarm, because of the frequency of its practice in this country," wrote Mazzoni in his judgement. "In fact, it is necessary to end the notion of impunity which animates such criminals. Moved by avarice, they do not hestitate to maintain their victims in captivity in sub-human conditions, imposing upon them physical and moral afflictions that are communicated to the families."

The judge went on to quote Brazilian legal thinker Nelson Hungria to justify the harsh punishment:

Punishment continues to have as its foundation the moral responsibility, but it is not only retribution or ethical–juridicial reaction, following Hegelian thought: it is also a social defence. Its imposition remains conditioned to psychic imputability, but its objective is not only the re-establishment of the violated law: it is, in the same step, the protection of life in society, the idea of justice allied with the policy of social defence.

In an interview in his São Paulo office nearly three years later, Nahum told me that the twenty-eight-year sentence had destroyed his faith in Brazilian justice. "There is no justice in this country," said the middle-aged lawyer, whose pastel linen jacket matched the peach-coloured walls in his exquisitely decorated office. These did not look like the digs of Latin American human rights crusaders. With expensive watercolour paintings on the walls and modernist black-lacquered furniture, Nahum's office looked more like a high-powered corporate law firm in Toronto than a human rights advocacy centre in Brazil. "The sentence was too severe for the crime," he said. "This case started out and continues to be a highly charged political issue in this country."

The Lamonts and their supporters were devastated when they heard the decision. "I can't believe it," said Marilyn Lamont. "So this is Brazilian justice? God help us." Indeed, many even in Brazil were shocked by the sentence. Two years earlier, Darli Alves da Silva and his son Darci Alves Pereira, Amazon ranchers who had murdered internationally respected environmental activist Chico Mendes, had received nineteen-year sentences.

A week after Christine and David's new sentence was announced, the Lamont and Spencer families formally petitioned the Secretary of State for External Affairs to request that Canada ask for the expulsion of Christine and David. As a back-up, the Canadian government began the lengthy process of finalizing an exchange of prisoners treaty with Brazil that would allow Christine and David to serve out the rest of their sentences in Canadian jails. Both these options, however, required that the Brazilian government, and more specifically the Brazilian president, intervene. Although the Lamonts and Bill Spencer were becoming expert in their lobbying efforts on Parliament Hill, Brazil was another matter.

Still, the Lamonts, with the help of the Department of External Affairs, were making friends in high places. At the Lamonts' request, in February 1992 Cardinal Arns sent a letter to then prime minister Brian Mulroney, stating that Christine and David were innocent and requesting the Canadian government to intervene on their behalf. "I've got the intimate conviction that Christine Lamont and David Spencer didn't participate of [sic] that grave criminal act." The Cardinal noted that "expulsion from Brazil will be the best and prompt remedy."

In the same year, consular officials in São Paulo arranged for the Lamonts to meet with Brazil's justice minister Jarbas Passarinho, who said that he would definitely recommend that President Collor sign an expulsion order. During the Earth Summit in Rio de Janeiro in June, Mulroney met with Collor in an off-the-record, closed-door session and reportedly asked the Brazilian president to release the Canadians. He did this despite the fact that McDougall had sent a letter on April 14 to the Lamont and Spencer families saying that she was not prepared to petition the Brazilian government for an expulsion. She noted that although she found the twenty-eight-year sentences excessive, she would only seek an expulsion once "local remedies" in Brazil, such as legal appeals, had been exhausted. Christine and David's lawyers had launched appeals to the Supreme Court to have the case re-tried as a political crime and to reduce the sentences. Collor, who would be impeached in a few months' time, reportedly said that he would study the case.

"We couldn't believe it. Not only was the Canadian prime minister asking the head of state of a foreign country to release two convicted kidnappers, but he was going against his own foreign minister to win a few political points. It was disgusting," said a Canadian consular official, based in Brazil, who did not want to be identified.

During question period in the House of Commons after his return to Canada, Mulroney admitted he had brought up the issue with Collor, but that a request for expulsion by the Canadians was not something that was automatic in Brazil because in this particular case the issue was so politically charged. In his reply to NDP member Svend Robinson, Mulroney said: "I examined with Brazilian officials... the concept that they were sitting around waiting for a request for an expulsion to which they would respond immediately. This is not the case. This is not an accurate assumption, and people ought to set it aside. What I did raise with the President is the opportunities under their constitution available to him and to the government of Canada considering the plight of these two prisoners, for whom we all feel a great deal of concern and anxiety."

In Canada there was a flurry of activity. The Lamonts hired the Toronto law firm Davies, Ward & Beck to make the case for an expulsion to McDougall. An all-party hearing of the parliamentary justice committee was held in June 1992. Five members of the Progressive Conservative party presided along with four Liberals and one New Democrat. After two days of tearful testimony from the Lamonts, Bill

Spencer, and Marco Antônio Nahum, the members of the justice committee unanimously agreed to recommend that the Canadian government seek an expulsion.

Like everything else in this case, the decision was based on a number of misconceptions spread in the Canadian media. One of those misconceptions was that "prison conditions in Brazil constitute a serious threat to the health and safety of Christine Lamont and David Spencer." Marilyn Lamont described in graphic detail what prison conditions were like for her daughter. "One month in solitary confinement when you can't even speak to anyone else, when there is a solid door and they close the slot so you can't even see anybody going by, where you are sleeping on a cement bed and they rip up your mattress in one of the searches that they do routinely and don't replace it for nine months — I don't know. How do you compare that? How do you equate that? I just have no way of equating it." The committee members all accepted this at face value even though much of Mrs. Lamont's description seemed to be a misconception.

There was much earnest hand-wringing by the committee members on political corruption in Brazil and irregularities in the trial proceedings. In fact, the entire two-day affair was characterized by huge leaps of logic and ludicrous generalities about the case and about Latin America.

When asked to explain why her daughter and David were travelling on false passports, Mrs. Lamont referred to the documents as "alternative identification" and gave an explanation that mixed Cold War generalities about Latin America with incredible ignorance. The statement was made with such authority and passion, though, that nobody dared question it: "If you're working in the human rights area in Central America, where they were previous to going to South America, if you are familiar with the Amnesty International information you will recognize that you're at risk not only for your life but for torture or for simply disappearing. If you enter a country using a false name, a false passport, and you establish your identity under that passport, and then you become aware that you're being followed, there's a death squad on your trail or you're in danger in some way, you get out your real passport and exit the country. This is how it protects you." Nobody bothered to consult Amnesty International or any of the other established human rights organizations to find out if this was true.

In addition to officials at Amnesty International, I spoke to individual human rights workers who said that they had never heard of anyone using false passports to protect themselves in Latin America. "It's simply too risky," said Amanda Hopkinson, a British translator who worked in the human rights field in El Salvador during the civil war. "If you get into trouble on a false passport, it's much more difficult for you to get out of the country."

For his part, Bill Spencer offered a ridiculous analogy to explain how his son could definitely have been in the safe house in São Paulo but not be considered a member of the gang: "My parents and I were evicted out of a run-down slum tenement because we couldn't pay the rent. My parents found a couple of rooms in a large, slummy tenement building in Saint John near the docks. The building was largely a brothel. . . . The sailors from the nearby docks would come to that house and the girls would perform their duties in the rooms and in the hallways and all that sort of thing. I grew up in a brothel. Please believe me, gentlemen, I am not a prostitute."

Despite the presence of Nahum, there was much ignorance about Brazil. Jennie Hatfield-Lyon, a law professor who had acted as a consultant on the brief presented by the Lamont and Spencer families' lawyers, told the justice committee that the Canadian government should have provided a trained Brazilian lawyer, "speaking Brazilian," to observe the trial proceedings.

Nahum, playing on the ignorance of the Canadians, made much of the fact that the kidnapping was used by the forces of the right in Brazil to discredit the left.

Everyone ganged up on Barry Mawhinney, a legal advisor for the Legal Affairs Branch of the Department of External Affairs. Mawhinney noted that "the case is both complex and difficult" and that McDougall had reviewed the case "thoroughly" and found that there had been no miscarriage of justice. "We decided at the outset that it would be totally inappropriate to retry the case. Therefore, our recommendation to the minister was not based on any conclusion about the guilt or innocence of Christine and David. Instead, we reviewed whether the trial judge and the appeal court had enough evidence, properly, to make the findings that they did. We also reviewed the trial process."

Concerned about the "harshness" of the twenty-eight-year sentences, McDougall had instructed the Canadian ambassador to express this concern to the Brazilian foreign ministry, but Mawhinney also noted that hostage taking by anyone — including Canadians — is a serious crime. The Montreal Hijacking Convention of 1971 and an international convention against the taking of hostages drafted in New York in 1979 both flatly condemn hijacking and hostage taking as grave offences and require states to make it an offence for their nationals to commit such acts, wherever they may be," said Mawhinney. He added that Canada implemented both conventions and that "our extradition treaties also clearly reject the notion that political motivation could be a legal defence to a crime involving the threat or use of force."

Mawhinney's remarks that Canada would lose its credibility abroad if it requested expulsion in this particular case would prove to be prescient a year later, when Canada was to become the laughing-stock of Brazil. "The minister examined this and her decision was that, given the seriousness of the crime involved, unless there was a serious miscarriage of justice in this case there would not be a basis for her [to recommend expulsion]," said Mawhinney. "The concern here is that if we simply make it a request for expulsion in a case like this, how can anyone take Canada seriously when we talk about basic human rights and respect for human rights and the matters related to the hostage-taking convention?"

Despite the unanimous recommendation of the justice committee to request that the Canadian government seek an expulsion, McDougall flatly refused. "I felt desperately sorry for the families, but we couldn't take this crime lightly. It was a serious crime," she told me. "Foreign ministers in government cannot protect nationals. There's only so much your government can do for you no matter how just your cause."

McDougall told *The Fifth Estate* that expulsion wasn't automatic because all legal avenues in Brazil had to be exhausted and it depended very much on the Brazilian president's political will. Besides, she noted, two intelligent adults "People who are in their late twenties have to take responsibility for their actions no matter how innocent, and when people are abroad they are subject to the laws of that country in which they travel."

The Lamont and Spencer families were appalled by what they took to be McDougall's indifference. "It's infuriating that your own country is doing this for God knows what reason," said Keith Lamont in an interview with *The Fifth Estate*. Marilyn Lamont said that McDougall must be "devoid of any compassion."

Bill Spencer was outraged. In a heart-wrenching interview on the same program he criticized McDougall and said he felt abandoned by his country. "I asked the government of Canada to intervene on behalf of a member of my family. They did nothing. Among thousands of my peers, I devoted five years of the prime of my life in defence of this democracy and on one of my first requests on behalf of a member of my family, I get nothing. Nothing."

A year earlier, just before his sentence was handed down, David had commented that the bureaucrats in Ottawa were just too pigheaded to understand how the Brazilian legal system works. "It's like they think Brazil is Canada, only with a nicer climate. The Canadian government doesn't understand the problems with the judicial system here after 25 years of dictatorship. . . Like, I'm in jail for 10 years for renting a house," he said in an interview with Bolan of the *Vancouver Sun*.

Right after the appeal court's sentence was pronounced in Brazil, David Humphreys wrote an opinion piece for *The Globe and Mail*. Entitled "When Ottawa Washes Its Hands," the article was a diatribe against the Canadian government's inaction on Christine and David's behalf.

> *The case of the two Canadians who unwittingly played bit parts in a Brazilian kidnap drama should serve as a lesson for any of us who get in trouble abroad and expect help from our government. . . . The Lamont and Spencer families have been advised to forget about Canadian assistance and to concentrate instead on the Brazilian end — an expensive proposition. This should not be necessary. Canadians have an obligation to show concern for fellow citizens in distress. Just because people have been indiscreet, naive or even foolhardy is no reason for the rest of us to sit back and say that "they deserve what they get."*

Humphreys couldn't resist taking a few shots at Brazil. "A dictatorship until 1986, Brazil remains high on the list of human rights violators kept by Amnesty International." (Nobody wrote a letter to *The Globe and Mail*, however, correcting Humphreys' knowledge of Latin American history. Brazil's military regime stepped down in 1985.) "It is interesting that Mrs. McDougall seems to find its system of justice acceptable. . . . The Lamont and Spencer families have documented a range of fabrications and distortions in the case. Both the RCMP and U.S. authorities have searched in vain for evidence of any criminal activity on the part of Mr. Spencer and the American-born Ms. Lamont."

Ordinary Canadians across the country were outraged by the "heartless" actions of their government. In a letter to the *Vancouver Sun*, Constance Doan of Mount Lehman wrote: "I am continually appalled by the apathy of the Canadian government in refusing to request the expulsion of Christine Lamont and David Spencer from Brazil. Why do we so often protect behind our border convicted U.S. criminals who, in a country with a system of common law similar to ours, presumably had a fair trial, yet we repeatedly refuse to bring home to Canada our own citizens from a country internationally infamous for human rights violations and political corruption. . . a country where children are known to be murdered in the streets of São Paulo by police to protect merchants from their petty thievery. . . a country where environmental activist Chico Mendes was murdered for his efforts to save the rainforest and no effort was made by Brazilian authorities to prosecute those who ordered his execution." Like Humphreys and the Lamont and Spencer families, Doan didn't really bother to get her facts right about Brazil. Brazilian authorities did indeed prosecute the murderers of Chico Mendes, although they escaped from prison in the Amazon state of Acre in February 1993.

Following the sentencing, the Lamont and Spencer families gained even more support across the country. New Brunswick premier Frank McKenna was outraged at the federal government for not doing more for David and Christine. "My heart bleeds at what these families are going through. . . knowing that their children are in danger in a foreign country, that they've been sentenced for a crime there's every real chance they never committed," he told Victor Malarek.

Barbara McDougall became the enemy of the Canadian people for standing by her principles on the case as the Progressive Conservative government trailed in the polls on the eve of a federal election.

A group of young lawyers at the University of Saskatchewan released an independent legal study in January 1993 suggesting that Christine and David should sue McDougall because she had failed to protect the lives of the jailed pair as guaranteed under the Charter of Rights and Freedoms. The forty-four-page brief was prepared by Blaine Donais, then a third-year law student at the University of Saskatchewan and president of the Saskatchewan chapter of an organization called Lawyers for Social Responsibility, a national advocacy group devoted mainly to environmental issues. Donais's brief, which used information culled from biased Canadian media reports on the prison conditions of the two Canadians, urged the two families to sue the Canadian government in order to force it to take action on an expulsion. The brief was based on the premise that Christine and David are protected by the Charter even though they are living abroad. Donais suggested that they could claim protection under Section 7, which guarantees "life, liberty and security of the person" and Section 12, which protects against "cruel and unusual treatment or punishment." Although the Charter could not "correct injustices committed in Brazil" it does cover action by a Canadian cabinet minister, argued Donais. He also noted that McDougall's inaction on the case exposed Christine and David to cruel and unusual punishment abroad and deprived them of liberty beyond the principles of fundamental justice.

"The Secretary of State for External Affairs has violated the rights guaranteed under Section 7 of the Charter. . . and the minister's refusal to make the expulsion request in light of the dangerous and appalling prison conditions (and in light of the clear miscarriage of justice) violates the rights of Lamont and Spencer to liberty and security of the person."

Although the brief presented an interesting legal argument and had the support of several senior faculty members at the University of Saskatchewan's College of Law, it was not taken very seriously by the Canadian legal establishment, many of whom argued that the Charter cannot be applied to Canadians in a foreign country. Had the case ever gone to court, a judge would have had to decide whether the Charter could be applied to citizens living outside Canada.

Nevertheless, the Lamont and Spencer families were pleased that many in Canada were in solidarity with them to get David and Christine out of jail. "It's really gratifiying to have something like this legal opinion pop up independently of ourselves," Mrs. Lamont told a reporter from *The Globe and Mail*. "We've found much of what we say is discredited by External Affairs because we are Christine's parents."

In the end, the Lamonts did not take legal action against the Canadian government, but their plight as honest Canadians fighting injustice in Brazil and indifference in Ottawa was given a huge boost. The media-smart Humphreys had done a wonderful job whipping up popular support for Christine and David, and the campaign might have worked had it not been for a mysterious explosion in Nicaragua that sent shock waves around the world.

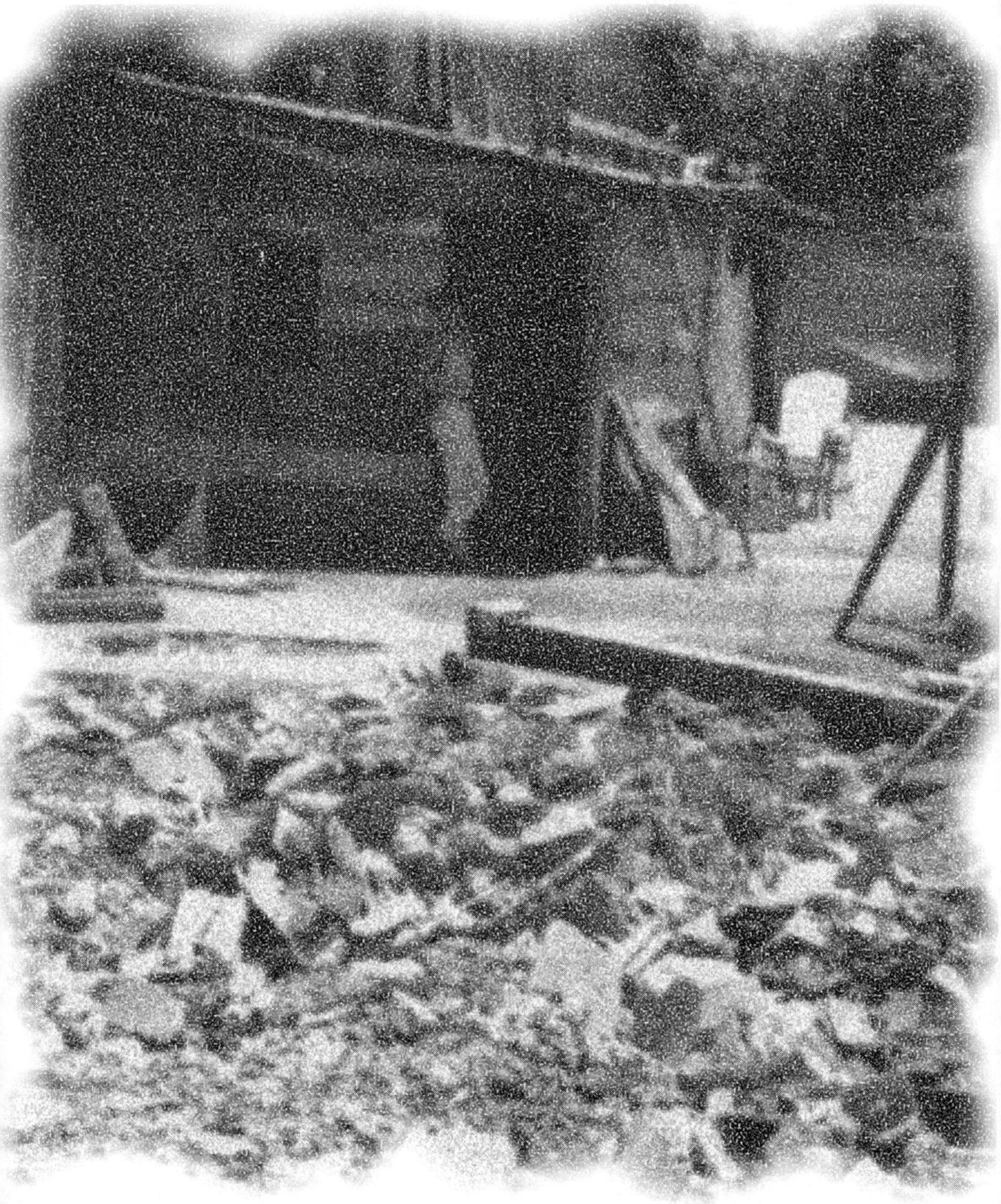

Six

Juan Carlos Rosales isn't very good with dates, but he does remember the night that his plywood shack came crashing down around him and his family as they slept. It was May 23, 1993 when a neighbouring auto repair shop exploded in Managua's industrial Santa Rosa district, levelling the area around it.

"It completely destroyed my house. I woke up buried under debris and found I had nothing left," said Rosales, a twenty-nine-year-old father of four, who has recently built a patchwork plywood and corrugated tin shack on the explosion site. The area now is a sun-blistered expanse of rusted oil drums, broken shingles, and shards of glass that nobody bothered to clean up after the blast and the subsequent police investigation.

Minutes after the explosion rocked the neighbourhood just after 2 a.m., a horde of journalists, police, and government officials began to arrive to photograph the site. Rosales remembers thinking that "something important" was going on because for weeks afterwards so many brand-new jeeps would slowly drive by, with their mysterious occupants lowering their tinted windows and peering from the upper rim of their Ray Bans to get a good look at the destroyed auto repair shop.

During the lengthy police investigation, the entire area around the explosion site was cordoned off, and Rosales, who, ironically, used to work in a fireworks factory, was kicked off his land. He recently set up as a squatter on the blast site, which has been converted into a mini dump. Residents throw their garbage there, including dead cats and dogs whose putrid remains swarm with flies, baking in the relentless afternoon sun around Rosales' tiny shack.

Rosales, who was unemployed when I spoke to him in March 1994, said that he and his neighbours wanted to clear the blast site and start a small communal vegetable farm. But it was hard going, he said wearily, surveying the piles of rubble around him. He said he wasn't really worried about being kicked off the land because he heard that the owner of the repair shop was a *terrorista* who probably wouldn't be coming back to Nicaragua to claim the property for a long time. However, there was a rumour that Managua city hall officials wanted to turn the site into a basketball court. Nevertheless, Rosales said that he was waiting for his sister and her family to arrive from the interior to set up a shack on a tiny plot of land he had managed to clear next to his house.

All he knew about the blast, which the Nicaraguan press dubbed the *"buzón de Santa Rosa"*, was that in the debris police had discovered a huge arms cache belonging to Salvadoran rebels. There were some other things too — false documents, lists of prominent Latin Americans — but Rosales didn't really pay that much attention after a while.

"I was just trying to provide for my family and survive," he said, adding that his children sometimes woke up screaming in the middle of the night, afraid that pieces of wood and tin were falling on them as they slept.

"The *buzón* changed my whole life."

■

The *buzón de Santa Rosa* also shook up the Latin American militant left. The blast revealed a subterranean chamber 4 metres deep and 2.3 metres wide, stocked with hundreds of assault rifles, tons of explosives and at least nineteen surface-to-air missiles, all belonging to the Popular Forces of Liberation (FPL—Fuerzas Populares de la Liberación), a radical faction of El Salvador's FMLN.

The blast damaged seventeen homes in the Santa Rosa neighbourhood and killed three people. Although no one is certain just what triggered the explosion, investigators believe that it may have occurred as the users of the bunker loaded part of their explosives cache into the trunk of a Volkswagen Beetle. Police believe a detonator may have accidentally fallen to the ground, setting off the explosion. Dominique Reugsegger, a Swiss citizen and the owner of the Beetle, was arrested by police right after the explosion, but said he knew nothing about the blast. He said his car, which was completely destroyed, had been undergoing repairs at the mechanic's shop.

The explosion made just about everyone on the Latin American militant left very nervous. The FMLN, who admitted to the ownership of the arms in the Santa Rosa bunker, had signed a UN-brokered peace accord with El Salvador's rightist government in January 1992 to end the brutal twelve-year civil war that claimed more than 75,000 lives. Stockpiling arms, even in a foreign country, was in direct violation of the accord. What was worse, the FMLN's former military strategist Joaquín Villalobos was forced to apologize to the Nicaraguan government and admit that in addition to the one in Santa Rosa, there were fifteen other bunkers scattered throughout Managua. Weapons were found at ten of the FMLN sites and in a cache belonging to the Guatemalan Unidad Revolucionaria Nacional Guatemalteca (URNG) rebels. In addition to the weapons seized at the Santa Rosa bunker, Nicaraguan police found a total of 823 machine guns, 1,359 grenades and 1.1 million rounds of ammunition.

The Managua explosion, which also linked the FMLN to terrorism and kidnapping, was to have grave implications for the coalition's chances of winning the elections in El Salvador. ARENA, the ruling rightist party, used the Managua blast in propaganda against the FMLN-dominated coalition. After the 1992 peace accords, the FMLN had become a legitimate political party in El Salvador and had helped to mount a leftist coalition to run in the country's first post–civil war elections in March 1994. The FMLN's opponents seized on the weapons discovery, saying it proved that the former rebels were not sincere in their support of democracy. The blast also led to divisive criticism within the FMLN itself, which operated as an alliance of five rebel groups that held together reasonably well during the civil war. The group's largest faction, the FPL, admitted to the ownership of the weapons found in Managua only to be bitterly criticized by the leader of the next-largest faction, who charged that the FPL was "eroding public faith in the alliance."

The blast also made the Nicaraguan Sandinistas look bad. While it was a well-known fact that the Sandinista government had given the FMLN rebels support during the civil war in El Salvador, many were surprised to find proof that it actually allowed them to build sophisticated bunkers in Managua. "This wasn't about storing arms in a basement. These were actual reinforced, steel bunkers. You just don't build one of these things overnight. Whoever built that bunker knew a lot about war," said a U.S. intelligence official, who is still investigating the Managua blast.

When asked how the arsenals could exist without the knowledge of the Sandinista party and the army, which is still largely controlled by the Sandinistas, former Nicaraguan president Daniel Ortega tried to avoid the issue. "This kind of thing happens in any country, including the United States," he said. "In this country, a lot of caches were planted here as a result of the politics of President Reagan."

The blast came right after revelations that radical Sandinistas had continued to help Latin American guerrillas in Managua and were still using the state security apparatus to keep a close eye on their enemies. This loosely defined group of radicals within the Sandinista party is suspected of having worked clandestinely since the mid-1980s with Latin American and Middle Eastern terrorists.

U.S. intelligence officials have long speculated that much of the terrorist activity in the region was controlled by the general directorate for state security (DGSE), which under Sandinista rule was controlled by the interior ministry. When they lost power in 1990, the Sandinistas managed to keep control of the DGSE by transferring its operations to the army. Many say that former interior minister Tomás Borge and former secret police chief Lenin Cerna were personally aware of the existence of the bunkers. Witnesses said that Borge even showed up on the night of the explosion of the Santa Rosa bunker in his pyjamas. A Nicaraguan journalist told me that one of the cars in the garage at the auto repair shop was a jeep belonging to Borge.

It is a well-documented fact that the DGSE had used European and Latin American terrorists for activities in the past, such as the 1980 assassination of former Nicaraguan dictator Anastásio Somoza in

Paraguay and the 1984 attempt against contra leader Eden Pastora at La Penca, a jungle outpost in Costa Rica. The bomb explosion at La Penca left three journalists dead and seventeen other people injured. Several years later, Pastora, a former Sandinista, said he recognized the bomber from a Sandinista guerrilla training camp. Until 1993, investigators suspected that the architects of the La Penca bombing were right-wing terrorists connected with the CIA. However, a private investigator found evidence suggesting that the bombing was a Sandinista plot.

The DGSE contracted with many *internacionalistas*, terrorists from other parts of Latin America and overseas. Argentine terrorist Enrique Gorriarán Merlo was employed by the Sandinistas on several occasions, and Nicaraguan police found a pamphlet on Gorriarán's guerrilla philosophy in the bunker. Investigators say he is an important link for Central American left-wing extremists and their South American counterparts.

Gorriarán was the ultimate internationalist revolutionary. Born in San Nicolas, a small town in the province of Buenos Aires, in 1942, Gorriarán worked with pro-Cuban groups in Argentina. In 1979 he travelled to Nicaragua where, like many Argentine revolutionaries, he joined the Sandinista National Liberation Front (FSLN). In 1980, he organized *Operación reptil*, the commando raid that killed Somoza with a single bazooka shell in Asuncion. Investigators believe that he was also behind the La Penca bombing in 1989. Also in 1989, Gorriarán's Movimiento todos por la patria (MTP, or the All for the Fatherland Movement) organized the attack on the La Tablada military barracks outside Buenos Aires. Gorriarán is believed to be at large in southern Brazil, and many intelligence officials have linked him to the multinational terrorist group that kidnapped Abilio Diniz in 1989.

In addition to Gorriarán, Nicaragua's DGSE regularly employed exiled members of the Chilean MIR for intelligence gathering operations abroad. Nicaraguans preferred to recruit foreigners such as Argentines and Chileans to carry out intelligence gathering missions because they were "better educated, whiter, and more cosmopolitan" than their Central American counterparts, said a Latin American diplomat stationed in Managua. According to Spanish press accounts, Basque terrorists were also recruited by the Sandinistas in the 1980s to assist in building bunkers, to train other *internacionalistas* in guerrilla tactics and to conduct intelligence operations.

"The general directorate (for state security) was a lot like the Comintern in the 1920s. Young revolutionaries would be sent to the Communist home state, in this case Nicaragua, to learn proper ideology and then sent out undercover to work in countries other than their home country," said a U.S. security expert, adding that terrorists trained in Nicaragua would often set up their bases of operation in quieter countries bordering those that were the real focus of their activities. For instance, many terrorists working in Brazil or Argentina set up in neighbouring Uruguay, and many FMLN guerrilla commanders would spend extended periods in Mexico or Nicaragua during the civil war in El Salvador.

As Nicaragua's national police continued to collect information on the bunkers, critics of Nicaraguan president Violetta Chamorro were calling for an end to the power-sharing agreement that she made with the Sandinistas after her election victory in 1990. Under that arrangement, the Sandinistas still maintained a significant amount of control over the the army and the state security intelligence forces, which are reportedly still made up largely of former Sandinista soldiers and spies trained in the former Soviet Union. In order to appease her critics, Doña Violetta, as she is known in Nicaragua, burned the weapons collected from the fifteen bunkers in a huge crater, under the watchful eye of UN officials. Despite Doña Violetta's public actions, U.S. State Department officials feared that the Nicaraguan police would be prevented from conducting a proper investigation into the explosion for fear of implicating former high-ranking Sandinista officials.

"In addition to a lack of professional training and resources, which impedes the government of Nicaragua from carrying out a comprehensive investigation, there is concern that Army and police officials do not want the investigation to move into areas where FSLN figures might be implicated," noted an official in a report from the U.S. State Department's Bureau of Inter-American Affairs.

In addition to a sizeable cache of arms, the blast unearthed 306 travel documents, including blank passports from Britain, El Salvador, Germany, Grenada, Italy, Switzerland, Venezuela, and the United States. In the bunker itself and in the house of the auto repair shop's owner, investigators found credit cards, false press credentials, drivers' licences, and 96 rubber stamps depicting entry and exit visas for various Latin American countries. They also found detailed notes on how to enter South American countries surreptitiously. In an annotation on crossing the Colombian border into Brazil, the writer notes that the best way to go is to cross the border at Letícia in the Amazon jungle, then to take a boat to Manaus from Benjamin Constant, a small Brazilian town on the Colombian/Peruvian/Brazilian border. The writer carefully notes that Brazilian immigration is open Monday to Friday from 8:00 a.m. to 12:00 noon and from 2:00 p.m. to 6:00 p.m. Similar routes are outlined for crossing the border into Peru and Venezuela from the Brazilian Amazon.

In addition to a list of detailed routes in and out of Latin American countries, police discovered notes on political party structures and military installations in various Latin American countries. The files clearly showed foreign leftists how to infiltrate left-wing political parties and human rights groups in foreign countries. Analysts say that terrorists forge links with these groups in order to establish a base of operations in a foreign country. The *Folha de São Paulo* reported that many of the reports found in the bunker referred to forging links with the Brazilian Worker's Party (PT), and the newspaper concluded from the find that the Chilean, Argentine, and Canadian kidnappers in the Diniz case in 1989 must have tried to take advantage of PT connections to set up an operating base in São Paulo.

> *The purpose was to obtain information about a place where a kidnapping was going to take place. The international gang planned to infiltrate their militants into left-wing parties and human rights groups and sometimes in the organizations operated by the kidnap targets themselves. This is demonstrated by the documents prepared by the group. There are details like the daily routine of the executives, police habits and the internal division of political parties (all of the factions of the PT are noted, for example).*

The article pointed out that many of the kidnappers passed themselves off as refugees under the protection of the United Nations High Commission on Refugees (UNHCR). But it also observed that the PT was probably not knowingly involved with the kidnapping. The PT is known for its open structure, analysts say, but has rejected any links with criminal activity in the past. In April 1986, for instance, the PT rejected illegal activity when one of its factions robbed a bank in Salvador a city in northeastern Brazil. The faction was immediately expelled.

Among the most suspicious items found in the bunker were lists of Latin American industrialists, detailing their daily movements and sources of income. Based on the lists, Nicaraguan police and Interpol officials immediately concluded that they were dealing with a highly organized international kidnapping ring. There were lists of more than 100 potential targets scattered throughout Latin America. Although much of the financial information about the executives appears to have been compiled from press clippings and company reports, their personal and family information was the result of espionage by members of the gang. Hand-scrawled annotations on the daily lives of these potential kidnap victims were extremely precise. Mexican hotel magnate Antonio Gutierrez Prieto was observed while attending a mass to commemorate the second anniversary of his wife's death. His son was later abducted and held for eight months. Among those observed in the late 1980s in Ecuador were relatives of current president Sixto Duran-Ballen. In addition to a listing of the family's banking, leasing, insurance, and commercial interests, police found very specific handwritten notes regarding Thomas, Ronald, and Sidney Wright Duran-Ballen that illustrate the intentions of the group:

1. *Objective: Thomas or Ronald, heads of the group and those with the greatest personal fortunes.*
2. *City: Quito*
3. *Possible worth of family: between $200 million and $250 million*
4. *Amount to negotiate: $10 million (could be higher, depending on the negotiations)*

Investigators were impressed by the amount of detail that went into the files on the potential victims. For instance, one note says that a garbage truck goes to the Lomas de Chapultepec mansion of Lebanese immigrant Carlos Slim Helu, who lives in Mexico City, every day at 10 a.m. and that a guard opens the gate for it.

"We have discovered an enormous operation," said Alfredo Mendieta, Nicaragua's interior minister and chief of internal security. "And we have only reached the tip of the iceberg."

On March 15, 1994, a cousin of Slim Helu, Alfredo Harp Helu, who was also on the list found in Managua, was kidnapped by eight armed men as he left his house for work. Harp, who is the president and a major stockholder of the Banamex–Accival financial group in Mexico, was eventually released in June 1994 after his family reportedly paid $30 million U.S. in a cash ransom to the kidnappers. Negotiations were tense because the kidnappers had originally demanded $124 million and had insisted that they would kill Harp if the ransom was not paid.

The *Los Angeles Times* reported that Harp's kidnapping was probably the work of a professional kidnap gang organized by Basque terrorists. "The efficiency and professionalism of the kidnapping — including the immediate blindfolding and drugging of Harp — indicated that the abductors had a surprising level of sophistication."

In April 1994, Angel Losada Moreno, vice-chairman of Grupo Gigante, Mexico's second-largest supermarket chain, was kidnapped in Mexico City. His abductors originally demanded a $30 million U.S. ransom and threatened to kill him if his family refused to pay. Losada was eventually released on August 5, 1994 after his family paid an undisclosed ransom. Both Losada and his father Angel Losada Gomez were on the Mangua list.

"This is a huge international terrorism network. You really have to be concerned about anyone whose passport was found in the bunker," said a spokesman for Kroll Associates, a U.S. security firm. Following the explosion, the well-regarded private investigation firm was swamped with calls from Latin American businessmen whose names had been found on the list.

Interpol said that the lists of these potential kidnap victims were probably compiled by a gang of international terrorists, working together from a base in Managua — "the control centre for terrorists in Latin America" as one Brazilian terrorism expert put it. Brazilian investigators traced the kidnappings of Abílio Diniz, Brazilian banker Antônio Beltran Martinez, Brazilian executive Geraldo Alonso Filho and Brazilian media guru Luis Salles to the Managua list. In the documents related to the Diniz family fortune found in the bunker, Abílio Diniz is not specifically mentioned but is referred to in passing simply as "Carmelo." This is the codename that the ten kidnappers used to refer to Diniz when he was kidnapped in 1989.

Investigators suspected that the Managua gang was led by Basque separatists exiled in Latin America. For nearly three decades, the ETA has conducted a bombing and assassination campaign to win independence for nearly 3 million Basques living along the Spanish–French border.

Hundreds of ETA members fled Spain in the 1980s to avoid capture by Spanish authorities and were given a warm welcome in Nicaragua by the leftist Sandinistas. In the Santa Rosa bunker police found a long dissertation on ETA strategy, dated May 12, 1992. Moreover, the repair shop that housed the bunker was owned by a Basque terrorist to whom the leftist Sandinista government had given Nicaraguan citizenship. Eusébio Arzalluz Tapia, known by his alias Miguel Antônio Larios Moreno, reportedly escaped after the explosion. Tapia, whose Interpol file is more than two metres thick, is a leading member of ETA, wanted in Europe for at least twenty bombings. Interpol officials say he was recruited by the Sandinista secret service to aid in intelligence gathering operations in the 1980s. A week after the explosion a former member of the Sandinista state security apparatus revealed to authorities the identities of three top-ranking ETA members living in Managua under assumed names. The three, who had all worked for interior minister Tomás Borge, were deported to Spain where they were immediately arrested.

Under questioning by Spanish authorities, José María Larreategui Cuadra, one of the ETA members deported from Nicaragua, said that many of the ETA members in Nicaragua had trained in guerrilla tactics in South Yemen along with members of the German Red Army Faction, France's Direct Action, and the Irish Republican Army. Larreategui, known as Pedro in Managua, had been sent to the Central American country in 1980 to establish links with the Sandinista government. Part of his work in Nicaragua was to pass on to his Latin American counterparts guerrilla tactics that he had learned in South Yemen.

It's clear that during the rule of the Sandinista government, ETA members established a secure base in Nicaragua, many of them working for the DGSE and helping run guerrilla training camps in the country. Before he left the presidency in April 1990 after his government was defeated, Daniel Ortega issued approximately two thousand Nicaraguan passports to foreigners. Of that group, eighty-eight were issued to members of the ETA in Spain. After the Sandinista election loss in 1990 and a crackdown on ETA leaders in Europe two years later, many Basque separatists reportedly set up bases in Mexico. In the 1970s, Basque terrorists were allowed into Mexico as political refugees. Spanish authorities believe that more than one hundred ETA members took refuge in Mexico over the last twenty years. Mexico and Spain are currently in the process of negotiating an extradition treaty that would include terrorist crimes.

In addition to Basque separatists, police believe other European and even Middle Eastern terrorist groups may be linked to the Managua bunker. The FBI reportedly investigated the Managua explosion for possible links to the February 1993 bombing of the World Trade Center in New York City because Arab suspects in that explosion were travelling with forged Nicaraguan passports.

"The blast proves that Nicaragua was a sanctuary for people who had been burned abroad and the headquarters for coordinating assistance to guerrillas and terrorists all over Latin America," said a Latin American diplomat stationed in Managua, who did not want to be identified.

The documents found in the Santa Rosa bunker pointed to a group of Latin American and European terrorists who had been brought together by sheer necessity. Former CIA operatives who conducted independent investigations of the explosion believed that the group was behind several kidnappings in Mexico and Brazil meant to raise money for weapons and for Marxist and separatist causes throughout Latin America and Europe. With the fall of the Berlin Wall in 1989, the collapse of the Eastern bloc, and the economic decline of Cuba, militant leftists had been forced to seek out alternative sources of funding to further their causes.

In September 1988, militant leftists from Latin America and Europe met in Hamburg at the same time as a series of World Bank/IMF meetings. There they staged demonstrations and forged a plan of action to obtain new sources of funding. Under cross-examination in São Paulo, one of Diniz's kidnappers, Chilean Pedro Lembach, said he met in Hamburg with more than 150 members of the MIR to hammer out a plan of attack. U.S. intelligence officials say that the meetings were held in Germany because the country tends to be lax about security in regard to Latin American extremists. Also, the World Bank/IMF meetings provided a great cover for holding a convention to discuss new strategies for a number of militant leftist groups. Pedro Lembach confessed to São Paulo police that the plan for the Diniz kidnapping was largely put together at the Hamburg meeting.

The meeting was reportedly organized by Germany's Rote Armee Fraktion or Red Army Faction (RAF), a twenty-four-year-old Marxist–Leninist terrorist group that has strong ties to the ETA and

Latin American extremist groups. Many RAF militants, who had made contact with Latin American exiles living in Germany, reportedly trained in Nicaragua in the 1980s. Like most of their Latin American and European urban guerrilla counterparts, the RAF targeted businessmen, politicians, government officials, and the U.S. military in their terrorist attacks. Just before the IMF/World Bank meetings, which were held in West Berlin, the RAF tried to assassinate West Germany's deputy finance minister, Hans Tietmeyer, in Bonn.

"These people needed to find their own way to fund the revolution," said one former U.S. intelligence official, adding that strong linkages still exist between European and Latin American terrorists, who regularly exchange information. "They're like-minded critters, separated only by geography."

Kidnapping to raise money for arms and political causes is nothing new in terrorist circles. In the 1970s, Italy's Red Brigades kidnapped for ransom money and as an effective tool of political pressure — by terrorizing the state and by coercing management of the industrial sector into concessions during labour unrest.

Brazilian revolutionary Carlos Marighella, a leading member of the Brazilian Communist party until 1967 and founder of a pro-Cuban guerrilla group called the Action for National Liberation(ALN), advocated kidnapping as an effective weapon in the urban guerrilla struggle.

"Kidnapping is capturing and holding in a secret spot a police agent, a North American spy, a political personality, or a notorious and dangerous enemy of the revolutionary movement," he wrote in *The Minimanual of the Urban Guerrilla*.

For Marighella, as for the Diniz kidnappers, the enemies of the revolutionary movement are members of the police, judiciary, and industry, and therefore all of them are logical targets for kidnapping.

Like their European counterparts, terrorists in Latin America followed Marighella's kidnap plan: "To compensate for his general weakness and shortage of arms compared to the enemy, the urban guerrilla uses surprise. The enemy has no way to fight surprise and becomes confused or is destroyed. . . . To insure a mobility and speed that the police cannot match, the urban guerrilla needs the following prerequisites a)mechanizations; b)knowledge of the terrain; c) a rupture or suspension of enemy communications and transport; d)light arms."

SEE NO EVIL

In all of the most recent high-profile kidnappings in Latin America, the plan of attack has been the same: terrorists surprise the victim, usually in the morning as he is on his way to work, cut off his car at a quiet intersection, hold a gun to his head, and bundle him into another vehicle. To ensure mobility and speed, the kidnappers in the Brazilian and Mexican kidnappings meticulously studied "the terrain" — in these cases, the daily habits of the executives they planned to kidnap. They also carefully documented the movements of the enemy, in these cases the police, with the aid of police-band radios.

But today, while all of Marighella's tactics still survive, much of the ideology is gone. Analysts say that revolutionary idealism actually plays a small role in the crime of kidnapping in Latin America. Since the 1970s, kidnapping has been the best way to raise quick cash for militant leftists in the region. However, the question of just how the ransoms should be divided has sparked heated arguments and splits within the Latin American left.

On September 19, 1974 a group of Montoneros, Peronist urban guerrillas, kidnapped Jorge and Juan Born, heirs and managers of the Bunge y Born grain fortune and conglomerate. The company was founded by Belgian immigrant wheat merchants in the nineteenth century and has since become one of the biggest symbols of wealth in Argentina. The Montoneros raised $64 million U.S. in ransom from the Born kidnapping alone. Much of the money was quickly spread throughout numerous banks in Europe, the United States, and Latin America while the guerrillas engaged in two more kidnappings that generated an estimated $8 million U.S. in ransom. The entire sum, which totalled more than $70 million U.S., was finally entrusted to a third party — Cuba. However, towards the end of 1977 the Cubans asked the Montoneros to donate a significant amount of the kidnap funds to Nicaragua's Sandinistas. The Argentines refused, arguing that the funds were earmarked for their final offensive and the disruption of the World Cup soccer finals in Buenos Aires in June 1978. While the Argentines fought it out among themselves, the Cubans kept the money and donated small amounts to other Latin American guerrilla groups, such as the FMLN, the Unidad Revolucionária Nacional Guatemalteca (URNG), the Honduran Cinchonero and Lorenzo Celaya Fuerzas Populares Revolucionárias, and the Chilean MIR.

"The story of the Montoneros' money illustrates the Latin American left's extreme complexity, internal contradictions and ongoing metamorphoses," writes Mexican historian Jorge Castañeda. "The right wing of the left, as exemplified by Argentine Peronism, ended up funding, arming, or organizing the extreme left of the Central American revolutionary movement."

There are several versions, all of them convoluted, of what finally happened to the Montoneros' funds. According to Castañeda, the issue of the rightful ownership of the Montoneros' funds was settled when Juan Martín Romero Victorica, the Argentine prosecutor in charge of the Born kidnapping case, filed an injunction in a Buenos Aires court demanding the freezing of $100 million allegedly deposited in the National Bank of Cuba. The Cuban Embassy in Argentina notarized the freeze, but there were rumours that Fidel Castro would return the money only if the warring factions of the Montoneros decided what they were going to do with it.

Today, Jorge Born III and one of his kidnappers, former Montonero strategist Rodolfo "El Loco" Galimberti, are business partners. In one of the strangest chapters in recent Latin American history, the two have teamed up to try to recover the lost "guerrilla gold" that should be worth at least $240 million U.S. today. Born says that while he's certain the money is in Cuba he expects no concessions while Castro is still in power. He is hopeful that a post-Castro regime might return the money.

Galimberti, former military chief of the Montoneros' Northern Column, now counsels Born on his security needs and carries a cellular phone on his rounds in the fashionable Recoleta district in Buenos Aires. Born, who was held for nine months when he was kidnapped in 1974, recently told a reporter for the *Miami Herald* that his brother Juan is concerned about his sanity.

"He thinks I'm crazy to be even talking to a guy like Galimberti," said Born. "But I've done a lot of risky things in my life. I figure what's life for if you can't take risks?"

■

Managua's Fifth Criminal Court is located in a dusty strip mall of government offices off one of the city's main highways. The entrance, through a large wrought-iron gate, is crowded with grimy street vendors selling clear plastic bags full of water. Some of the bags contain

SEE NO EVIL

dubious orange-, purple-, and yellow-coloured liquids. A crowd of lawyers and other court officials cluster around the gates, balancing legal texts and briefcases as they sip the colourful liquids through little plastic straws.

When the gates open at 8:00 a.m., there is a frenzy of activity as the civil servants and lawyers discard their plastic bags and push to be the first into the fly-infested court building. Everyone is in a hurry, and, as is typical with civil servants in Nicaragua, nobody will stop to give you directions.

Martha Quezada is one of those arrogant civil servants who despise foreigners, especially foreign journalists. She is also the judge leading an inquiry into the blast at the *buzón de Santa Rosa* and the custodian of the documents found there. She's tough talking and flashy, with a penchant for large, gold-plated earrings, and she's not in the least impressed by credentials or business cards.

I visited her office on four occasions when I was in Managua in March 1994 before she would allow me to see the forty-five manila envelopes packed with the charred passports and other documents found after the Santa Rosa explosion.

One of those dusty manila envelopes contained travel documents, credit cards, cheque-books, Ontario and international drivers' licences, personal correspondence, letters of reference, and even library cards belonging to David and Christine.

Much of the ID, which is now neatly pasted into official scrapbooks, is a study in deception. For instance, there are several passport-sized photos of Christine, each taken with her in different poses and hairstyles to alter her look. There are doctored Ontario drivers' licences with Christine and David's photographs, but with the names Lisa Lynne Walker and Paul Joseph Gomes Mendes — the aliases they were using when they travelled to Brazil in mid-1989. On two of the Ontario licences, somebody has superimposed a Simon Fraser University crest. One of Christine's student cards from Simon Fraser contains a photograph of a man, possibly a Honduran guerrilla, according to Nicaraguan police officials. On a press pass for CKLN radio in Toronto, issued January 3, 1989, Christine has spelled her last name LaMont. Whether the spelling is intentional or not, the use of the upper-case "m" turns her into another person.

The bulging envelope at the Fifth Criminal Court also contained several pieces of blank stationery from businesses in Toronto and Vancouver and numerous reference letters from Canadian student organizations and alternative media outlets. In one letter, dated December 28, 1988, the writer praises Christine's organizational skills and attests to "her upstanding personal character." The letter, written on letterhead from the Winnipeg offices of Canadian University Press (CUP), a largely left-wing Canadian student newspaper collective, was signed by Ronald Newton, a professor of Latin American history whose classes Christine attended at Simon Fraser. In an interview in Vancouver, Newton said the letter is a forgery. A spokesman for CUP said that no one at the organization knew how Christine and David got hold of their stationery. He conceded that taking the stationery would not be difficult to do, since the organization was very much involved with left-wing student activists across the country. In addition to the letter signed by Newton, there were five other letters on CUP stationery found in the house which belonged to ETA member Tapia.

Another letter, from Darlison Associates, a computer consulting firm in Toronto, says that David and Christine are on assignment for the company and authorized to act as its agents "in all manner of contracts and other binding agreements." The date on the letter is February 21, 1989. In an interview in Toronto, Mr. Darlison said he did not write the letter. Still another letter says both Christine and David worked for the Teknos Career Institute in Vancouver, and another that David was on assignment for the International Council for Adult Education in Toronto.

Christine and David's original passports (not the false ones they were using to travel to Brazil in 1989) were also included in the manila envelope. Both Christine and David were issued Canadian passports on November 2, 1988. On November 28, Christine's passport was used to enter the United States, but it was reported lost a few days later. A second passport was issued to her on December 6, 1988. Both passports turned up in Managua. However, the original one, still bearing Christine's name, has a photo of Honduran citizen Carlos Hernandez Riviera, whose national identification document and photos were also found in the banker.

Nicaraguan police also discovered Christine's U.S. passport, which was issued on December 12, 1988, and David's Canadian passport, which was last used April 10, 1991, fully a year and a half after his arrest.

SEE NO EVIL

Among the most damning documents found after the blast are fourteen personal letters written to family members in Canada. The letters, all of them postdated over a period from July 1989 to July 1990, are full of vague generalities about life in Nicaragua, and all contain yellow Post-it notes on the airmail envelopes, with neatly printed mailing instructions in Spanish. Along with the letters is a handwritten list on a separate sheet of notepaper with the heading "Stories told in letters." The list appears to be a monthly log of what Christine and David would say in their letters home — what books they were reading, how they spent their holidays, and what the weather was like. Under the entry for May 1990, Christine wrote:

-*possible trip — summer or Christmas*
-*rainy season coming*
-*intimate we are in different house*
-*Semana de Santa [sic] — beach for weekend*
-*congrats to H on grad*

Under the entry for January 1990 Christine notes, among other things, how they spent Christmas and New Year's Eve. The corresponding letter, which was probably written sometime in May or June 1989, describes a happy Christmas spent with friends at the beach when in fact Christine and David had been in jail for a week nearly half a continent away. "As I had predicted, I missed you all very much at Christmas, but all the same Dave and I had one we won't soon forget," Christine presciently noted. The letter, never posted, would probably have reached Langley, B.C. sometime in mid-January 1990 just as the Lamonts were returning home from their first trip to São Paulo to visit their daughter after her arrest.

If Christine and David hadn't been arrested in São Paulo, Dr. Lamont might have received the following Father's Day card in June 1990: "Bone, I want to wish you a Happy Father's Day. I wish I were better able to convey how I feel about this but I want you to know how much I love you and what a great friend you are to me! I'll be thinking of you on Father's Day and be missing you as I am right now. I love you very, very much."

Upon examining the letters and other documents belonging to the Canadians, one U.S. counter-terrorism expert said, "Those two are in it up to their eyeballs." The expert noted that David and Christine had to have made preparations in Canada in order to go underground. He also said that false drivers' licences are easy to obtain once you have another false piece of identification, such as a student card. "It's obvious they already arrived in Nicaragua with all of the tools to assume a clandestine life."

Back in Canada, Christine and David's families and supporters struggled to come up with an explanation. Christine's older sister Elizabeth told the *Miami Herald* that there might have been a legitimate reason for her sister to write so many postdated letters. "I just don't believe it," said Elizabeth Lamont. "I still look at it all and say 'What do you think those letters prove?' She knew we were worried to death. [It may have been] in case she were anywhere she couldn't phone or write, she'd have them as a back-up."

When I called David Humphreys in Ottawa right after the discovery of the phony letters and documents in Managua, he said he had hired a U.S. freelance journalist in Managua to conduct an independent investigation of the blast. He seemed at a loss for words, as did David and Christine. In a confusing statement made by one of their São Paulo lawyers, David and Christine said they did not know how their documents ended up in a bunker in Managua. David said that he remembered handing all of his documents to "an American Sandinista named Steve" when he was in Buenos Aires in the fall of 1989, but he did not know what had become of them. Why David and Christine should have been carrying phony letters and ID and letters from Christine's parents that began "to our dear Christy, Wisty" while they were supposedly on vacation in Buenos Aires nobody ever asked.

When I spoke to Christine, she told me that she had never been to the Santa Rosa neighbourhood and knew nothing about a bunker. Indeed, Nicaraguan police believe that the bunker was built and stocked between late 1990 and early 1991 when Christine and David were already in jail. But the defence was poorly applied because nobody was accusing the pair of being involved in the building of an FMLN bunker. Investigators simply wanted to know what their documents were doing alongside others from well-known European and Latin American terrorists and with notes for major kidnapping operations in Latin America.

In a letter to her parents from prison Christine wrote, "Four years later we simply have no way to know. Our papers could have fallen into the hands of those who would use them against us."

The statement sounds as if it had been lifted from a cloak-and-dagger thriller. Just who were those who would use the papers against Christine and David? In an interview with *The Toronto Star* Marilyn Lamont wondered if her daughter had been brainwashed.

In Brazil, the *Folha de São Paulo* sent a correspondent to Managua to investigate the documents and follow the movements of Brazilian Interpol chief, Romeu Tuma, Sr., who had also been dispatched to Nicaragua to investigate the explosion. Based on his findings in Nicaragua, Tuma concluded that ETA members had participated in the January 1993 kidnapping of Brazilian advertising executive Geraldo Alonso Filho, president of Norton Publicidade.

The *Folha* ran a series of articles on the blast over several weeks, concentrating on David and Christine's background and movements in Latin America. *Folha* reporters Fernando Rodrigues, who was sent to Managua, and Claudio Júlio Tognolli, who had been covering the Diniz case since 1989, reported that Christine, David, and Raimundo Roselio Costa Freire, the Brazilian member of the group that kidnapped Diniz, had received military training in Nicaragua.

Costa, a left-wing militant and history student, joined a Nicaraguan solidarity group in the northeastern Brazilian city of Fortaleza in 1988. On May 22, 1988, he left for Managua, via Panama City. He told a São Paulo police officer that he spent part of his days in Managua cultivating manioc, an edible root, and the rest of the time training at a guerrilla camp. Costa said he returned to São Paulo in January 1989 and left again for Nicaragua in March, when he reportedly received instructions to work on the Diniz kidnapping.

"He said that a lot of Brazilians were being trained by the guerrillas in Nicaragua and that there were people from all over the world. He also said that there were a lot of Europeans, especially Swiss and Germans," said Antônio Fernando Costa, a São Paulo Civil Police officer who interrogated Costa about his training in Nicaragua in January 1991.

Tognolli told an interviewer from *Canada AM* that Christine and David's documents found in the Managua banker proved their guilt in the Diniz kidnapping.

But the ten kidnappers in the Diniz case later denied that they had any kind of preparatory training in Nicaragua in the 1980s. "They were part of human rights committees in Nicaragua and they didn't get involved with guerrillas," lawyer Marco Antonio Nahum told the *Folha*. "There were a lot of people there [in Nicaragua] at that time, even some Chinese, who supported [Daniel] Ortega." Moreover, Nahum said that David and Christine's identification had nothing to do with the explosion. He noted that the story about the kidnapping list appeared in a Nicaraguan newspaper on June 2, 1993, nine days after the explosion. "Police had time to plant all this information."

In a matter of days, Christine and David's photos appeared on the front pages of newspapers throughout Brazil, and practically overnight their role in the Diniz kidnapping was elevated from mere participants to the "brains" behind the operation. Romeu Tuma, Jr., a São Paulo police officer and assistant to his father at Interpol, told me in an interview after the blast that "David was one of the big heads of the Diniz operation" and that Christine had received specialized training in wartime emergency medical procedures.

Waldomiro Bueno, one of the investigating officers in the Diniz case, also told me that David was one of the brains behind the kidnapping operation. He said that David was in charge of the group's logistics and of setting up all of the clandestine meetings at which the kidnapping was planned. The accounting records for the Diniz kidnapping, which were found in a night-table in the bedroom used by Christine and David at the Praça Hachiro Miyazaki house, were in David's handwriting, said Bueno, who had the records analysed by an expert.

Whether or not any of this was true, the damage was done in Brazil. Photos of their phony drivers' licences became an important graphic link between the 1989 Diniz kidnapping and the Managua blast. In Managua, the left-wing daily *Barricada* plastered photos of Christine and David's fake drivers' licences on the front page. São Paulo police and Interpol decided to reopen the file on the Diniz kidnapping case based on the documents found in Managua. Brazilian journalists all asked the same question: what were the two Canadians doing in Nicaragua in 1989?

O Globo, the country's most influential daily, sent reporter Askanio Seleme on a three-week visit to Canada to report on the reaction to the Managua blast and its effect on the lobbying effort. Seleme linked Christine and David to Central American solidarity groups in Canada, and his stories made much of David's connections with Canada's only terrorist organization, Direct Action. *Folha de São Paulo* even provided a chart of the world's terrorist organizations connected with the Managua blast, among them ETA, the Chilean MIR, Germany's Red Army Faction, and Canada's Direct Action, which by 1993 had been largely disbanded. Again, it didn't matter that there was much extrapolating and playing with the truth in these newspaper accounts. For Brazilians, the image of Christine and David as ruthless international terrorists was solidified.

In Canada, many of their diehard supporters began to turn against them. Barbara McDougall said she received letters of apology from former supporters of David and Christine. McDougall, who was on her way out of External Affairs by that time, said that the incident severely damaged David and Christine's case in Canada.

"If ever there was a chance for expulsion, the Nicaragua blast put paid to it," she said. "It made for a very unfortunate situation."

Marilyn Lamont agreed: "The Managua blast was terrible for us. Just terrible," she told me.

However, the Department of External Affairs issued a statement that the question of whether any offences had been committed by David and Christine in regard to the Managua bunker was a matter for the RCMP to investigate, and External Affairs officials said that the explosion would not affect the government's handling of the case in Canada.

For the first time since the story had hit front pages across the country, a major Canadian newspaper got tough with Christine and David. In a landmark report that was very influential in changing the tenor of the debate on the case in Canada, *The Toronto Star* published a long front-page story on July 24, 1993, which included photographs of the false documents and the phony letters that Christine and David wrote to prepare an alibi. The story, "Trail of lies connects Canadians to terrorists," appeared in Southam newspapers across the country and made it very clear that Christine and David had lied to their parents and to the Brazilian authorities. In short, they'd wandered down "a murky trail of lies, deceit and unanswered questions."

The tone of the story left no doubt: Christine and David were guilty. *Star* reporter Caroline Mallan asked the same question the Brazilians had aready asked: just what were Christine and David doing in Nicaragua between January and June 1989 before they returned to Canada for a brief three-week visit? And what were they doing between July and December of that same year? The standard answers that they were working as translators/human rights workers in Managua during the first half of the year and vacationing in South America didn't wash. Canadians started to weigh the evidence against these two nice "do-gooder kids" locked up in a Brazilian jail, and facts that had been buried under all the lobbying hype of the past began to surface.

How, for instance, could they be working as translators in Managua if they couldn't speak very good Spanish at the time?

Vancouver Sun columnist Trevor Lautens, who was one of the few Canadian journalists to be skeptical about Christine and David's innocence since the kidnapping in 1989, seized upon the Managua blast: "I'm more satisfied than ever that former External Affairs minister Barabara McDougall and her staff acted correctly and courageously in the face of intense, often abusive pressure. And that Christine and David are guilty beyond any reasonable doubt. Only a mother, and I guess a father, could believe otherwise."

Letters to the editor of newspapers across the country started to attack Christine and David. In one responding to Lautens's column in the *Vancouver Sun*, Pru Zerny wrote:

> *I am a Canadian business person with close ties to South America, having lived in Colombia since 1989. As a result I have met journalists, including Brazilians, all who informed me at least two years ago that Christine Lamont and David Spencer were never the 'innocent young victims,' as their parents would have us believe, but guilty of breaking the law in Brazil. If you are foolish enough to do this, remember that in the eyes of the Brazilian law you are 'guilty until proven innocent.' Let this be a lesson to naive Canadians who visit Central or South America on goodwill missions that get out of control. If you break the law and, heaven forbid, end up in jail, be prepared to accept the severe consequences.*

Stung by the reports coming out of Nicaragua and Brazil, the families nevertheless decided to soldier on and crank up the lobbying effort. They tried to convince anyone who would listen that the blast in Nicaragua was some kind of CIA plot to discredit the left in Central America in general and David and Christine in particular. The old Cold War demons were dragged out of the closet and the rationalizations for

SEE NO EVIL

what David and Christine's documents were doing in a bunker in Managua started to sound a lot like something from Evelyn Waugh's satirical novel *Scoop*. The characters in the book, most of whom are confused journalists, chase complex global conspiracy theories that are often of their own design.

"From our own experience in Latin America, we're pretty sure the whole thing is a plant," said Eric Robinson, who heads the White Rock, B.C. chapter of the Committee for Justice for Christine Lamont and David Spencer. Robinson, a retired professor of labour management studies, and his wife, a retired nurse, had travelled through Central America in the mid-1980s. They got involved in the Lamont/Spencer support group because "we saw how easy it was to go to jail in the Third World," said Anne Robinson. While she was living in Honduras she knew of four people who were "disappeared" by government forces.

Blaine Donais, the Toronto lawyer who had prepared a study of the case, admitted that the biggest problem with Christine and David's arguement "is lack of knowledge of the Managua situation." He added, "The CIA is involved in this kind of stuff all the time. I don't think the blast connects Lamont and Spencer at all to the kidnappings."

Despite the Managua explosion, Cardinal Arns remained Christine and David's most loyal supporter in Brazil. "David and Christine are innocent until somebody can prove otherwise," he told the *Folha de São Paulo*. But perhaps even the cardinal, who received a great deal of media criticism in Brazil for his support of the pair, is having doubts. In 1994, I made repeated requests to his office in São Paulo for an interview regarding Christine and David. Cardinal Arns refused to see me in person, but asked that I fax him my questions. In his written answers, which he faxed back to my office in Rio de Janeiro, he said that the Managua explosion itself, and more specifically David and Christine's false documents found near the blast site, didn't prove the existence of a central terrorist network.

But it was when I asked him if he still thought David and Christine were innocent that the way he worded his answer surprised me. Unlike in his previous statements regarding the pair, which were issued before the Managua blast, the cardinal did not say outright that Christine and David were innocent. He seemed to be choosing his words very carefully: "the conversations I have had with Marilyn and Keith Lamont have led me to the intimate conviction that

Christine Lamont and David Spencer did not want to participate in that serious crime." Still, for the cardinal, Christine and David's case was very much an important human rights issue in Brazil because of the length of the sentence. "They are from good homes and have good conduct. Even if they are guilty, the charge suggests that they were involved in a minor way and therefore should have gotten a lighter sentence."

If, in the wake of the Managua blast, the cardinal had to choose his words carefully when talking about the jailed pair, the supporters of Christine and David in Canada were completely tongue-tied. The Managua blast and its aftermath practically destroyed the Canadian campaign to free David and Christine. Their supporters were so shocked by the events that it took them quite a while to marshal their forces and respond to the allegations. The problem is that, to this day, they haven't dealt with the content and meaning of the documents found in Managua. They have skirted the issue, blaming journalists for their biased coverage or insisting that the bunker explosion had nothing to do with Christine and David or with a conspiracy by many of the world's terrorist organizations to raise money through kidnappings.

The supporters wasted much of their time attacking *The Toronto Star* story and reporter Caroline Mallan. "I still think we could have made it back then if it hadn't been for that *Star* story," David Humphreys confided to me.

The Lamonts mumbled about taking legal action against the paper, but settled for lodging a complaint against it with the Ontario Press Council based on their allegation that Mallan "made many factual errors, as well as misinterpretations." The Lamonts called Mallan's account of the Managua blast "substandard journalism" and accused the *Star* of not printing a full-fledged review of the Lamont/Spencer case and not of taking up their offer to arrange an interview with the pair in São Paulo. The Lamont and Spencer families also attacked the credibility of the Nicaraguan police sources used in the article, criticizing Mallan for "quoting them as if they had the same credibility as Canadian police."

The complaint also accused the *Star* of hurting the parents' efforts to get the two out of jail. The newspaper replied that it set out to tell a true story, "not to advance or hurt lobbying efforts." Moreover, Mallan said that she had been told there would be no chance for an interview with Christine or David.

The complaint was not upheld. "The Council was thus faced with two diametrically opposed positions based on differing interpretations of available evidence. . . ." In declining to uphold the complaint, the council said it believed the story followed "normal and acceptable practice" and found no evidence to suggest that it affected the campaign for Canadian government intervention.

In an impassioned opinion piece in the *Vancouver Sun*, Marilyn Lamont argued once again for the Canadian government to intervene on behalf of Christine and David and bitterly attacked the *Star* story. Interestingly, Mrs. Lamont's emphasis has no longer on the innocence of Christine and David but on the fact that no matter what they did they had surely suffered enough. It was time, she said, for the Canadian government to bring them home.

> *I don't doubt that after recent reports from Nicaragua there are those saying that perhaps she (Barbara McDougall) was right all along. Was there not more to the story? We always conceded there were false passports involved and we invited Canadian authorities to lay charges if they thought them appropriate. The personal papers and documents found in Nicaragua may have some bearing on that matter. They don't alter the facts in Brazil. Two experienced reporters in Managua have confirmed that there is not one shred of evidence linking Christine and David to any organization in Nicaragua except the FMLN, at the time fighting a repressive government in El Salvador. We are disgusted by the Toronto Star's reporting imputing motives to Christine and David as a result of letters they are purported to have written. They were in direct touch with us by phone at a time we were supposed to be getting the phony letters from them. We never got any letters. We are taking steps to get the answers the Star declined to get. We offered to arrange for the Star to go to the prisons to discuss its findings with Christine and David. The Star, in a hurry to publish its sensational innuendoes, declined. The Star reporter does not embrace the concept "innocent until proven guilty." She has set up public court in her newspaper, and they have been sentenced in the headlines. The Star has caused unnecessary additional anguish to our family. But we know Canadians to be fair-minded. We are counting on them at this difficult time to accept the central issues in this case which remain unchanged. Mistakes were made. Two young Canadians went to*

prison and paid their price. Nothing has happened to make them deserving of more time behind bars when a remedy exists to get them home now.

The Lamont and Spencer families were grasping at straws. They hired Managua-based freelance journalist David Dye to investigate David and Christine's articles found in the *buzón*. When I spoke to him in San Salvador in March 1994, he told me he had agreed to conduct the investigation "for humanitarian reasons" but could find nothing that other reporters had missed.

A few months after the explosion in Managua, the families and David Humphreys seized on a *Washington Post* story, which appeared on October 29, 1993, that state U.S. investigators could find "no evidence to support suspicion of a terrorism and kidnapping ring operating throughout Latin America." A team of U.S. State Department investigators believed that Sandinista agents, who continued to control the Nicaraguan army after Chamorro's election, set up the arms cache for possible use by El Salvador's FMLN if UN-sponsored peace talks failed to end the civil war. The story went on to say that the documents found in the bunker were probably provided by the Nicaraguan DGSE, which was controlled by Tomás Borge. However, in the last paragraph of the story, the writer reported that U.S. officials said the investigators were unable to establish links between the documents and recent terrorist acts and that "only one of the people under surveillance... was kidnapped." But as many as four Mexican high-level executives and at least one Brazilian — Diniz — noted on the list have in fact been kidnapped by professional gangs and millions of dollars in ransom demanded. Two of the Mexicans on the list (Harp Helu and Losada Moreno) were kidnapped in 1994, a year after the publication of the *Washington Post* report.

David Humphreys handed me a copy of the report with an air of triumph when I went to visit him in his Ottawa office on a clear, bitterly cold spring day in April 1994. Over a mug of instant cappuccino, he told me about his new strategy. With the Canadian press becoming more skeptical about the case and no longer on his side, the only thing left to do was to lobby quietly and not give any more interviews to anyone.

During the course of our lengthy discussion, I related a conversation I had had with one of my editors at *The Globe and Mail*, who had said that the newspaper wasn't particularly interested in the story anymore because "everyone knows Christine and David are guilty."

The comment seemed to pain Humphreys, who gave me a wounded look. "What do they mean, 'guilty'?" he asked, but I knew he didn't expect an answer from me. "How do they know that?"

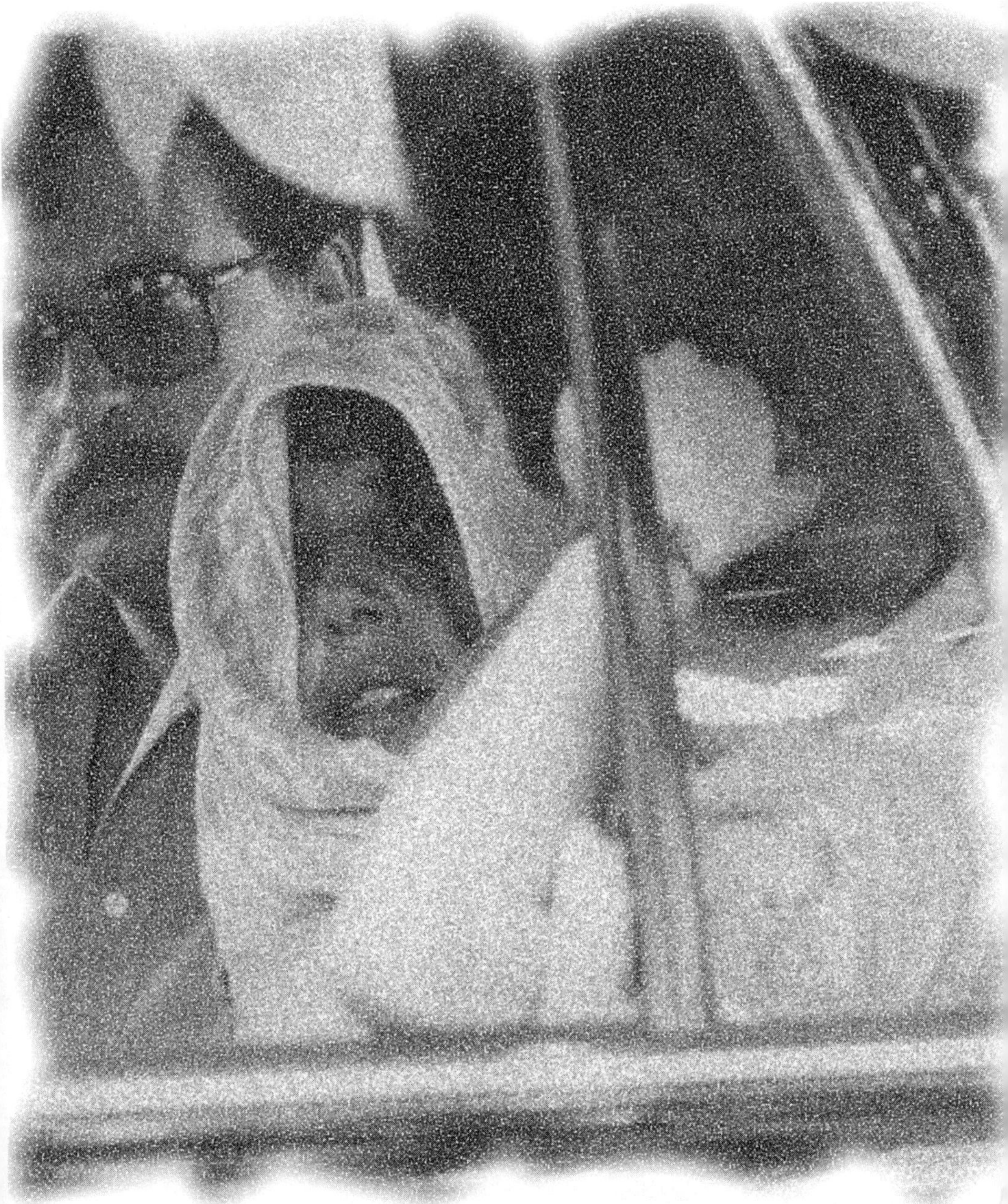

Seven

Bóris Casoy is paid to get angry. Every night, Brazil's most outspoken newscaster whips himself up into a rage about some pressing national issue like government corruption or the pitiful state of Brazil's educational system.

But when viewers tuned into the prime-time *Telejornal Brasil* newshour in late August 1993, many were bemused to see Casoy turning red in the face over something as innocuous as, well, Canada. For a whole week, the imposing, bespectacled television commentator raged against a country that few Brazilians knew anything about.

Historically, Brazilians have had good relations with Canada. A Canadian company was largely responsible for the modernization of the country's two most important cities, Rio and São Paulo in the early years of this century. The giant Canadian utilities company originally known as the Brazilian Traction, Light and Power Company and later as Brascan, provided most of the electricity needs in the country's major cities and helped build the huge infrastructure that allowed Rio and São Paulo to experience explosive growth in the twentieth century. In Rio the company built the famous *bondes* or trams at the turn of the century that still wind their way around the hillside Santa Teresa neighbourhood, which overlooks the city's downtown core.

"These two cities were but miserable colonial towns, infested with yellow fever and malaria, when the Canadians came in. They [the Canadians] brought not only a business, but a mission," wrote Brazil's most well-known journalist, Assis Chateaubriand, in 1962.

Today, although Brazil is the third-largest recipient of direct Canadian investment (after the United States and Great Britain), most Brazilians rarely think about the frozen land north of the United States. Canada rarely makes it into the headlines in the Brazilian press except when there has been a truly monumental event, like a record low temperature in Montreal or fans rioting after a hockey game in Vancouver. Occasionally at a party you'll meet a cosmopolitan Brazilian who has visited Canada. Once when I suggested to a Brazilian journalist I know that he should visit the country, he said he'd been to Toronto and quite enjoyed it, but added, "Why would I want to go there? There's nothing happening."

So it was with some shock that Brazilians tuned into the *Telejornal Brasil* to see Casoy staring squarely into the television camera and barking his familiar refrain to viewers across the country, "*É uma vergonha*" (It's shameful) about a place few of them knew anything about.

Casoy, like many of the country's journalists at the time, was upset about the exchange of prisoners treaty that would allow Christine Lamont and David Spencer to serve out the rest of their sentences in a Canadian prison where they would likely be eligible for parole after serving one-third of their sentences. The treaty, approved by Canada in the summer of 1992, would also allow Brazilians serving time in Canadian prisons to complete their sentences in Brazil.

The treaty had been passed by the Brazilian Senate on August 12 and needed to be ratified by then president Itamar Franco to have force in law. Casoy accused the Canadian ambassador Bill Dymond of "unabashedly lobbying on the floor of the Brazilian Senate" to push through the treaty specifically on behalf of the two Canadian kidnappers. He charged him with improperly interfering in the internal affairs of Brazil, and for five nights in a row he repeated that Ambassador Dymond should be expelled from Brazil. This was what enraged Casoy the most: that the treaty was not, in fact, a routine agreement between two friendly countries, but a ploy, a trick the Canadians had designed to dupe Brazil into setting David and Christine free.

Indeed, allegations that the ambassador had vigorously lobbied Brazilian legislators were reported in newspapers throughout the country. The *Folha de São Paulo* reported that it had obtained a "classified" memo from the Department of External Affairs in Ottawa, listing everyone the Canadian ambassador would need to lobby in Brazil to push the treaty through the Senate. The *Folha* claimed that over the course of a year the ambassador lobbied, among others, an aide in Itamar Franco's office, then foreign affairs minister Celso Lafer, the president of the Supreme Court in Brasília, and public prosecutor Ribeiro de Bonis to expedite the appeals process for Christine and David and to press for the exchange of prisoners treaty.

During the negotiations for the treaty, Brazilians quickly became aware of the massive Canadian lobbying effort, set in motion by the Lamonts, to pressure the Canadian and Brazilian governments to get Christine and David out of jail. Citing an unnamed Brazilian diplomat in Canada, the *Estado de São Paulo* erroneously reported that the Lamonts had lobbied External Affairs and even Canadian Prime Minister Kim Campbell to get the treaty approved. The Lamonts, who had been pushing for an expulsion, denied lobbying for the treaty, which would not allow Christine and David to go free in Canada.

But Barbara McDougall and the Canadian government clearly saw the treaty as an easy way out — a workable political alternative to what would probably be in Brazil a very politically contentious expulsion — and lobbied accordingly. In an article that appeared on October 1, 1993, *The Toronto Star* reported that Ambassador Dymond had launched "a massive lobby for the treaty shortly after his arrival in Brasília in September 1992." The *Star* quoted from briefing notes prepared by External Affairs, dated November 24, 1992, and cited by the *Folha de São Paulo*: "The embassy has also undertaken an extensive lobbying campaign to ensure that the treaty, which, under Brazilian practice requires ratification by the Congress, received expeditious treatment in the legislature."

According to the same report, Ambassador Dymond lobbied several high-ranking Brazilian government officials, including the speaker of the upper house, "to get ratification of the treaty through the Senate in 10 days. . . . In the Brazilian context such lobbying of legislators by foreign ambassadors is considered quite proper."

Alfredo Campos, then president of the Senate Commission on Foreign Relations, admitted that Bill Dymond had gone to see him twice to ask him to vote on the treaty as quickly as possible, according to a report in O *Globo*. "The Canadians pressured us by saying that in their country, the public was demanding that Christine Lamont and David Spencer be freed because they were suffering torture and horrible conditions in jail," said a Brazilian diplomat quoted in the article.

Although officials at the Canadian Embassy in Brasília denied that they had mounted such a full-scale lobby to get the treaty approved in the Brazilian Senate, few Canadian observers in Brazil actually believed them. With the expulsion option looking less and less likely for Christine and David, the treaty seemed the most obvious way for the unpopular Progressive Conservative government to get them back to Canada and score some political points on the eve of the federal election in October 1993. After all, the prime minister had said in June that the country would do its utmost to make sure the treaty was approved in Brazil. "We are pressing with every degree of energy to have this legislation passed. . . because we plan to invoke it as quickly as we possibly can," said Brian Mulroney.

In an interview in Toronto nearly a year after the Canadian lobbying, Barbara McDougall admitted to me that "lobbying actions were indeed taken" by the Canadian government "to keep the treaty moving and not to let it die. We were frustrated the whole thing was taking so long. It just eventually took on a life of its own."

In a letter to MP Robert Horner, chairman of the Standing Committee on Justice and the Solicitor General, McDougall indicated that the Canadian government had embarked on a vigorous campaign to speed up Christine and David's appeal process and the ratification of the treaty:

> *The Embassy has undertaken an extensive lobbying campaign to ensure that the Transfer of Offenders Treaty between Canada and Brazil signed on July 15, 1992 receives expeditious consideration by the Brazilian Congress which under Brazilian law must give its approval before the Treaty can enter into force. The Ambassador has called on the Speakers of both the Senate and the Chamber of Deputies, the Chief of Staff in President Franco's office and the Chairmen of both the committees of the Chamber of Deputies which will review the Treaty. All expressed optimism with regard to the early approval of the Treaty and undertook to assist in having it dealt with*

quickly. The Minister of Justice has undertaken twice in the past week to speak to the Government House Leaders in both Houses to expedite its passage.

The vigorous lobbying effort on the part of the Canadian government helped the treaty to be passed in record time. Signed in Brasília on July 15, 1992, it was ratified by the Chamber of Deputies, the lower house of Brazil's bicameral legislature, in late June 1993 and by the Senate on August 12. On August 24, Humberto Lucena, the president of the Senate, signed a legislative decree on the treaty, which was then sent to the president's office for final approval. In a country where it is not unusual to wait two years for a change-of-ownership document for an automobile, the speed with which the Brazilian congress ratified a bilateral accord was nothing short of revolutionary.

But the whole thing turned into a political time bomb, especially when Brazilians found out that in addition to Ambassador Dymond, Cardinal Arns and PT Senator Eduardo Suplicy had also been conducting a strong lobby on behalf of the Lamont and Spencer families to get David and Christine out of jail. In fact, an intense lobbying effort had been going on for years under the Brazilians' noses. In 1992, the National Conference of Brazilian Bishops had asked the justice minister to expel the Canadians. For the first time, Brazilian newspapers also reported that in 1991 Cardinal Arns had faxed the Brazilian minister of justice, Jarbas Passarinho, asking that he meet with the Lamonts.

Former justice minister turned senator Jarbas Passarinho said he signed the treaty because Cardinal Arns had asked him to do it: "I took action based on a request from the archbishop of São Paulo, Dom Paulo Evaristo Arns." He later admitted that he had sent a fax to Cardinal Arns right after the Managua explosion, saying that the Canadian couple "isn't so innocent."

In addition to reporting all this on *Telejornal Brasil*, Bóris Casoy also attacked several members of the Brazilian Senate for not realizing that the treaty would benefit only Christine and David, two of the ten kidnappers who had been caught red-handed in the country's most notorious kidnapping. While Casoy read his commentary, Brazilian viewers were shown an artist's rendering of Christine pointing a gun at a man's head. Humberto Lucena admitted he didn't even know about the Canadian prisoners when he signed the treaty, and he told the *Folha de*

São Paulo, "We would have been in error if we had known beforehand that the treaty would only benefit the two Canadians in São Paulo. Not even in the lower house [of congress] did the deputies know about the case."

"It was a mistake," said Rio de Janeiro senator Darcy Ribeiro of the Senate's approval of the exchange of prisoners treaty. Senator Ribeiro, however, admitted to having signed it. "I demand that the president veto the treaty and reestablish juridical order." Since there were no other Canadian prisoners in Brazilian jails at the time, Christine and David would indeed have been the only direct beneficiaries of such a treaty, which Canada insisted, perhaps too often, was a "routine" agreement that the country had already established with many other nations.

"I was ashamed to be Brazilian," Casoy later said in an interview with me. "It was a matter of principle. The Brazilian congress was kneeling before Canada, one of the world's seven richest countries. I just couldn't stand by and watch our country be pushed around so badly by an arrogant First World nation."

Brazilians were up in arms after Casoy's broadcasts. The media created an image of the Lamonts as the most influential citizens in Canada. Keith Lamont was depicted as one of the country's most important surgeons, a man who had spent millions trying to get his daughter out of jail. Moreover, the *Folha* reported that David Humphreys was one of the richest and most influential men in Canada. With such seemingly powerful interests backing them in Canada, David and Christine lost the sympathy of the Brazilian public. Brazilians are highly nationalistic, and they had little compassion for two convicted kidnappers with apparent ties to some of the world's nastiest terrorist organizations.

Moreover, the treaty itself was so distorted in the Brazilian media that many newspapers were reporting that it would allow David and Christine to go free once they returned to Canada. The senators' ratification of the treaty was viewed as completely irresponsible. Police inspector Carlos Alberto Costa, director of the State Department of Criminal Investigation in São Paulo, said that repatriating David and Christine to Canada would constitute "a stimulus to more crime" in Brazil.

"Kidnapping is one of the worst crimes and they are professionals. . . . They rented the house for the kidnap victim and when we surrounded the house, Christine stood the whole time with a gun pointed at Diniz's head," said Costa in an interview with the *Estado de São Paulo*.

Nelson Guimarães, the São Paulo police chief who had led the investigation of the Diniz kidnapping and helped with the negotiations for the surrender of the kidnappers in 1989, called the treaty immoral.

"This is a blow to Brazilian sovereignty," said Guimarães, now head of the homicide department for the São Paulo Civil Police. "We shouldn't sell out our national dignity. What does the Canadian government think this is? A banana republic? They're treating us as if we were a colony without any of our own laws. If we take down our pants for Canada, we'll have to keep them down for the rest of the world."

Romeu Tuma, Sr., vice-president of Interpol, called the treaty a national disgrace. Like Guimarães, he insisted that Christine and David stay in Brazil to complete their twenty-eight-year sentences.

"They are professionals in crime, calculating criminals with the ability to maintain people in panic and desperation during several months until their families pay a ransom," said Tuma. "They eat well, they sleep soundly, while their victims are holed up in tiny cells."

At a press conference in September 1993, Brazil's justice minister Maurício Correa said, "If I find that it was put together to favour the two Canadians I'll recommend that President Itamar Franco veto it. The crime that these two Canadians committed is very serious and we would be risking a serious precedent if the minister of justice would agree to this transfer. They should complete their sentences in Brazil." Correa admitted to journalists that he had been visited by Canadian parliamentarians lobbying for his support in getting the treaty passed. Correa, who would not name the Canadian politicians, said he turned them down.

Things got so out of hand that on September 10 Senate president Lucena had to make a special broadcast on television and radio across the country to reassure the Brazilian public that the Senate had not been swayed by Canadian lobbying efforts. However, Brazilian newspapers reported that Lucena lifted a key paragraph of his speech from a press release issued by the Canadian Embassy. Lucena's political opponents accused him of plagiarizing a press release issued by a foreign government in order to explain the Senate's actions on the treaty. The press release noted that Canada currently had prisoner transfer treaties with some forty countries, including Mexico, Bolivia, Peru, and the United States, and that more than five hundred prisoners had been successfully transferred to Canada under the treaties. "The treaty," ran the press release and Lucena's speech, "has a humanitarian purpose: to permit the prisoners to serve out the remainder of their sentences close to their families and to take full advantage of rehabilitation programs and reintegration into society."

"This kind of plagiarism makes the congress look ridiculous," said PT deputy José Genoíno. "In spite of that he [Lucena] wasn't able to explain anything properly and didn't convince anybody. This whole incident shows that the senator doesn't know what he's doing."

In addition to the treaty, now Brazilians started criticizing Lucena for wasting expensive air time to defend the Canadian government and Brazil's senators, many of whom were caught completely off guard and mechanically signed the treaty without weighing its political ramifications. In an article perhaps appropriately entitled "Bla, Bla, Canada," newsmagazine *Isto É* pointed out that there was no reason for Brazilians to worry about the treaty, since it had to be pushed through a few other legal hoops before it could be applied to Christine and David.

> *Those opposing the treaty are making much ado about nothing: it's up to Itamar Franco and the justice ministry to say whether David and Christine can go home and even in that case, the transfer is not automatic. A Brazilian judge could authorize it or not, and demand guarantees that the sentence not be reduced in the country of origin of the prisoner. The next time the president of the Senate decides that he wants to enter by force into Brazilian homes, it would be good if he had something more important to discuss.*

But few Brazilian journalists bothered to come to grips with the ins and outs of the treaty, officially known as the Treaty on Transfer of Offenders Between Canada and the Federative Republic of Brazil. Under its terms, Christine and David would have to apply to the Brazilian authorities for permission to serve out the rest of their sentences in Canada. Brazil would then have to approve the request. However, the treaty specifies that "the completion of the sentence of an offender who has been transferred shall be in accordance with the laws and procedures of the Receiving State." The Brazilian press rightfully noted that with the provision for parole in Canada, the two could see their sentences reduced from twenty-eight years to just seven in Canada.

At the time that the treaty was being negotiated, both David and Christine said they were not interested in applying to serve the remainder of their sentences in Canadian prisons. Both maintained their innocence and said that they wanted to wait until a final appeal to reduce their sentences had been heard in the Brazilian courts.

"At the end of the day, Lamont and Spencer didn't care if the treaty went through or not because they never had any intention of fulfilling the legal obligations," McDougall told me.

But the pressure was on Canadian diplomats to get the treaty ratified because Christine and David had already lost two important appeals. On June 3, 1993, appellate court Judge José Candido refused to reduce or "individualize" the sentences based on different levels of culpability of the ten convicted kidnappers.

Marilyn Lamont charged that there was a great deal of political interference in the case because one appeal court judge broke the rules by presenting the other judges with new evidence related to Christine and David's false identification papers found in Managua. However, just where Mrs. Lamont was getting her information was unclear because none of the appellate court judges mentioned the Managua discovery in their written judgements.

Less than a week after the appellate court denied the sentencing appeal, Judge Haroldo Ferraz da Nóbrega, the Substitute General Republic Attorney, refused an appeal that the kidnapping be retried as a political crime. "It goes beyond the question to talk about political crime when the crimes under judgement, however politically motivated, slide, when executed, towards nefarious common criminal practices, one of which is nowadays considered in the category of heinous crime."

The appeals were rejected without recourse to a full court hearing. However, on June 30 the Supremo Tribunal de Justiça in Brasília, the Supreme Court, decided it would hear the appeals on the reduction of the sentences. The appeals were heard in November of the same year, but again the court decided, by a three-to-two vote, not to reduce the sentences.

Canadian diplomats in Brazil, stunned by the backlash in the Brazilian press, wondered whether they were the victims of a media conspiracy.

"Bóris Casoy and the Brazilian media in general have spread nothing but lies about this case," said Marco Antônio Nahum, Christine and

David's attorney, when I went to see him in October 1994. "They're not to be trusted."

One Canadian diplomat wanted to know who was paying Bóris Casoy to mount such heated attacks against Canada. I put the question directly to Casoy when I visited him in the SBT studios in a working class district of São Paulo where he tapes the *Telejornal Brasil*.

Casoy, a veteran newsman and former lawyer and an editor of the influential *Folha de São Paulo*, was extremely offended by the question. Well-read and intelligent, he told me that his purpose on the show was to keep Brazilian democracy alive by exposing high-level corruption. Although he described himself as "right of centre" in terms of his politics, he prides himself on not being a partisan. Described as Brazil's national conscience, Casoy is highly respected in the country, even by his critics.

"We need more journalists like Bóris Casoy in Brazil," wrote the country's leading anthropologist, Roberto Damatta, in a column in São Paulo's daily *Jornal da Tarde* in early 1994. "We need more ethical journalists — people who, like Casoy, know their limits. . . and who don't use the media to further their own political ends."

When I went to visit Casoy, Luis Inácio Lula da Silva, the PT presidential candidate in the 1994 elections, was preparing to go on the air for a live interview. Unlike its rival network Globo, SBT prides itself on presenting all sides of the political debate in Brazil. Fernando Henrique Cardoso, the social democratic candidate in the 1994 presidential race, also appeared on Casoy's show before the October elections.

"There are no outside interests guiding me in anything I do," whispered the stout Casoy, who was suffering from a nasty bout of laringitis. "I had followed the kidnapping very closely in 1989, and I was always of the opinion that there were other more powerful interests behind the kidnapping. I was extremely upset when I saw what the Canadians were doing. If the situation were reversed and we were talking about two Brazilians who had done the same thing in Canada, how would Canadians respond?"

I asked whether or not he thought the Canadian government would ever be successful, through an expulsion or the treaty, in getting the two out of jail in São Paulo. Casoy replied that either way would be political suicide for the Brazilian president, no matter what party he belonged to. Indeed, by the time the Treaty on the Transfer of Offenders made its way to the Palácio do Planalto, the presidential offices in Brasília, it was clear that given the negative uproar in the media, President Itamar Franco was not going to touch it.

Casoy was categoric in his political assessment of the case in Brazil: "The president will be lynched if he signs the treaty. Short of mounting an escape or a kidnap operation, I don't know how your government is going to get them out of jail." He added that with everything that had happened to further complicate the case — the bunker explosion in Managua, the Canadian lobby in Brazil — the Brazilian press was not about to let the issue die. Casoy assured me that if the Canadians pulled any more stunts, they would be hearing from him and his colleagues in the Brazilian media.

Casoy had been planning a trip to Montreal to visit a friend. "I guess this means I won't be getting a visa to visit Canada any time soon," he said with a smile.

■

After the Managua explosion and the Brazilian media uproar about the treaty, the Lamonts and their lobbyist decided to tone down their efforts. Despite these major setbacks, they still counted on a substantial support base in Canada but decided, as we have seen, to concentrate their lobbying efforts less on the guilt or innocence of Christine and David and more on the harshness of the sentences. "Surely, they've already paid the price for whatever they may or may not have done." This became the rallying cry of the new phase of the campaign to free David and Christine. "We're no longer operating on the issue of innocence or guilt. We're operating on the humanitarian issue of the twenty-eight-year sentence," said a senior bureaucrat in the Department of Foreign Affairs. Even conservative politicians in Canada started to pressure their own government to do something for the jailed pair.

Having nearly exhausted all appeals for reduced sentences in Brazil, Christine and David were waiting to hear if they would be granted day parole. As of late 1994 things looked bleak for Christine. São Paulo public prosecutor Osvaldo de Oliveira Marques argued against giving her "a semi-open" sentence even though she had already served one sixth of her sentence and had high marks for good behaviour. The prosecutor said that granting Christine parole might, among other things, facilitate her escape from the country.

"Finally, the crime in which she was involved caused a huge outcry across the country, and granting her parole now would give society the message of impunity for criminals and would discredit our system of justice," said de Oliveira, adding that Christine was "a dangerous person," and by not granting her parole, the court would be promoting national security.

But while things looked bleak for Christine and David, they were starting to look very good for their Chilean colleagues in prison. In mid-1994, a Chilean television crew and a delegation of Chilean politicians, most of them members of the Socialist party, visited the Chilean prisoners and promised them that they would lobby President Eduardo Frei to seek an expulsion, on the grounds that Maria Emília, Ulisses, Pedro, and Sérgio had been tortured by São Paulo police in 1989.

Their request for expulsion from Brazil was also based on the fact that Tânia Maria Cordeiro Vaz, a Brazilian psychologist living in Chile, had been granted permission to leave the country in 1993 after suffering torture at the hands of Chile's infamous Policia de Investigaciones she was also later discriminated against by Chilean authorities, who committed several legal irregularities in her case.

Vaz, who allegedly had ties to the radical arm of the MIR, had been detained by police along with her thirteen-year-old daughter in March 1993. Vaz said that during her eight or nine days of detention in Santiago (she can't remember the exact number of days), she was repeatedly raped, had electric shocks applied to her vagina, and at one point was forced to eat her own excrement. She said police wanted information about the MIR's terrorist activities. Although Vaz was sharing a house with several radical members of the MIR in Rancagua, a city seventy-eight kilometres south of Santiago, she maintained that she had no knowledge of their activities. Hector Salazar, one of Chile's leading human rights lawyers, took up her case, which immediately became a cause célèbre in Chile. For the first time since the end of the Pinochet regime in 1989, Chileans had proof that Chile's law enforcement officials were still using torture against alleged subversives and leftists, said

Salazar, who was receiving payment from the Brazilian government to defend Vaz.

Brazil's president Itamar Franco was so shocked by the reports of torture that he hinted he would cancel a state visit to the country if the Chilean authorities did not reopen their investigation into the case. Vaz, who had been cleared of terrorist charges by Chilean authorities, was at the time serving a jail sentence for robbery in Chile. But according to the Brazilian ambassador in Chile, Guilherme Leite Ribeiro, the judge who sentenced Vaz based her decision on a report compiled by the eight police officers who were responsible for her torture.

"The charges against her are based on some very serious errors of investigation. Moreover, there were some severe irregularities in legal procedure," Leite told a reporter for the *Jornal do Brasil* in January 1994. Leite added that Vaz was never informed of the charges against her and that none of the workers at the telephone post, where the robbery she was charged with was supposed to have taken place, recognized her. Furthermore, the presiding Chilean judge would not allow Vaz a translator as prescribed by Chilean law for foreigners whose first language is not Spanish. On appeal, the case was retried at the Supreme Court level and thrown out for lack of evidence. In an interview, Vaz's lawyer Salazar said that her case was groundbreaking for Chile because for the first time in its recent history, law enforcement officials were being taken to task for human rights abuses. "Things are finally changing in this country," said Salazar from his office in Santiago. In the past, law enforcement officials had enjoyed almost complete impunity from prosecution for human rights abuses.

Legal experts in Santiago said that without diplomatic pressure from the Brazilian government, Vaz might still be in jail. She returned to Brazil in early 1994.

The Vaz case was a ray of hope for the Chilean kidnappers, who felt they had endured many of the same legal irregularities on the Brazilian end. However, unlike the Vaz case there was no possibility that their case would be retried in Brazil. The only option would be a government-sanctioned expulsion. With Chile's government beginning to consider asking for the Chilean kidnappers expulsion from Brazil, Christine and David were hopeful that the Canadian Liberal government, which was very sympathetic to their case, would follow suit.

In the meantime, with the exception of *The Toronto Star* and *The Globe and Mail*, much of the Canadian press was still on the side of the jailed Canadians, even after the Managua blast. Although Christine and David had been convicted of kidnapping, an editorial in the *Ottawa Citizen* in 1993 insisted upon calling them "accessories in a kidnapping." The editorial, which presented David and Christine yet again as victims of harsh Third World justice, went on to attack Brazil's then justice minister Maurício Correa.

> *Correa is wrong — wrong to obstruct ratification of a good treaty with the excuse of a single case, and wrong to interfere in a case [while appeals are under way] that has already suffered too much political interference. . . . Guilty or not, Lamont and Spencer have suffered a nightmare. Their punishment is grossly disproportionate to the crime they are supposed to have committed. Instead of correcting the injustice done, Correa threatens to make it worse.*

But such comments only infuriated the Brazilians, who started sending journalists to Canada to report on the lobbying effort. Reports of what the parents were saying in Canada filtered back to Brazil. Carmen dos Santos, the warden at Christine's jail, had told me she was infuriated by the comments that Mrs. Lamont made about Christine's prison conditions. Canadian consular officials in São Paulo confirmed that as a result of the negative publicity in Canada about Christine's jail situation, dos Santos started to refuse Christine any more special privileges. Indeed, Mrs. Lamont complained to me that she couldn't understand why the warden was being so strict about family visits. Although the Lamonts travelled such a long distance to be with their daughter, they now found that they were only allowed to stay a few minutes beyond their daily allotted half-hour visits. On previous visits the Lamonts said they had been able to be with Christine for longer periods of time.

The lobbying effort picked up speed with the prospect of a Progressive Conservative defeat in the October 1993 federal elections. In a campaign speech in New Brunswick in July 1993 Liberal leader Jean Chrétien promised to do everything he could to get David and Christine out of jail. "We are very curious why the Canadian government has not asked for expulsion," said Chrétien at the end of a pre-election bus tour through northern Nova Scotia and New Brunswick. He added that Christine and David had not been treated fairly by Ottawa or Brazil. But as an afterthought, he noted that he hadn't been fully briefed on the details of the case.

When the Liberals swept to victory in October, the Lamont and Spencer families were confident that they would finally make some inroads in Ottawa. Marilyn Lamont went so far as to speculate that the overwhelming Liberal majority was due in part to her daughter's case. She told the *Vancouver Sun* that their supporters across the country had helped defeat the Progressive Conservatives because of the latter's negative response to the plight of Christine and David. "Although we don't think our case is a major national issue, it does have a lot of support across the country and more than 30,000 people have signed petitions that are now in the House of Commons."

The new government's strategy in dealing with the case was official silence. Nobody was commenting on the case at the RCMP or the renamed Department of Foreign Affairs. Indeed, Lily Campbell, a spokeswoman for Foreign Affairs, seemed disappointed that I wanted information on the case when I called her early in 1994. "Because this is such a sensitive case it's being handled very carefully. We're looking at every angle," she said, adding that the department was trying to prevent any more negative stories from appearing in the Brazilian press.

Burned by their experience with *The Toronto Star* in July 1993, the Lamonts stopped giving interviews unless they could somehow guarantee that the journalist would be sympathetic to their case. They began to toy with the idea of renewing their lobbying efforts in Brazil during the 1994 election year. Perhaps, went the logic, they could somehow sneak through an expulsion or the presidential ratification that the exchange of prisoners treaty needed to have force in law. Maybe Brazilians would be too preoccupied with their own affairs to notice the two Canadians.

"We're working to try to push the case in Brazil. Strategically, for us the best time would be between the election and the inauguration of the new president," said David Humphreys, noting that the departing president Itamar Franco would have little to lose politically by signing the treaty or an expulsion order.

The Lamonts also began a much more discreet lobbying effort in Canada to renew calls for a request for expulsion. They began to press for a meeting with new Foreign Affairs minister André Ouellet, who had said that he would not pursue expulsion with the Brazilian government but would instead concentrate the ministry's efforts on pushing for the exchange of prisoners treaty. By mid-December, Ouellet said he was willing to speak to them on the telephone, but that wasn't good enough for the Lamonts, who wanted to meet him face to face. Mrs. Lamont insisted that the complex, four-year history of the case could not be relayed over the telephone. At one point she got so frustrated that she said, "This is even worse than [Barbara] McDougall." In November, George Rideout, a Liberal MP from Moncton, wrested a commitment from Ouellet to assign somebody at the department to the Lamont and the Spencer families to hammer out a new strategy for the case.

This ensured that the Lamonts were treated like royalty by the new government. Although they didn't have a direct line to Ouellet, they did have one to his senior policy advisor, Michael Pearson, who seemed to be on the phone to them in Langley every week to consult on the case.

In April 1994, I met with Pearson and two aides in his comfortable Ottawa office. Over cups of weak coffee in china emblazoned with Canada's official crest, Pearson told me that the department's aim was to bring the Canadians home before the end of the calendar year. There was so much self-assurance in the claim that I found myself asking if the new Liberal government had discovered some kind of secret formula to get Christine and David out of jail. Perhaps, I suggested to Pearson and his two aides, Foreign Affairs would arrange Christine and David's escape. Pearson was not amused and replied that the government was still counting on either expulsion or the exchange of prisoners treaty.

"It's not in anyone's interest to allow this case to fester. We've indicated to the Brazilians that we want expulsion, but we're prepared to push any button necessary to get them out of jail. We're going to work hard to resolve this case by the end of the year, cooperatively and quietly."

I pointed out that both options were virtually impossible because of the negative publicity associated with the treaty and the Canadian lobbying effort in general in Brazil. No Brazilian president, not even a Marxist, was likely to sign an expulsion order or ratify the treaty, I said. President Itamar Franco was unlikely to make any move on the Canadians before his term expired at the end of 1994 because in so doing he would risk jeopardizing the chances of his own candidate in the federal elections in October. The case was a hornet's nest in Brazil and no politician in the country was about to stir it up by allowing two convicted kidnappers to walk out of jail.

Pearson noted that the Managua explosion wasn't an issue. He followed the McDougall line when he said that the government of Canada was not really interested in retrying the case. It seemed to me that the biggest fear the department had was that Christine and David's case was going to turn into a huge bilateral issue (some would argue that it already has) that would cripple future relations between the two countries. Pearson stressed that for humanitarian reasons it was imperative that Christine and David be set free. When I asked him what he meant by humanitarian reasons, other than the harshness of the long sentence, he looked me squarely in the eyes and said that Christine and David's prison conditions were like something out of Alan Parker's film *Midnight Express*, which details a young American's nightmarish ordeal in a Turkish prison.

I asked Pearson if he had read the consular reports on David and Christine's conditions. He assured me that he had, but perhaps he really meant that he'd read the Canadian press reports about the prison conditions instead.

"It's disgusting the way Ottawa has chosen to handle this case," said a Canadian diplomat based in Brazil, who has been following the case for years. "We send Ottawa reams of reports and information on Christine and David, and I don't think anybody bothers to read them."

The consular reports are not the only documents that officials at the Department of Foreign Affairs seem disinclined to read. Senior bureaucrats in the ministry told me they had no interest in the reports from the Managua explosion, nor did they care about whether or not there was a CSIS file on Christine or David. "We've made a deliberate decision not to make an issue out of Nicaragua or anything else for that matter. Managua's raised a lot of circumstances that we could talk about until the cows come home. The first order of business is bringing the two back home. We're not going to complicate that with other discussions," said Pearson.

Christine Stewart, deputy minister for Latin America and Africa, had much the same response when I spoke to her in June 1994 at an Organization of American States (OAS) conference in Belem, a port city at the mouth of the Amazon River. For someone who should have read the consular briefings on the case, she seemed terribly surprised to hear about David and Christine's prison conditions. She repeated the Liberal government's policy on the case and, like Pearson, she too was convinced that Christine and David would be back in Canada at the end of the calendar year, although she seemed to have no real grounds for such a conviction.

I asked Stewart the same questions I had asked Michael Pearson. What about the evidence from Managua? What about the false passports and the evidence that came out during the trial in Brazil? Had Foreign Affairs spoken to the RCMP or CSIS? Flustered, Stewart responded that the Canadian government was doing everything it could to get them out of jail. "We have to get them out of jail because they say they're innocent," she said, rushing off to give a speech before the OAS general assembly on Canada's relations with Cuba.

I was left with the impression that in one way the Canadian government is not so different from a terrorist organization. Both work in cells in which each part of the organization is kept in ignorance of what the other parts are doing.

■

The coffee at the Brazilian Embassy in Ottawa is stronger than the weak, watered-down liquid they serve at Canada's Department of Foreign Affairs. At the Sandy Hill mansion that houses the embassy offices on a quiet, tree-lined street, the *cafezinho* is served as it is in Brazil, in tiny cups with a huge dose of sugar. Two *cafezinhos* will jolt you awake and keep you that way no matter how tired you might be.

And much of the conversation at the Embassy is like the coffee. It's a jolt of reality.

When I visited in 1994, the Lamont/Spencer case didn't really seem to be the first thing on anybody's mind. I had the feeling that these diplomats would rather talk about something more important than the fate of two convicted kidnappers stuck in São Paulo jails. The Brazilians were more concerned with improving commercial relations and trying to prove that their country was finally getting its economic house in order and opening its borders to foreign investment. The Lamont/Spencer case was for them a non-issue that was to be handled directly through the *Itamaraty* or Foreign Ministry in Brasília.

They refused to admit that this was the biggest diplomatic issue between the two countries, and they were puzzled that the Canadian public was still insisting that the two were innocent victims of Brazilian injustice. "They were caught in flagrante," shrugged one diplomat, echoing the response that I have heard from just about every Brazilian I've ever spoken to about this case. I asked the Brazilians if they thought the two could be classified as terrorists, but nobody was willing to risk an answer.

"If Christine and David were Argentine or Brazilian, you would never be asking that question," warned a Canadian diplomat in Brasília. "But because they're two nice Canadians nobody can believe it. It's a racist argument and if I were Brazilian I would be incredibly insulted."

But the Brazilians were beyond being insulted by the case. They just seemed vaguely amused by all the fuss it had generated in Canada. They were even more amused by the determination of the Liberal government to get the two out of jail in a hurry. In Brazil, with its Byzantine bureaucracy, few things ever happen in a hurry.

"How are they going to do that?" asked a Brazilian diplomat when I mentioned that the Liberal government was convinced they would get the two out before the end of the year. "This is going to be a lot of fun to watch."

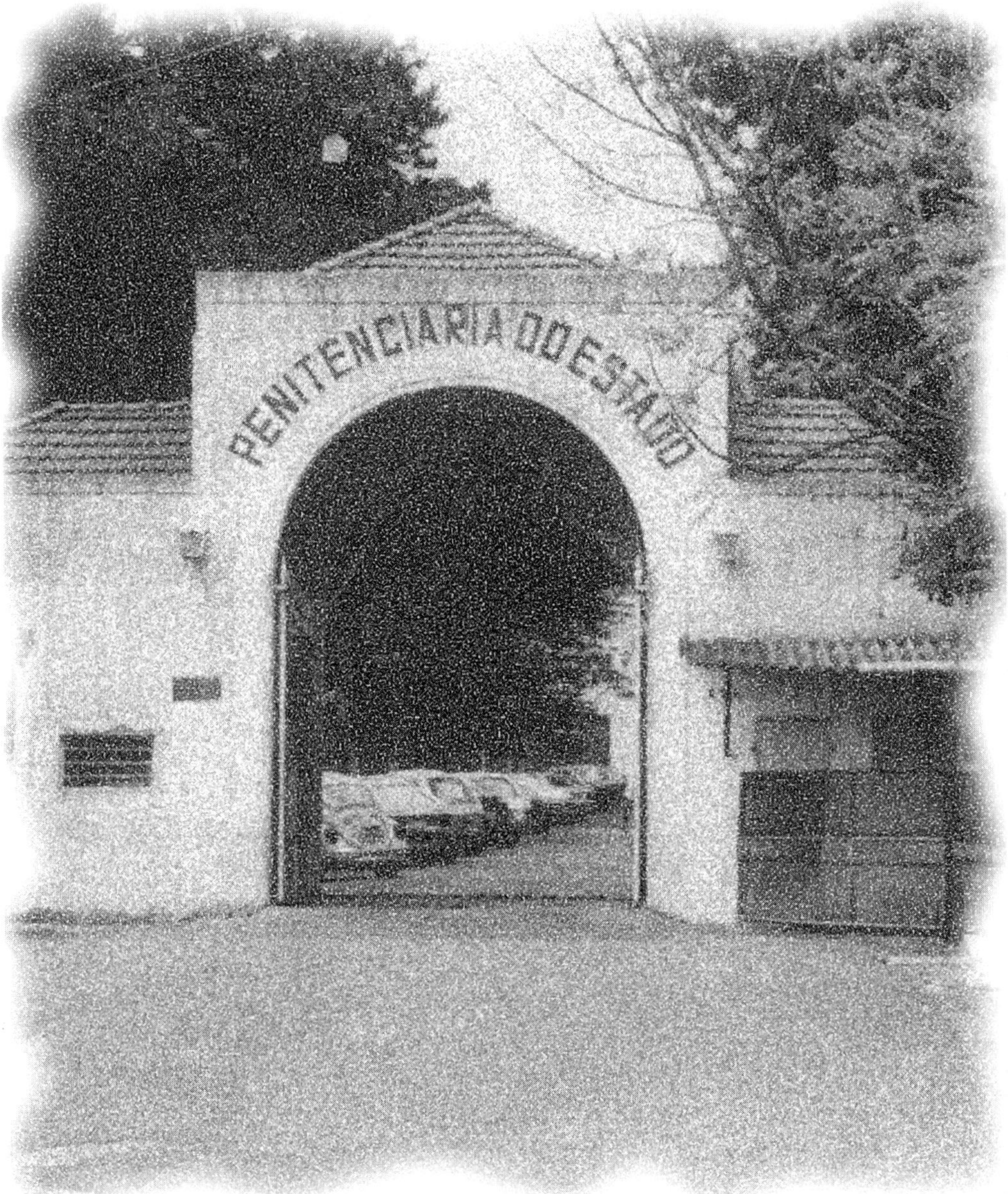
PENITENCIARIA DO ESTADO

Eight

Christine Lamont absently twirls the ponytail that juts out awkwardly from one side of her head and butts her cigarette in a clear glass ashtray in the warden's office at the Penitenciária Feminina.

It's a sun-drenched spring afternoon and we've been talking for more than four hours about Latin American politics. We haven't been discussing her case because she has made a pact with her parents, David, and perhaps her lawyers not to give any more interviews to the Brazilian or Canadian media. She doesn't trust journalists, and she is guarded in her responses to my questions. But although she has told me she won't cooperate with me on this book, Christine craves conversation, and occasionally her guard disintegrates and she becomes confessional.

She doesn't want to apply under the terms of the exchange of prisoners treaty to return to Canada because she doesn't want to serve any time in a Canadian jail. She wants expulsion and is now putting all of her hopes in the Liberal government's submitting the request to the Brazilian president.

"I've read lots of articles on Canadian jails — everything I could get my hands on — and it really scares me," she says, fishing a sleek black box of John Players Special out of the pocket of her prison-issue khakis.

SEE NO EVIL

Although a new women's prison is nearing completion in Joliette, Quebec, Christine would likely have to serve her time at the antiquated Prison for Women in Kingston, Ontario. Built in 1934, the federal penitentiary is sorely lacking in treatment facilities and rehabilitation programs. On a general level, women in Canadian jails get substandard treatment compared with men because they make up a very small percentage — 7 per cent — of the prison population in the country. A 1991 government report on conditions at federal prisons for women in Canada found that women "have been offered little training or treatment appropriate to their needs. The effects of separation from their families both on them and their children has received little attention. . . . They have been kept in conditions of security which bear little relationship to the risk which they pose to society." The report, which concentrates specifically on the women's prison in Kingston, says that "the problems which have been created for women have remained largely untackled for. . . . 150 years."

Life is not perfect at the Penitenciária Feminina in the working-class Carandiru neighbourhood of São Paulo, but it just may be better than anything waiting for Christine in Canada. In addition to receiving private medical and dental care, Christine, who had just turned thirty-five when I first went to visit her, seems well treated by prison officials, who refer to her with respect as Doña Christine. She participates in theatre workshops and helps with English classes for the other inmates.

Carmen dos Santos, the warden, says that Christine is extremely cooperative and well behaved, but that she is not the exceptional and heroic prisoner her parents have made her out to be in the Canadian media. According to the Lamonts, Christine and Maria Emília Badilla, the other convicted Diniz kidnapper and her best friend in the jail, pioneered theatre workshops, many of them educational exercises to teach inmates about such issues as AIDS. But according to dos Santos, the workshops had been in place long before Christine and Maria Emília arrived. The same goes for the English classes, said dos Santos. "She's very nice, but she's just like the other prisoners."

I mentioned that the Lamonts had been upset that they were not allowed to bring a cake on Christine's birthday in April 1994. Dos Santos replied that none of the other prisoners are allowed to have cakes brought from outside on their birthdays for security reasons, so why should Christine? In Brazil, it seems, birthday cakes are still common hiding places for files and other tools traditionally used in prison escapes.""We can't bend the rules just because she's Canadian," said dos Santos, adding that Christine probably receives the greatest number of visitors, compared with the other prisoners, and that someone from the Canadian consulate in São Paulo visits several times a month to make sure that everything is all right.

"She's a celebrity," said dos Santos, fishing through a stack of letters on her desk from church groups and individuals requesting interviews with Christine. "We get so many requests that I have to refuse a lot of them. It's not fair to the other prisoners."

At first sight, dos Santos, or Doutora Carmen (Dr. Carmen) as she is known at the jail, appears a bit rough around the edges. But she's probably one of the most professional and fair-minded people I've met in Brazil. The middle-aged warden, who is fond of lace curtains and bouquets of plastic flowers in her otherwise spartan office, has had to fight against possibly the worst type of prejudice in Brazil: she's a woman, she's from a poor family, and she's black. In a country where few black women ever attain positions of power, dos Santos's career is a stellar exception. If the Penitenciária Feminina is considered a model prison for women in Brazil, that is largely thanks to the dedication and professionalism of Doutora Carmen.

Prison life is monotonous in any country, but other than boredom and loneliness, I really couldn't find much that was negative about life at the Penitenciária Feminina. When I first visited Christine in May 1994, she was working in one of the prison workshops sewing zippers onto bright orange uniforms to be used by São Paulo's public works employees. (When she first entered the general prison population in 1990, she worked making clothespins and then cutting the threads off truckers' hats and pasting fabric samples into catalogues. Many articles were written in the Canadian press about her allergic reaction to the dyes, after her mother reported it.)

I recognized her right away and instantly liked her. In contrast to the other prisoners, who ignored me, forcing themselves to concentrate on their sewing machines, Christine seemed genuinely interested. She had no idea at the time who I was or that I had come to visit her, but she looked up immediately and an easy smile spread over her face. She went back to work, but occasionally she'd look up again — hair spilling over her eyes — and fix me with that easy, infectious smile.

She's thinner than she appears in the few photographs I've seen of her and has recently started to dye her light brown hair auburn. Her teeth are stained from too many cigarettes and she has deep, dark circles under her eyes. At our first meeting, I asked if she was tired and she said that she always looked like that. "I get tons of sleep, but I always look tired," she laughed.

Christine told me she worked Monday to Friday at what she described as very dull menial tasks like sewing zippers onto uniforms, and that she had an hour and a half off for lunch. ("Did I say an hour and a half in our last interview?" she asked me anxiously when I went to see her again in October 1994. "Please don't print that. I only have an hour.") Work is usually over by late afternoon, and then she reads, writes letters, or listens to her shortwave radio until dinner time. During most of the day, she is free to wander around the grounds of the Penitenciária, where there are trees, neatly manicured lawns, and volleyball courts. After dinner, she can watch television in the common room in her cell block, an ugly concrete building next to a barbed-wire fence. But Christine told me that most of the women in her cell block are addicted to the *telenovelas* or soap operas, which air on Brazil's biggest network, Globo, from about 5:00 p.m. to 9:00 p.m. She says she hates the soap operas and would much rather read, write letters, or knit in her cell with its crocheted bedspread, stacks of books, and the shrine of photos of David on the wall next to her bed in neat, handmade, watercolour borders.

I was stunned when I first saw Christine's cell. I'm not sure what I was expecting — perhaps some tiny, dark, and dingy underground room without windows, much like the cell used to house Abílio Diniz that I had seen in the black and white police video. But Christine's cell is not only well lit and pleasant — with its potted plants and fruit basket — it's nearly three times bigger than Diniz's claustrophobic "tank."

Although Christine has barely seen David in her five-and-a-half years in jail, they write to each other regularly. Articles in the Canadian press have portrayed them as a modern-day Romeo and Juliet, pining for each other over the concrete walls and barbed wire fences that separate them. There are stories of the two glimpsing each other from afar, Christine clad in a bright red sweater to attract his attention at a prearranged time. Sometimes, the stories go, David can spot Christine from the top floor of the men's prison as he looks down into the women's exercise yard. But for two people who are supposedly so much in love,

I found it strange that neither of them spoke about the other. I asked Christine, whom I visited first, if she had any message she wanted me to pass on to David. She said no. When I told David that I had seen Christine the day before, he seemed uninterested. "How is she?" he asked me, more out of politeness perhaps than any genuine interest. But maybe he was in a disagreeable mood at our first meeting, because subsequently he specifically asked about Christine and told me to give her his love.

David's days aren't very different from Christine's. When I first went to see him, the trim thirty-year-old with the neatly cropped auburn hair was working as a janitor in the jail. He works during the day and spends his evenings reading, watching television in his cell, or writing. Unlike Christine, David seems fascinated by Brazil. He has written several articles for the *Ottawa Citizen* and *Conexiones*, the alternative newspaper he worked for in Vancouver. While his stories often deal with the "injustices" he has suffered in the Brazilian courts, there is also an attempt to analyse and condemn — quite arrogantly — Brazilian society as a whole.

David's reflections on Brazilian democracy, for instance, do not take into account just how far this country has come since the military regime ended in 1985. "In December 1989, Brazilians elected Fernando Collor de Mello, making him the first directly elected president since the 1964 military coup. But does one election a democracy make? Of course not. Brazil's public institutions, the pillars of any healthy, functioning democracy, are still wracked [sic] and hobbled by the pain of the last 25 years. The justice system is a pertinent example. Today's police officers, judges and public prosecutors learned their professions in the bad old days. One night they went to sleep in a dictatorship and the next morning woke up in a democracy. But old habits die hard."

While nobody denies that Brazil still needs to make a great effort to clean up government corruption and to work for the educational reforms that will further entrench democratic principles, the country is still Latin America's biggest democracy. In the 1994 election, more than 93 million people went to the polls. In 1992, Brazil's "wracked and hobbled" public institutions managed to come up with a democratic solution to a national crisis. Brazilians peacefully impeached Collor for his role in an influence-peddling scandal. In previous years, such a crisis would undoubtedly have been solved by a military takeover. Brazil also has one of the most complete and comprehensive constitutions in the Western world. The book-length Magna Carta, rewritten thanks to aggressive lobbying on the part of the Brazilian left in 1988, guarantees everything from civil rights to "sports justice" (guaranteeing fairness in sporting competitions) for every citizen in this nation of 150 million people. Although the constitution has presented several obstacles to economic reform in recent years, it is hardly the charter of an undemocratic, unsophisticated banana-republic.

Perhaps David is at his best when he leaves Brazilian politics aside and writes human interest stories. His most memorable one is a piece that appeared December 23, 1992 in the *Ottawa Citizen* about his first Christmas in Brazil. David describes how on Christmas Day he just felt like ignoring the holiday until three fellow inmates thrust Tupperware containers crammed with Christmas goodies into his cell.

Suddenly, Christmas broke out in my cell. I was happy, the happiest I'd been in more than a year. Just when the world starts looking like a bowl of lousy bean soup, someone shows up with a Christmas dinner. That's life for you. What possessed those three wise men bearing gifts in Tupperware containers? It would have been much easier for them to ignore my plight. But they didn't. Prison has at least one thing in common with life on the outside: it is easier to keep your hands in your pockets. Easier to do nothing than it is to, oh dear, do the right thing. But every so often the rules are broken and hands come out of their pockets... Maybe that's what this oft referred to Christmas spirit is all about. Once a year our hands come out of our pockets and the best part of our human nature is set free, only to be locked away again at day's end.

When I told David that I really enjoyed reading this work, he seemed embarrassed and said that he thought the Christmas story was particularly "soppy."

David told me that for his own protection he spends a lot of time with "the rest of the gang," the seven other convicted kidnappers who share his cell block. Some inmates at the Penitenciária do Estado, where David is incarcerated, say that the eight men are inseparable. "Nobody messes with them. They have a lot of money," said one inmate, an AIDS sufferer at the prison infirmary. David says they stay together to avoid getting into any trouble with the other prisoners. For instance, he told me that the eight rarely participate in organized sporting events, such as soccer games, in order to avoid potential riot situations.

Like Christine, David was reluctant to speak to me at first and refused to say anything about his case. But sitting in the large wood-panelled warden's office where the late afternoon sun spilled in through wide open windows, we spoke for nearly four hours about politics in Latin America and Africa, swapping the titles of books we'd recently read. David sat upright in a straight-backed chair and towards the end of the interview apologized for being on edge because he hadn't had a cigarette all afternoon. Walter Hoffgen, the warden, finally cut us off when he announced that he wanted to leave his office early. "It's Friday and I'd like to go out for a whisky now," said Hoffgen, tidying his desk. Like Doutora Carmen, Doutor Walter as he is known at the Penitenciária do Estado, is a consummate professional who seems genuinely concerned with the welfare of his prisoners. When I visited him in October 1994, David complained that he wasn't feeling well. Doutor Walter immediately arranged for a doctor to visit him.

I left my first meetings with David and Christine feeling that we had covered a lot of ground in terms of their interests in Latin American issues. These were not stupid people, and I could hardly believe that they were ever "unwitting dupes" in any situation. I recalled a conversation I had had with an RCMP officer, who was familiar with the case: "We tend to think that criminals are dumb," he said. "But many just exploit that side of the world. You cannot tell your neighbour just by living next door. You have to dig deeper."

David is still very committed to his Marxist beliefs, but he is a very critical thinker who craves argument.

"Despite everything, I make a separation between why I came here and what happened to me," David told *The Fifth Estate* in 1992. "And why I came here, I have no qualms about."

Although Christine is not as independent a thinker as David, she struck me as extremely intelligent and well informed. We spoke mostly about the recent changes in Central America, particularly in El Salvador, which she obviously knew a lot about. She is still in touch with some of her Central American solidarity contacts in Vancouver and receives a regular subscription to *Conexiones* from her friends on the editorial collective of the magazine. At one point in our conversation I asked her about the ERP, referring to the Ejército Revolucionario del Pueblo, now known as the Expresion Renovadora del Pueblo, the FMLN faction led by Joaquín Villalobos in El Salvador. Christine fixed me with an inquisitive expression and asked, "Which ERP are you talking about?" The question said a lot about her knowledge of Latin American politics. The other ERP was an Argentine guerrilla group that emerged from within the Peronist party in the late 1960s. Also known as the Montoneros, the ERP in Argentina was crushed in the dirty war that the Argentine military waged against leftists from 1976 to 1979.

After speaking to Christine and David, I found it difficult to believe that they could have been as naive as they claimed during the Diniz kidnapping. Many left-wing terrorist organizations pose as human rights groups and are highly organized units that are divided into cells. Often one cell or group of people are not told what the other cell is doing on purpose. This arrangement is made mostly for security reasons. If one or more members of the group are caught, they will not be able to give the authorities any information that might damage the rest of the group.

Still, even supposing a cell structure was used by the Diniz kidnappers and some of them were indeed in the dark about the whole operation, there are numerous unanswered questions about just what David and Christine were doing in Latin America in the first place. The story as told by Christine and David and the Canadian media is full of distortions, conflicting testimony, and huge gaps.

What were David and Christine really doing in Nicaragua? Although they say they were working as translators for Salpress, the fact is that in early 1989 they could only speak rudimentary Spanish, and no legitimate employee of the news organization remembers the two in Managua. Perhaps they had false credentials for Salpress, just as they had false credentials for alternative media in Toronto.

Interpol and the Brazilian authorities have suggested that they were doing solidarity work with the Sandinistas and undergoing guerrilla training at one of the many camps the Sandinistas had set up to train *internacionalistas* in using weapons, making explosives, and gathering information. This version of events would explain how it came to be that David and Christine were cited as expertly handling weapons during the thirty-six-hour seige in São Paulo. How else would a nice Canadian from an upper-middle-class home in Langley, B.C. learn how to clean, load, and handle a pistol?

Why were they travelling on false passports? Christine and David have maintained that human rights workers in Latin America had to use what Mrs. Lamont discreetly referred to as "alternative identification" in order to protect themselves. But nobody has really bothered to ask just what they were protecting themselves from. In 1989, all but two Latin American countries had made the transition to democracy. Although Nicaragua was still in the grip of a civil war, the Sandinistas were certainly receptive to *internacionalistas* and would have given human rights workers (most of whom were probably on the side of the Sandinista regime) little trouble. Brazil and Argentina, the other countries in which they spent lengthy amounts of time, were hardly the repressive Latin American societies of the 1960s and 1970s. Foreigners travelling to these countries, even foreigners working in the human rights field, were hardly targets for the military or the police, unless of course they were doing something illegal.

David and Christine claim they were tourists when they went to São Paulo in the summer of 1989, but since when do Canadian tourists find it necessary to lie to their neighbours about where they are from? How many Canadian tourists set off with enough money to put down several months' rent in U.S. dollars on two houses in Latin America and have cash left over to buy a van?

Were they human rights workers or tourists or perhaps a combination of both? Victor Malarek points out in his first documentary on them for *The Fifth Estate* that the two wanted to tour through some of Latin America's poorest places before settling down and raising a family in Canada. When they were interrogated by the police in São Paulo, they said they spent their days shopping, sightseeing, and looking for courses in Portuguese in the city. They said they left the house in the early morning and did not return until the evening. As interesting as some may find São Paulo, probably Latin America's most industrialized and smog-filled city, it's hardly a foreign tourist's paradise. I can think of few things more stressful or depressing than spending more than a month in São Paulo, a city of some 17 million people, as a tourist.

SEE NO EVIL

Why did they write fourteen postdated letters to their parents? Christine and David have never properly addressed what their documents and the letters were doing in Nicaragua. Their supporters say that the letters were written so that their parents wouldn't worry. But the whole letter-writing operation was carefully orchestrated so that both of them could tell their families essentially the same story. Why write phony letters, spread out over a year, unless you don't want somebody to know what you're really doing?

If Christine and David maintain their innocence, why do they insist upon being defended with the eight other members of the group? If you're searching for legal transcripts of this case at the São Paulo courts, you must look up those which refer to "Humberto Paz and others." If their defence has rested on each member of the group having a different level of culpability in the crime, then why be represented together as a group?

Furthermore, David and Christine have remained faithful to their fellow kidnappers in the group. They are inseparable in jail and look out for each others' interests. Yet, if these are the people who got David and Christine into trouble in the first place, by pressuring them to rent the houses in São Paulo and assist in the plot to kidnap Diniz, then why be so friendly with them? Journalist Kim Bolan explained it to me this way: "Maybe Christine and David can't talk about what really happened, because they would implicate the others. The dynamics in these types of groups are very strong."

Who is paying the legal fees for the ten kidnappers? This is by far the most interesting question in the case. Lawyers at the Bandeira Mello e Associados firm in São Paulo, one of the country's most prestigious law firms, do not come cheap.

About two years ago, I called Marilyn Lamont in Vancouver and asked her about the legal bills. I said that it must be a huge financial burden, paying for such expensive lawyers. At the time, Mrs. Lamont told me that she didn't know how much the lawyers were being paid or who was paying them. She said in no uncertain terms that she and her husband were not paying legal fees in Brazil at that time. (The Lamonts also reportedly told Canadian consular officials in São Paulo that they did not know who was paying Christine and David's legal fees.)

"Who *is* paying the lawyers?" I asked again.

"I don't know," said Mrs. Lamont matter-of-factly. But she must have realized the importance of that question in winning sympathy for her daughter's plight, because several months later I read that she was concerned about being able to pay the high legal fees in Brazil.

Lawyers Marco Antônio Nahum and Belisário dos Santos are not saying who is paying their fees. Perhaps they just don't know, but one thing is for certain: they're not working for free. Brazilian journalists who have followed the case since 1989 say that the legal fees are probably being paid by members of the kidnap group who are still at large in Brazil. Two years ago, the *Folha de São Paulo* speculated that the kidnapping of Geraldo Alonso Filho in Brazil was carried out specifically to raise money for the legal defence of the ten. Others take it one step further and suggest that Enrique Gorriarán Merlo, the Argentine terrorist whom many suspect to be the brains behind the wave of kidnappings throughout Latin America in the last few years, is "taking care of his people."

This list of maddeningly unanswered questions casts a great deal of doubt and suspicion on the two Canadians. In the course of researching this book, I've talked to many people who have asked me the same question over and over again: are Christine and David guilty? While it is quite obvious that they are indeed guilty of participating in a kidnapping (they were, after all, convicted in a Brazilian court), the question of whether they are guilty of being terrorists puts us in murkier waters. Perhaps Christine and David have steadfastly maintained their innocence because they were working for a cause they felt was just. Perhaps they really believed that they were helping Latin America's poor and downtrodden masses when they were busy acquiring false documentation and preparing to join the underground struggle. When you're fighting for such important issues as social justice, and when you've exhausted all possible democratic means to achieve your goals, why shouldn't you break the law?

"Why are Lamont and Spencer regarded as terrorists for allegedly resorting to violence to tackle grave economic and social injustices in Brazil, while Nelson Mandela who called for armed struggle to overthrow apartheid in South Africa is now considered a hero?" asked Bill Warden, executive director of the International Centre at the University of Calgary.

Many still see Christine and David as modern-day Che Guevaras. However, the big difference between the Argentine revolutionary and the members of the group that kidnapped Diniz is that Guevara had a set of clear revolutionary goals and ideals. The kidnappers, although ideologically motivated, had only a vague notion of helping the poor throughout Latin America, or so they'd like us to believe. If they had managed to raise $30 million U.S. in the Diniz kidnapping, what were they going to do with the money? Was it for personal enrichment? Was it to buy arms for the struggle, and if so, what were they struggling for?

Only David and Christine know for sure what their level of involvement really was. But based on the evidence gathered in Brazil, Nicaragua, and Canada, they are certainly not the innocent Canadian kids they've portrayed themselves to be.

In that case, are they terrorists or are they freedom fighters? Is it a hat or is it an elephant inside a boa constrictor? Christine and David, at least, would like us to think that it is all a matter of interpretation.

"It was my impression then and it is my impression now that these two are victims. That their crime was a crime of compassion and naiveté. A crime that Canadians are famous for Compassion is just a part of being a Canadian," wrote Andrew Moodre, an Ottawa actor and writer, in a letter to Barbara McDougall asking her to bring Christine and David back to Canada.

If compassion is indeed just a part of being Canadian, then so too are naiveté and ignorance. The Lamont/Spencer case showed us just how terribly naive and ignorant this nation as a whole can be. As presented in much of the mainstream media, the case had all the elements of an epic Canadian story: two nice Canadian kids, working to change the world, unwittingly get mixed up in international terrorism and are locked away in dank Third World jails, isolated from their families and each other, for nearly three decades. Everyone is against them, including their own government. But ordinary Canadians across the country sign petitions, light candles, and hold vigils to press for their release. The fight may be long and hard, but in the end justice will surely prevail.

Unfortunately, the real story is extremely complicated and it doesn't have a happy ending. If there's a moral here, it lies in the ease with which public opinion in this country can be influenced and directed, especially by using distortions and lies. The Lamont and Spencer families didn't need to spend a lot of money whipping up public opinion in their favour. They had all the elements of a ready-made campaign already in place: an evil foreign country, friends in the media, and a well-connected lobbyist.

Even if they don't know the capital of Latin America's largest nation, most Canadians assume certain things about Brazil — that it is a country notorious for corruption, where off-duty police murder street children in large urban centres and fat-cat ranchers burn down the rainforest. There is indeed much that is wrong with Brazil, but most of these issues have nothing to do with Christine and David's case. Still, Christine and David's supporters have mechanically cited Amnesty International reports on the murder of street kids in Rio, rural violence in the Brazilian northeast, and rampant government corruption as if they had a direct bearing on Christine and David's lives in São Paulo.

As much as Canadians want to believe otherwise, Christine and David were given a fair trial. Although the Lamont and Spencer families alleged that "a grave miscarriage of justice had occurred," the Canadian government discovered otherwise. Although she found that it would be inappropriate to retry the case, McDougall asked legal experts at the Department of External Affairs to review the trial judge's decision and the decision of the appeal court, saying that she wanted to know whether the judge and court had had enough evidence to make the findings that they did and whether the trial had provided a fair hearing. Based on her department's research, McDougall concluded that the decision taken by the Brazilian courts was made "in a proper way."

Christine and David's most prominent friends in the media were the *Vancouver Sun*'s Kim Bolan and the producers at *The Fifth Estate* who either failed to do their homework or chose to ignore salient information. The *Fifth Estate* documentaries were so popular with the Lamont and Spencer families and their supporters that they were used as propaganda material at vigils for Christine and David in Vancouver. Bolan's strident tone in her articles on the case and her willingness to report everything the Lamonts said without questioning it practically turned the pair into martyrs in the eyes of the Canadian public. It was largely from Bolan's reporting that Canadians became acquainted with the supposedly nightmarish prison conditions in São Paulo, and with the evil campaign by Brazilian politicians to use the kidnapping to discredit the left in that country.

SEE NO EVIL

Few journalists had the desire or the courage to question the Lamonts. Trevor Lautens, writing in the *Vancouver Sun*, was one of the first Canadian journalists to note, as early as 1991 that the media were being "grotesquely manipulated."

> *Is Canada properly checking the prison where the two are held? I asked External Affairs Department spokesman Scott Mullin. He said Canadian consular staff had made dozens of visits. Dozens? Dozens. An extraordinary amount of time has been devoted to monitoring the condition of the pair. They're in individual cells at their own request. They have television and common room privileges. They have books. They've given interviews. I doubt if it's pretty. I doubt if it should be. It's prison, not Club Med.*
>
> *Mullin is no fool and no flack. He's a career diplomat whose tough postings have included two years as chargé d'affaires in Tehran and previously in Lebanon just before the roof caved in. "Images are sometimes created that are difficult to refute," he said. "We're also constrained about what we can say by privacy legislation. The families of the pair are not so constrained." My favourite* Sun *headline to date on this hyped-up tear-jerker is: "Bleak Prison Life Bars Lovers' Plan to Marry, Raise Family." Thanks, for that style of journalism I can get the* National Enquirer.

The same sort of obliviousness beset many Ottawa bureaucrats, who either refused to read consular reports on the case by diplomats in the field or ignored the facts. How else can it be explained that some five years after Christine and David were locked up in jail, a high-ranking bureaucrat like Michael Pearson could say that their prison conditions smacked of those in Alan Parker's *Midnight Express*? Moreover, the case, which took on a political life all of its own, was used by some career diplomats to further their own careers at the expense of the truth.

If there's a hero in this story, it's Barbara McDougall, former secretary of state for External Affairs. Despite what the Lamont and Spencer families may feel about her, she was the only high-ranking Canadian government official who refused to be swayed by political considerations. She could have taken the easy way out and scored big political points by demanding expulsion for the two, but she stuck by her principles. And, as she pointed out time and again, expulsion is not an automatic process. Even if Canada were to have asked for an expulsion, there is no guarantee that the Brazilians would have granted it.

Prior to her refusal to ask the Brazilian government for an expulsion, McDougall and her staff spent months reviewing the case and concluded that David and Christine had indeed been treated fairly in Brazil. Later, she admitted that the twenty-eight-year sentences were too harsh. But after communicating her disapproval to the Brazilian government and pushing for the exchange of prisoners treaty, there was little else she could do. After all, Christine and David had broken the law in a foreign country and as a result were subject to the laws of that country. Despite their protestations of innocence, the evidence was unassailable, and Canadian courts and the Canadian government could not interfere in another jurisdiction.

"I felt that we went the extra mile on this case. We investigated every single complaint. Whatever we could do we did," said McDougall, adding that the Managua blast turned many in Canada against Christine and David and seriously damaged their credibility. "I felt badly for the parents because the facts coming out of the Managua blast were so incontrovertible."

The Lamonts maintained throughout that McDougall's decision not to ask for on expulsion on humanitarian or legal grounds was political, even though it was obvious that she had nothing to gain politically from taking a hard-line approach on the case. Mrs. Lamont called External Affairs "a whole bureaucracy that adopted a 'guilty verdict' at the beginning of the case, well before the courts did."

With hindsight, McDougall and others say that the Lamont and Spencer families lobbied too hard when they should have sought quieter diplomatic solutions. In fact, this is precisely the strategy the families have adopted in the last year to get Christine and David out of jail. Many now say that the parents made tactical errors in the case by not coming clean from the very beginning about what it was that Christine and David were really doing in Latin America.

"They kept the pot boiling on the issue in such a way that maybe it hurt their cause," said McDougall. "They relied on the advice they got from Humphreys and others, but you often get the advice you're looking for. But if it were your kid, wouldn't you do the same?"

For their part, the Lamont and Spencer families say that they decided on an all-out media campaign only because they were getting nowhere in the early days with quiet diplomatic lobbying. Maybe they didn't intend for the issue to explode the way it did, but the information they gave the Canadian press and their demonization of Brazil, and the rest of Latin America for that matter, turned the case into a twisted, exaggerated tale.

In addition to castigating Barbara McDougall, the Lamont and Spencer families severely criticized the Canadian government, in particular the Department of External Affairs, for not doing enough for the imprisoned pair. One of Christine and David's supporters in British Columbia went so far as to suggest that the federal government's treatment of the case constituted an anti-West bias. In Vancouver, people mumbled under their breath that if David and Christine had been from Toronto, they would surely be out of jail by now. Indeed, in our first interview in São Paulo, David remarked that *The Globe and Mail* wasn't more interested in reporting on the case because he and Christine were not from Toronto.

Yet the truth is that the Canadian government has spent more time on this case than probably any other of its kind in recent history. Although they deny that the case has taken on the status of a major diplomatic issue between the two countries, Canadian diplomats in Brasilia and São Paulo will tell you in private that they spend more time on this case than any other issue. There are more than five hundred Canadians serving time in foreign jails, but it is doubtful that they receive anything like the kind of treatment that David and Christine do from the Canadian government. High-ranking consular officials visit the two on a regular basis. David has been known to phone the Canadian consul general in São Paulo at home, a practice that is highly unusual and beyond the call of duty for Canadian diplomats abroad. Whenever there is the remotest chance that one or both may be ill (even if it's just a cold) or that they may be in any danger, a Canadian diplomat is dispatched post-haste.

David is probably the only Canadian prisoner abroad who is allowed long-distance telephone privileges at the expense of the Canadian government. Every three months, Bill Spencer, his father, is given the opportunity to talk to his son for forty-five minutes at the Canadian taxpayers' expense. (This privilege, instituted under the Progressive Conservative government, is being maintained by the Liberals.) These are hardly the actions of a cruel and unfeeling federal government that, as the Lamont and Spencer families would have us believe, has abandoned its helpless citizens in Third World jails.

Although the parents and the Liberal government have adopted a quiet strategy to get David and Christine out of jail, the issue is not about to go away. Perhaps, however, with more pressing foreign policy issues at stake in Latin America, such as NAFTA and Cuba, officials at the Department of Foreign Affairs will not have the luxury of spending so much time on this particular issue. Still, the Lamonts report that Michael Pearson calls them just about every week to consult on "strategy." The truth is that thanks to the dogged persistence of the Lamonts the case won't be resolved until David and Christine are either set free or return to Canada to serve out the rest of their terms in Canadian jails. Liberals have painted themselves into a tight political corner over this case and are doing everything they can to get Christine and David out or at least back to the dubious comfort of a Canadian jail.

In Brazil, the Diniz kidnapping case remains very much a political issue. During the 1994 presidential campaign, the PT used images from the kidnapping in television ads, suggesting that their right-wing foes had tried to discredit the party by tying them to criminal activity during the 1989 campaign and that they would stop at nothing to make sure they lost the 1994 race. It didn't matter that Fernando Henrique Cardoso, their closest rival in the 1994 race, was a committed social democrat and one of the most articulate spokesmen for the left in Latin America. As in the 1989 presidential campaign, the PT was all set to blame its loss on a right-wing plot to discredit them.

It's little wonder that the Lamonts' attempt to export their aggressive lobbying strategy to Brazil fell flat. Brazilians, who are for the most part a fervently nationalistic bunch, don't respond well to having their country portrayed as a corrupt banana-republic. Unfortunately the Lamonts, who have by now paid numerous visits to the country, never quite picked up on the Brazilian *jeitinho* or trick — the national ability to solve the impossible, sometimes through quiet lobbying and making the right contacts. Anything is possible with the *jeitinho*, but you've got to be patient. Before I went to live in Brazil in 1991, a Brazilian friend gave me a piece of advice that has served me well. He said that whenever you get frustrated by Brazilian bureaucracy, never get angry, never raise your voice and never make a fuss. "If things get really bad, just start crying. Brazilians respond really well to that."

The Lamonts and their supporters, who never questioned that their cause was right and just, never really bothered to understand Brazilian political or legal culture. They just assumed that it was all corrupt. As one Canadian diplomat put it, "There's no place as frustrating as Brazil. The impossible in Canada gets done in Brazil whereas the mundane in Canada becomes impossible in Brazil."

Still, the Lamonts, who have for the most part been treated sympathetically in the Brazilian media, have not been completely unsuccessful in Brazil. They did manage to get people like Cardinal Arns, PT senator Eduardo Suplicy, and former justice minister Jarbas Passarinho on side, but in the end their political influence meant nothing. The earnest Cardinal Arns says he is convinced they didn't want to participate, but, given all of the evidence against them, the cardinal has turned himself into an object of ridicule in his own country for his outspoken support of the two Canadians. He has actually said he reached his conclusions about the innocence of the pair based on his conversations with the ten kidnappers.

"He [Cardinal Arns] believes that from the bottom of his heart," Nelson Guimarães, the police inspector who headed the investigation into the Diniz case, told *The Fifth Estate*. "I use my head."

Others, including Canadian government officials, have also criticized Cardinal Arns for getting involved in the lobbying effort to free Christine and David. Although he means well, it is doubtful whether he has ever examined the facts of the case in any depth. Furthermore, he is hardly an objective analyst in this case, since he is a committed supporter of the PT in Brazil and helped to promote the theory in 1989 that the kidnapping was used as a vehicle to discredit the Marxist party on the eve of the presidential election.

But if the Diniz kidnapping was supposed to be used as a vehicle to discredit the Brazilian left or somehow undermine Brazilian democracy, it was a miserable failure. In 1994, the two main contenders in the presidential race were both candidates from the Brazilian left. A less radical Lula, who was now sporting double-breasted suits and ties, was back. His main rival was Cardoso, a former sociologist who was a strong opponent of Brazil's military regime and fled to Chile to avoid arrest after the Brazilian military junta seized power in 1964. Cardoso, along with co-author Enzo Falletto, wrote *Dependency and Development in Latin America*, which broached the ground-breaking thesis that Latin American development had been hampered by the demands of the world's big economies, such as the United States.

Cardoso, a committed social democrat, won handily in the first round of voting in October thanks to a successful anti-inflation plan he had instituted while he was finance minister in Itamar Franco's government. The *Plano Real* or Real Plan saw inflation drop from 45 per cent per month to 2 per cent per month with the introduction of a new currency, loosely pegged to the U.S. dollar, and the de-indexing of wages and prices. As in 1989, Brazilians were confident that their fortunes were beginning to change for the better, and they put a great deal of hope in their new president. Unlike Collor, Cardoso is not a demagogue, and he is perhaps more sincere about working for social and economic change in Brazil. However, he has many obstacles ahead of him. His biggest problem will be overcoming congressional deadlock in order to push through much-needed constitutional reforms to ensure the continued success of his economic plan.

But perhaps under Cardoso there is finally hope for Brazil, a country that the Lamonts have told us is corrupt, evil, and completely unsophisticated. They have pointed to the corruption of Brazilian law enforcement officials and the press to prove their points. The São Paulo police are corrupt, they say, because after the stand-off, all of Christine and David's personal belongings and about $200,000 U.S. in cash and travellers' cheques belonging to the kidnap gang mysteriously went missing from the house on Praça Hachiro Miyazaki. Many Brazilians share the Lamonts' suspicion that the items were indeed taken by members of the force. Furthermore, Christine and David's false passports, which were used as evidence during the first trial in 1990, have also disappeared. A few years ago, U.S. customs authorities reported that two people had entered the United States using those passports. Many suspect that the passports were stolen and sold on the black market by São Paulo law enforcement officials, who earn as little as $200 U.S. per month. But despite corruption in the São Paulo Civil Police force, their special anti-kidnapping squad did handle the Diniz kidnapping and subsequent investigation efficiently and without any loss of life.

Similarly, the Brazilian press is by no means blameless in its reporting of the Diniz kidnapping. Although there was hardly a media conspiracy to cover anything up, some of the reporting was sensationalistic and not as accurate or as well-researched as it could have been. The reporting in the Brazilian press about the exchange of prisoners treaty is a case in point. I had the feeling that many Brazilian reporters didn't even bother to read the treaty and, for the most part, erroneously reported that the treaty would allow David and Christine to go free in Canada. Many Brazilian journalists also made much of David having been a member of the Squamish Five Support Group in Vancouver. However, few had any understanding of what the Squamish Five was all about and what the term "terrorist group" meant in a country that had only dealt with two such organizations (the Front de Libération du Québec and Direct Action) in its recent history. After the Managua blast, newspapers such as O *Globo* and the *Folha de São Paulo* were ludicrously reporting that Canada was a hotbed of terrorism.

But it was really a case of quid pro quo. Canadians, who had been engaging in a mud-slinging campaign against the Brazilian media for more than five years, deserved exactly what they got in return. Reporting in both countries was characterized by ignorance and racism. But the lies and distortions seemed worse at the Canadian end, largely because journalists in Canada, an advanced First World nation, probably should have known better. Instead, the reporting in this country on the case merely served to show us how little we know about Latin America. In light of the North American Free Trade Agreement, which has brought Canada closer than ever to Latin America, Canadians should be forging stronger links and building a better understanding among their Latin American neighbours. In addition to Mexico, Canadians may soon find themselves trading with Chile, Argentina, and Venezuela, which are already standing in line to join NAFTA. But if nothing else, this case has shown how parochial we are — how terribly unprepared we are to join in any meaningful way with our neighbours in the Southern Hemisphere.

Like Christine and David, most Canadians tried to impose their beliefs on a part of the world they knew nothing about. In their naiveté, Christine and David worked to bring about the revolution in Latin America, to institute the ABCs of militant leftism on a continent that had already graduated to neoliberal economics. Nobody had to tell them the revolution was dead or the Cold War over. All they needed to do was look around them. In Chile, former left-wing militants who had spent the 1970s throwing rocks and Molotov cocktails at the military were working in the finance ministry helping to open the country's markets even wider to foreign investment. In El Salvador, former guerrilla fighters were driving around the capital in Nissan Pathfinders, equipped with cellular phones, talking about how the left needed to be more social democratic, less militant, less left-wing.

Christine and David really believe that the answers to Latin America's problems with poverty lie in socialist economic policies, but they fail to remember that it was these very policies that brought about many of Latin America's problems in the modern era. Salvador Allende's nationalist economic policies in Chile just ended up fuelling inflation and worsening the plight of the poor. In Brazil, Mexico, and Argentina, corrupt, nationalist, spendthrift governments in the 1960s and 1970s brought about hyperinflation and helped usher in the 1980s debt crisis. These misguided policies only worsened the plight of the poor, for inflation is the worst kind of burden on them. When inflation was high in Brazil, as recently as 1994, currency was devaluing by 2 per cent per day. Those making one minimum wage or less than one minimum wage per month (at the time $65 U.S.) had no way of saving their money and had to spend it quickly before inflation rendered it useless.

There's no doubt that David and Christine are guilty of being naive. They're guilty of being misguided and relying a bit too much on the kindness of strangers — ruthless, calculating strangers who exploited their commitment, energy, and naiveté to get much of their dirty work done. But the two Canadians are guilty of carrying false identification and participating in a kidnapping. They are adults and responsible for their own actions. Perhaps their case was used for political purposes in Brazil, but that's not a legal defence and it doesn't get them off the hook.

If they insist that the kidnapping was used for political purposes by right-wing elements in Brazil, then they have nobody to blame but themselves. The fact is that the kidnapping, which occurred on the eve of Brazil's first free elections in nearly three decades, showed an awful lack of political savvy on the kidnappers' parts. In short, they did it at the wrong time and thereby played directly into the hands of the so-called right wing. But for me what is most annoying about the case can be summarized in one more unanswered question. That is, if you're really committed to the struggle for democracy and liberation in Latin America, why kidnap a man in a country struggling hard to be a democracy after nearly thirty years of military rule? Doesn't that undermine the struggle?

Perhaps David and Christine don't deserve to spend twenty-eight years in prison, but it is unlikely they will, even if they remain in Brazil. In handing down the stiff sentences, the appellate court judge noted that the prisoners would be allowed out after serving a fraction of their sentences, either through parole or through the seemingly constant appeals process.

The Canadian government has had no luck convincing two Brazilian presidents to sign an expulsion or the exchange of prisoners treaty. Neither Fernando Collor de Mello nor Itamar Franco would touch Christine and David's case. Franco, a fervent nationalist, refused to oblige the Canadians just before leaving office in December 1994. During that month he had been approached by both Prime Minister Jean Chrétien at the Summit for the Americas in Miami, and by Deputy Prime Minister Sheila Copps, who represented Canada at the inauguration of President Cardoso in Brasília on January 1, 1995. "I heard the arguments of the [Canadian] prime minister but I was clear: in my government the deportation of the two Canadians will not be authorized," said Franco in an interview with *Globo* newspaper on December 30, 1994. "They were condemned by Brazilian justice and they should serve out their sentences in Brazil."

But perhaps things will change. Perhaps Cardoso, the country's new president, will be swayed by his good friend Cardinal Arns and sign either an expulsion order or the treaty.

However, in January 1995 when Jean Chretien broached the issue of the release of Lamont and Spencer with the Brazilian president, Cardoso was polite but firm. "There's no way Fernando Henrique is going to release the authors of the biggest kidnapping in Brazilian history when we are experiencing a wave of kidnappings in Brazil," said a high official in the Itamaraty or Brazilian foreign ministry. "Don't the Canadians have anything else to worry about?"

■

I was startled the last time I went to see David in jail. He looked so pale and thin that I immediately asked him if he was ill. He said he had had a high fever and chills for several days and was worried. He had seen the prison doctor, but the doctor had only prescribed strong antibiotics and didn't tell David what had provoked the fever in the first place. "That's the way they deal with everything here. They just give you antibiotics. They're a kind of cure-all," he told me.

David was worried that the fever was a flare-up of a bout of malaria he had had in Nicaragua in 1989 and asked me to call the Canadian consulate so that they could arrange for a private doctor. Although he is reluctant to ask for help, he seemed desperate enough at the time to ask me to bring him some milk powder and papayas. "I need to put the weight back on," he smiled. "Please don't tell Christine I'm sick. I don't want her to worry."

The next day, I packed up the groceries in a plastic bag and stood in line with the prisoners' families at the grimy kiosk in front of the Penitenciária do Estado. It is here that you can leave groceries and books for the inmates. The guards, a group of gum-chewing women, some in tight blue jeans and sporting colourful decorative combs in their hair, felt the bags of milk powder, which were clearly labelled "David Spencer, matrícula [prisoner number] 68861." Maybe they were checking for files or weapons; I don't know. I asked if they were going to open the papayas, just in case I had managed to sneak something inside the fruit. They smiled, but didn't respond.

Christine França, who works at the Canadian consulate in São Paulo, snapped into action as soon as I told her of David's medical problems. In a few hours, she was able to provide a doctor to take a look at David. It turned out it wasn't malaria after all, just a nasty case of the flu.

"Thank God," I said to França, who echoed my relief. "I was really worried about David."

It was then I realized just how much respect I have for David Spencer. I admire his quick wit and intelligence and truly enjoyed the time we spent together talking about politics. He always seemed genuinely happy to see me and one day he told Doutor Walter that I was the only journalist in the world he would ever talk to.

"I like you a lot, but you know I can't cooperate with you on your book," he told me one day at the end of our visit. The late afternoon sun spilled into the tiny wood-pannelled waiting room where we sat in leather armchairs, chatting about the future of the militant left in Latin America.

I told him I didn't want to pressure him to do anything he didn't want to do and was content to spend an afternoon talking.

Just then he lit a cigarette, took a long drag, and moved his chair closer to mine. "One day, when I'm out of this place, I'd like to take you out for a beer and tell you the whole story," he said.

He took another long drag on his cigarette, smiled, and lowered his voice to a conspiratorial whisper:

"It's a great story."

List of Political Parties and Organizations

ALN — Aliança Libertadora Nacional/Alliance for National Liberation (Brazil) — A Brazilian, pro-Cuban, urban guerrilla group founded by Carlos Marighella in the late 1960s to fight against the country's military regime. The ALN began military activities in 1968 and provided military support for the kidnapping of U.S. ambassador Burke Elbrick. They kidnapped the Swiss ambassador in 1970.

ARENA — Alianza Republicana Nacionalista/Nationalist Republican Alliance (El Salvador) — An extreme right-wing party founded in 1981, committed to nationalism, individualism, free enterprise, and national security. The party, which ruled for much of the 1980s, clandestinely supported death squads in the 1980s and early 1990s and won the 1994 elections, the first democratic elections following the end of El Salvador's civil war in 1992.

ERP — Ejército Revolucionário del Pueblo /People's Revolutionary Army (El Salvador) — One of the leading factions of the FMLN coalition, formed in 1972 by middle-class Christian Democrats, and headed during the civil war by the FMLN's foremost military strategist, Joaquín Villalobos. Last year the group changed its named to the Expresión Renovadora del Pueblo (the People's Expression of Renewal).

ERP — Ejército Revolucionário del Pueblo /People's Revolutionary Army (Argentina) — An Argentine leftist movement influenced by Trotsky and

Che Guevara and one of the two main guerrilla organizations in the country in the 1970s. The ERP began a campaign of attacks during military rule in Argentina in the 1970s. After the 1976 coup the movement was defeated during the military's "dirty war" against leftists.

ETA — Euzkadi Ta Askatasuna /Basque Homeland and Freedom (Spain) — One of Europe's best-organized terrorist organizations, the group has conducted a bombing and assassination campaign for thirty years to gain independence for nearly three million Basques living along the Spanish/French border.

FMLN — Frente Farabundo Marti para la Liberación Nacional /Farabundo Marti National Liberation Front (El Salvador) — A guerrilla front originally founded in El Salvador in October 1980 by the People's Liberation Forces (FPL), the People's Revolutionary Army (ERP) and the Salvadoran Communist Party (PCS). By December 1980 two other Salvadoran guerrilla groups had also joined — the National Resistance (RN) and the Revolutionary Party of Central-Americanist Workers (PRTC). The FMLN, which is named after a Communist Party leader executed in 1932, waged a twelve-year struggle against the rightist U.S.-backed government forces. With the transition to peace in the country, the Front has been the victim of political infighting among the five factions. However, members participated in the 1994 elections as part of a broad leftist coalition party.

FPL — Fuerzas Populares de la Liberación/Popular Forces of Liberation (El Salvador) — A guerrilla organization founded in 1970 by breakaway members of the Salvadoran Communist Party and one of the most radical members of the FMLN guerrilla coalition.

FPMR — Frente Patriótico Manuel Rodriguez/Manuel Rodriguez Patriotic Front (Chile) — The group, which is named for the hero of the resistance to Spanish colonial rule, is usually regarded as the armed wing of the Chilean Communist Party although it has always claimed autonomy and has forged links with other groups. It was founded in 1983 to create a nationwide military organization to lead popular resistance and work towards the collapse of the Pinochet regime. Its activities have ranged from armed propaganda to assassination. In September, 1986, twenty-five members of the group staged a machine-gun and rocket attack on President Augusto Pinochet in which five of his bodyguards were killed.

FSLN — Frente Sandinista de Liberación Nacional /Sandinista National Liberation Front (Nicaragua) — A Nicaraguan guerrilla movement founded in 1961 in Honduras by Carlos Fonseca, Tomas Borge, and Sílvio Mayorga to overthrow the Somoza family dictatorship in Nicaragua. The group took its name in memory of Augusto César Sandino, a Nicaraguan general who fought against the U.S. occupation of his country in the 1930s. Following a long guerrilla war, the FSLN toppled the Somoza dictatorship and took power in 1979. During the 1980s, the FSLN government fought a civil war against U.S.-backed Contra rebels. The FSLN, now a legitimate political party, lost in national elections in 1990.

MIR — Movimiento de la Izquierda Revolucionária /Movement of the Revolutionary Left (Chile) — Founded in 1965 by a group of university students, the MIR staged bank robberies to collect funds for its political work in shantytowns on the outskirts of Santiago. After the attempted coup of June 29, 1973, the group went underground to prepare attacks against the country's armed forces. In 1974 the group allied itself with Argentina's ERP. Now a legitimate political party, the MIR still has several underground armed splinter groups that engage in sporadic terrorist attacks.

MTP — Movimiento Todos Por la Pátria /All for the Fatherland Movement (Argentina) — An urban guerrilla group that often poses as a human rights group. In January, 1989 the MTP launched a disastrous attack on the La Tablada military barracks outside Buenos Aires. Thirty-two people died in the attack, which the group said was engineered to preempt a military coup. Enrique Gorriarán Merlo, one of Latin America's most powerful terrorists, is affiliated with the MTP.

OAS — Organization of American States — The main inter-American organization, founded to strengthen political, economic, and social ties. The OAS traces its origins to the First Congress of American States, convened by Simon Bolivar in Panama in 1826 and the International Union of American Republics, set up in 1890, later renamed the Pan American Union (PAU). The ninth International American Congress under the PAU in Bogotá formally set up the OAS in 1948.

ORA — Organización de Resistencia Armada/Organization of the Armed Resistance (Chile) — A terrorist splinter group of the Chilean MIR.

PT — Partido dos Trabalhadores /Workers' Party (Brazil) — Brazil's left-wing labour party which emerged from the trade union movement in the late 1970s in São Paulo's industrial sectors. The group is led by former union leader Luis Inácio Lula da Silva, who has made two unsuccessful bids for the presidency in Brazil (1989, 1994).

PRI — Partido Revolucionário Institucional/Institutional Revolutionary Party (Mexico) — The ruling PRI grew out of the Mexican revolution and has dominated the country's political system since 1929.

PMDB — Partido do Movimento Democrático Brasileiro/Brazilian Democratic Movement Party (Brazil) — The only permitted opposition party in Brazil during the military regime. In 1984, the party emerged as the driving force in the campaign to end military rule and work for direct presidential elections. In 1985, the party joined with the Liberal Front Party (PFL) to back the presidential candidacy of Tancredo Neves. In January, Neves was elected along with José Sarney as vice-president. Although Sarney was closer to the PFL he had to join the PMDB to satisfy the Brazilian constitution requirement that the presidential and vice-presidential candidates belong to the same party. When Neves died shortly after becoming president, Sarney assumed the presidency. The party has been characterized by its commitment to social reforms and economic nationalism.

PRN — Partido da Reconstrução Nacional /National Reconstruction Party (Brazil) — The political party had its origins in 1985 as the Partido da Juventude/Youth Party. In 1987, the name of the party was changed and its sole purpose became to launch the candidacy of Fernando Affonso Collor de Mello for the presidential elections in 1989.

RAF — Rote Armee Fraktion /Red Army Faction (Germany) — A German Marxist-Leninist group founded in 1970, which has targeted businessmen, politicians, government officials, and U.S. military installations in its terrorist attacks.

URNG — Unidad Revolucionária Nacional Guatemalteca /Guatemalan National Revolutionary Union (Guatemala) — A guerrilla front founded in 1982 by Guatemala's armed revolutionary groups to end repression, and domination by the rich, and to work towards equality for indigenous people.

Index

Acevedo, Ulisses Gallardo, 14, 102
Action for National Liberation (ALN), 144
AIDS, 111, 113, 182, 186
Allende, Salvador, 84, 201
Alonso, Geraldo, 141, 151, 191
Amnesty International, 11–12, 94, 115, 125–126, 128, 193
ARENA, 25, 135, 205
Arns, Dom Paulo Evaristo, 4, 165
Aylwin, Patricio, 46
Barricada, 15, 152
Basque terrorists, 16, 52, 137, 141–142
Berlin Wall, 16, 42, 49, 143
Bolan, Kim, 20, 33, 35, 53, 56, 107, 112–113, 190, 193
Borge, Tomás, 51, 136, 142, 158
Born, Jorge, 146
Born, Juan, 145
Brazilian Traction, Light and Power Company (Brascan), 161
bunker, 5, 14–17, 54, 56, 135–143, 150, 153, 155–156, 158, 171
buzon de Santa Rosa, 16
Carandiru, 23, 109, 182
Carandiru massacre, 111–112, 115
Cardoso, Fernando Henrique, 49, 96, 170, 197
Carreno, Manuel, 85
Casa da Detenção, 109–111, 115
Casolo, Jennifer Jean, 38
Casoy, Boris, 101, 161
Castañeda, Jorge, 27, 31, 42, 146
Castro, Fidel, 26, 42, 146
caudillos, 48
Cavallo, Domingo, 44
Cavallo Plan, 44
CASFUSA (Central America Simon Fraser University Students' Association), 29
Chamorro, Violetta, 15, 51, 138
Charter of Rights and Freedoms, 18, 129
Che Guevara, 24, 27, 206
Chiapas, 24, 30–31
Chrétien, Jean, Prime Minister, 202
Cold War, 19–20, 24, 42, 49, 125, 154, 200
Collor de Mello, Fernando Affonso, 3, 6, 45, 71, 208
Committee for Justice for Christine Lamont and David Spencer, 28, 95, 155
Contra, 48, 51, 137, 207
Correa, Maurício, 110, 167, 174
Cristiani, Alfredo, 49
CSIS, 32–33, 37, 177–178

Cuba, 16, 24, 26–27, 34, 42–43, 55, 84, 143, 145–146, 178, 197
da Silva, Luis Inácio Lula, 3, 13, 99, 103–104, 170, 208
death squads, 20, 25, 57, 205
debt crisis, 6, 201
democracy, 6, 43, 46–47, 128, 135, 170, 185, 189, 198, 201–202
Diniz, Abílio dos Santos, 3, 69–70
Direct Action, 32, 142, 153, 200
Donais, Blaine, 18, 129, 155
Dymond, Bill, 162–163
Earth Summit, 124
El Salvador, 9, 14, 16, 24–26, 29, 33–35, 37, 39, 48–50, 52, 56–57, 87, 126, 134–136, 138, 157–158, 187–188, 201, 205–206
Euzkadi Ta Askatasuna, (ETA), 15–16, 77, 141–143, 148, 151, 153, 206
exchange-of-prisoners treaty, 11
expulsion, 10–11, 18, 96, 119–121, 123–125, 127, 129–130, 153, 163–164, 170, 172–173, 175–176, 181, 194–195, 202
External Affairs, 7, 11, 32, 87, 97, 111–113, 120–121, 123, 126, 130, 153–154, 163, 193–196
favelas, 45, 57
Fifth Estate, The, 9–10, 12, 62, 64–65, 75, 88, 102, 106, 111, 127, 187, 189, 193, 198
Fleury, Luis Antônio, 13
Frente Farabundo Marti para la Liberació Nacional, (FMLN), 14, 16, 24, 26, 33, 37–39, 49–50, 52–54, 56, 87, 134–136, 138, 145, 150, 157–158, 188, 205–206
Foreign Affairs, Canadian Department of, 12, 163, 171, 175–178, 197
Fuerzas Populares de la Liberación, (FPL), 14, 16, 53, 134–136, 206

Franco, Itamar, 162–163, 167–168, 171, 173, 175–176, 199, 202
Frei, Eduardo, 172
Freire, Raimundo Costa, 57, 68, 77–78, 88
Friedman, Milton, 44
Fuentes, Carlos, 49
Fujimori, Alberto, 44
Galimberti, Rodolfo, 146
Garvin, Glenn, 48, 51
general directorate for state security (DGSE), 136
Globe and Mail, The, 13, 17, 28, 97, 128, 130, 158, 174, 196
Globo, 3–5, 7, 80, 104–105, 152, 164, 170, 184, 200, 202
Guillermoprieto, Alma, 47
"Haiti", 46
Hamburg, 16, 143
Helu, Alfredo Harp, 15, 140
Hoffgen, Walter, 111, 115, 187
human rights, 4, 9–12, 18, 20, 33, 47, 52–53, 56–57, 63, 65, 73, 86, 94, 105, 107, 110, 123, 125–129, 139, 151, 154, 156, 172–173, 188–189, 207
Humphreys, David, 10, 17, 19–20, 52, 97–98, 104, 116, 120, 128, 150, 156, 158, 166, 175
internacionalistas, 38–39, 42, 51–52, 54, 137, 188–189
International Monetary Fund, 16
Interpol, 14–16, 55, 82, 84–85, 87, 140–142, 151–152, 167, 188
Irish Republican Army, 16, 142
La Quena Coffee House, 23
La Tablada, 49, 86–87, 137, 207
Lamont, Christine, 5, 17, 19, 28, 36, 73, 91, 93, 95, 113–114, 123, 125, 129, 154–156, 162, 164, 181
Lamont, Dr. Keith, 7, 93, 113

Lamont, Marilyn, 7, 32, 52, 93–95, 98, 112, 114, 123, 125, 127, 151, 153, 157, 169, 175, 190
Lembach, Pedro, 59, 77, 85, 143
Liberal Government, Canada, 12–13, 173, 176, 178–179, 181, 197
Little Drummer Girl, The, 36–37
Lucena, Humberto, 165
Malarek, Victor, 10, 106, 129, 189
Manuel Rodriguez Patriotic Front (FPMR), 84, 206
Marighella, Carlos, 144, 205
Martinez, Antonio Beltran, 83
Mawhinney, Barry, 126
McDougall, Barbara, 87, 89, 112, 121, 129, 153, 157, 163–164, 176, 192, 194, 196
McKenna, Frank, Premier, 129
Mendes, Paul Joseph Gomes, 8, 75, 147
Menem, Carlos Saul, 44
Merlo, Enrique Gorriarán, 86, 137, 191, 207
Miami Herald, The, 17, 26, 56, 93, 146, 150
Midnight Express, 13, 177, 194
Military police, 58, 69, 110–111
Minimanual of the Urban Guerrilla, 144
MIR, 16, 84–87, 103, 137, 143, 145, 153, 172, 207
Missing, 18, 149, 199
Montoneros, 145–146, 188
Moreno, Angel Losada, 141
Movement of the Revolutionary Left (MIR), 84
Movimiento Todos por la Patria (MTP), 137
Mulroney, Brian, 123, 164
National Guard, 51
National Reconstruction Party (PRN), 100

Nicaragua, 8–9, 14–16, 30, 33–34, 48, 50–53, 55–57, 77, 82, 131, 134, 137–138, 140, 142–145, 147, 149–154, 157, 177, 188–190, 192, 203, 207
Operation Carmelo, 72
Organización de Resistencia Armada (ORA), 85, 207
Organization of American States (OAS), 52, 177, 207
Ortega, Daniel, 48, 52, 136, 142, 152
Ottawa Citizen, The, 31, 107, 174, 185–186
Paraguay, 87, 137
parliamentary justice committee, 124
Partido Revolucionário Institucional (PRI), 47, 208
Passarinho, Jarbas, 97, 123, 165, 198
Paz, Humberto Eduardo, 5, 86
Pão de Açucar, 3, 70–72
Penitenciaria Feminina, 181
People's Revolutionary Army (ERP), 87, 206
Pinochet, General Augusto, 43, 87
Plano Collor, 71
Popular Forces of Liberation (FPL), 134
Progressive Conservative Government, 11, 129, 164, 196
Radio Farabundo Marti, 33
RCMP, 32, 60, 82, 106, 117, 129, 153, 175, 178, 187
Red Army Faction, RAF, 143
Red Brigades, 144
reforms, neoliberal, 25, 44
Rideout, George, 113, 176
Robinson, Svend, 10, 124
Sachs, Jeffrey, 44
Salazar, Hector, 172
Salinas de Gortari, Carlos, 48
Salles, Luiz, 83
Salpress, 38, 52–53, 188

Sandinista, 15, 48, 51–52, 55, 77,
    136–138, 142, 150, 158, 189, 207
Saturday Night, 39, 56–57, 100–102,
    106, 108
social-democratic, 26, 32, 49
Somoza, Anastasio, 51
Soviet Union, 16, 42, 138
Spencer, Bill, 7, 30, 56, 111, 115,
    123, 126, 128, 196
Spencer, David, 5, 7, 19, 28, 61, 73,
    95, 123, 125, 129, 154–156, 162,
    164, 203
Squamish Five Support Group, 200
Stewart, Christine, 177
Suplicy, Eduardo, 100–101, 165, 198
Tapia, Hector Collante, 57, 61, 77
Tarver, Rebecca, 38
Telejornal Brasil, 161–162, 165, 170
Third World, 6, 12, 18, 24, 69, 87,
    91–92, 155, 174, 192, 197

Toronto Star, The, 15, 36, 74, 151,
    153, 156–157, 163, 174–175
torture, 11–12, 14, 18, 60–61, 63–64,
    101–102, 117, 125, 164, 172–173
Transfer of Offenders Treaty, 164,
    168, 171
Tuma, Romeu, Jr., 55, 152
Unidad Revolucionária Nacional
    Guatemalteca (URNG), 145, 208
Urtubia, Sergio Martin olivares, 58–59
Utopia Unarmed, 27, 31, 42
Vancouver Sun, The, 28–29, 33, 94,
    103, 107, 112–113, 116, 128–129,
    154, 157, 175, 193–194
Vaz, Tânia Maria Cordeiro, 172
Villalobos, Joaquín, 26, 135, 188, 205
Walker, Lisa Lynne, 8, 15, 147
Workers Party, (PT), 13, 102, 208
World Bank, 16, 143–144
Zapatista National Liberation Army, 24

Illustrations

The Publisher would like to thank the following photographers and organizations for their kind permission to reproduce the photographs in this book:

Front cover: Military Police in Riot Gear, Globo News Agency/Isabel Vincent, photo image from videotape; Front cover: forged passport photos of Christine Lamont and David Spencer, Globo News Agency/C. Duran, photo image from videotape; Page 2: Abílio dos Santos Diniz held at window by kidnappers, Marlene Bergamo/Banco de Dados, Folha de S.Paulo; Page 22; David Spencer and Christine Lamont shortly after their arrest, Globo News Agency/Isabel Vincent, photo image from videotape; Page 40: Humberto Paz taken from the kidnapping scene in a police bus, Juan Esteves/Banco de Dados, Folha de S.Paulo; Page 66: Abílio dos Santos after being released from confinement indicating he has been unharmed, Elena Vetorazo/Banco de Dados, Folha de S.Paulo; Page 90: Christine Lamont's prison cell, Photo by Author; Page 132: Ruins of exploded bunker in Santa Rosa, Photo by Author; Page 160: Tânia Maria Cordeiro Vaz looking out from the inside of a police car, Helcio Nagamine/Banco de Dados, Folha de S.Paulo; Page 180: Gates of David Spencer's prison, Photo by Author; Back Cover: Isabel Vincent, Photo by James Michael Cooper.

Every effort has been made to trace copyright holders. If, however, there are inadvertent omissions, these can be corrected in any future editions.

April Fool's Day
Bryce Courtenay

In 1984 Damon Courtenay, a haemophiliac, was diagnosed HIV positive. He died on April Fool's day 1991 at the age of twenty-five.

April Fool's Day is his story as told by the people who loved him, a modern love story. At times controversial, painful and heartbreaking, it has a gentle humour about it, reflecting Damon's love of life. Above all, it is a testimony to the incredible regenerative strength of love — how when we confront our worst, we can become our best.

Bryce Courtenay was born in South Africa but has spent the greater part of his adult life in Australia. He lives in Sydney and is creative director at George Patterson Advertising agency. He also writes a weekly column in the *Australian*. *The Power of One* and *Tandia* are his first novels.

Reed Books Canada   674 Pb
0 433 39710 1 $26.99

A Way in the World
V. S. Naipaul

We all know the parents or grandparents we come from. But we go back and back, forever; we go back to the very beginning; in our blood and bone and brain we carry the memories of thousands of beings. — V. S. Naipaul

In classical storytelling traditions, V. S. Naipaul draws on examples of Spanish and British imperial history in the Caribbean (especially El Golfo Triste), and upon a profound awareness of the modern, post-colonial experience, to construct a series of linked narrations of astonishing imaginative integrity. The reader in living witness to the shame of Raleigh's final expedition to the New World, and to the timeless ironies of Francisco Miranda's disastrous invasion of South America in the late eighteenth century.

V. S. Naipaul recreates the great dramas of the past within a context of echoing modernity, laying bare the unvarying impulses, the ambitions and delusions of each man.

V. S. Naipaul was born in Trinidad in 1932. His award winning novels include *The Mystic Masseur* (John Llewelyn Rhys Memorial Prize), *Miguel Street* (Somerset Maugham Award), *The Mimic Men* (W. H. Smith Award), and *In a Free State* (Booker Prize). He has also written a collection of short stories and nine works of nonfiction. He received a Knighthood in the 1990 New Year's Honours list for services to literature, and in 1993 was the first recipient of the David Cohen British Literature Prize.

Reed Books Canada
0 433 39711 X $15.99 Pb

Time only enhances V. S. Naipaul's clarity of vision
— *Montreal Gazette*

... a questing, poetic intelligence writing English prose as well as it can be written
— *Ottawa Citizen*

A Way in the World is one of his supreme triumphs
— *European*

Naipaul writes beautifully ... He is one of the finest writers working today and this large, various, artful book is among his best
— *The Times*

His own modern labour of love, loss and disquiet, this really is a book to treasure
— *Sunday Express*

John Steinbeck: A Biography
Jay Parini

When he died in 1968, John Steinbeck was perhaps the most popular of American novelists in the world, yet despite receiving the Nobel Prize for literature in 1964 he was no darling of the critics or the literary establishment. Born in a small town in Northern California in 1902, his career mirrors the highs and lows of this tumultuous century. A difficult relationship with his parents, his turbulent married life and his often tempestuous friendships with numerous celebrated writers, entertainers, intellectuals and politicians, from Charlie Chaplin to Lyndon Johnson, Ernest Hemingway to William Faulkner all played their part in the creation of some of the greatest works of fiction of the twentieth century. Works that inspired millions of Americans, as well as a devoted following around the world. Jay Parini's John Steinbeck is both an important reassessment and a fascinating portrait, offering a vivid portrayal of a driven and difficult man, who remains unfailingly attractive to readers of all ages and levels of sophistication.

Jay Parini, an American poet and novelist, is currently the Fowler Hamilton Fellow of Christ Church, Oxford. He is the author of numerous books, including *Anthracite Country, Town Life, The Last Station* and *Bay of Arrows*. His earlier biographical study of the poet Theodore Roethke was short-listed for a Pulitzer prize in 1979.

Reed Books Canada
0 7493 9652 0 $16.99 Pb

[Parini] has, after diligent research, written a readable, often engrossing biography of one of the most important writers of this century.
— *The London Free Press*

Parini, a distinguished poet and novelist whose biographical study of the poet Theodore Roethke was short-listed for a Pulitzer Prize, brings intelligence, insight and style to this important work.
— *Calgary Herald*

Truly excellent.
— *Sunday Express*

Precious and essential reading.
— *Daily Mail*

Dancing with a Ghost
Exploring Indian Reality
Rupert Ross

Canadians are increasingly aware of the immense gulf that separates Native from other Canadian cultures. Rupert Ross seeks to bridge this gap by examining the traditional Cree and Ojibway world view, and by showing why their philosophy so often places them in conflict with the Canadian justice system. Ross cites examples of Native ethics, such as a parent's belief in non-interference child-rearing, a victim's hesitation to make eye contact with a prosecutor, or a witness's reluctance to testify or comment on someone else's behaviour, that can lead to unfair judgements in non-Native courts.

In *Dancing with a Ghost* Ross develops an appreciation of Native philosophy and points to ways in which Native values can be incorporated into court processes and other aspects of mainstream culture. Written with encouragement and guidance from Native leaders across Canada, this timely book suggests how we, collectively, can build a nation which acknowledges and accommodates both societies.

Rupert Ross is an Assistant Crown Attorney for the District of Kenora, Ontario, where he works closely with the Ojibway and Cree peoples to make the court system more responsive to the needs of their communities. He has also written extensively on Native justice issues and speaks regularly at conferences across the country.

Reed Books Canada
0 409 90648 4 $15.95 Pb

> A poignant, delicately careful examination of the cultural roots and contemporary adaptations of Canada's Native people . . . crisply written and lasting in its impact. A necessary book.
> — June Callwood

> In *Dancing with a Ghost*, Mr. Rupert Ross has succeeded where most others have fallen short.
> — Basil H. Johnston